THE LITERATURE OF THE FILM

A Bibliographical Guide to The Film As Art
And Entertainment, 1936-1970

The Literature of the Film

*A Bibliographical Guide to the Film as Art
and Entertainment, 1936-1970*

By Alan R. Dyment

Distributed by
GALE RESEARCH COMPANY
Book Tower
Detroit, Michigan 48226

WHITE LION PUBLISHERS LIMITED
London, New York, Sydney and Toronto

ISBN 72850 0558

Made and Printed in
Great Britain
for White Lion Publishers Limited,
138 Park Lane, London W1Y 3DD
by
R. Kingshott & Co. Ltd.,
Deadbrook Lane, Aldershot, Hampshire

CONTENTS

INTRODUCTION

With the ever-increasing number of film-study courses being offered in schools, colleges and universities in North America, and with the voluminous amount of cinema literature being published, it is surprising that no major bibliography or guide to this literature has been produced in the English language since 1941. At that time The film index was published. (Entry # 1303) The first volume, The film as art, was the only one to be completed and provided references to more than 8600 books and periodical articles and to 3200 films. This major work, edited by Harold Leonard, was a project of the Writers' Program. Bibliographies in foreign languages have occasionally been published, but their usefulness is obviously limited. The most important is the Bibliografia generale del cinema (Roma, Edizioni dell'Ateneo, 1953) edited by Carl Vincent and compiled by a group of members of the Cinematographic Centre of the University of Padua with the cooperation of some foreign correspondents. English-language entries were included in this bibliography but few annotations were provided. Book lists have been issued at various times by libraries and institutions, and specialist bookstores such as Larry Edmunds in Hollywood and Cinemabilia in New York issue extensive catalogues, but often the bibliographical data is incorrect and lacking in essential information.

The present work provides a brief survey of film literature published since January 1936. This date was selected as The film index provides coverage up to that date. Circumstances dictated many limitations in its scope but it is hoped that it will be of assistance to librarians, educators, and all those who have an interest in the cinema as an art form or as an entertainment medium. All books included are in the English language, and most are available through the various library interloan systems or from specialist bookstores. Annotations are provided in nearly all cases unless the title is self-explanatory. The compiler has examined most of the volumes

listed, and information on the remaining items has been obtained from reliable sources such as the National Union Catalogue, the British Museum
Catalogue, and the British National Bibliography. All items have been checked
against these works for accuracy in establishing correct forms of personal
names. In the world of the cinema, widely varying birth dates abound, particularly for actors and actresses. The dates given by the Library of Congress
have been accepted wherever possible. Choice of author generally follows
current cataloguing procedure, and bibliographical data has been kept as suc-
cict as possible.

Entries are arranged by specialized categories, in many cases similar to
those used in The film index. Since many books could be expected to be found
in more than one category, complete added entries have been supplied to avoid
tiresome cross-references. Main entries are numbered in sequence and are arranged alphabetically within each category. Individual biographies, studies,
reminiscences and portraits are arranged alphabetically by name of subject,
and entries in the Individual screenplays and film studies category are arranged alphabetically by film title. As this bibliography was compiled in
Canada, the state of publishing and book distribution peculiar to that country
has resulted in a mixture of English and American editions. Wherever a title
change between editions is involved, this has been noted, otherwise the edition examined is the one listed in the bibliography. Abbreviations used are
those of standard cataloguing practice.

Certain categories of works have been excluded from the bibliography unless they were considered to be of exceptional interest or importance. Such
items include pamphlets of fewer than thirty pages; foreign language publications; publicity material; unpublished documents; biographies of stage actors
who may have made rare screen appearances or biographies with no film information; highly technical works; periodicals. The latter were excluded reluct-
antly due to the compiler's lack of access to the majority of titles. For-

tunately this particular branch of film bibliography is the only one already quite well researched. Two publications provide this information:- World list of film periodicals and serials (entry #1268) and Current film periodicals in English (entry #1293)

The bibliography may appear to include material which is clearly out of date for the practical purpose for which it was written. Such books may now be of value for their historical interest or as research material on the industry at the time of publication. A certain amount of apparently ephemeral material has also been included, particularly in the Personalities category. Film itself is a transitory medium; examples of the work of film directors and actors of the past have often been destroyed without thought for their value to future generations. Often a poorly written memoir may be all that remains for the film enthusiast interested in a particular film personality. Many film artists have been given fresh recognition. A bibliographer in 1940 may have considered Laurel & Hardy to be of little importance when discussing the film as an art form, but today many critics consider such artists to be major figures. Jerry Lewis, scorned in his own country by critical writers, is hailed by many in France as an artist of genius. This bibliography therefore includes ephemeral works if there is reason to suppose that they could have some merit or shed light on a personality or aspect of the cinema.

The difficulties faced by the compiler in obtaining access to material have prevented this bibliography from attempting to be in any way complete. It is hoped however that no major work has been omitted, and that at some time in the future, through a cooperative effort with specialist librarians in such cities as London, Los Angeles and New York, a worthy successor to The film index can be produced.

THE HISTORY OF THE FILM AND CINEMA

General works

0001   BARDECHE, Maurice   and BRASILLACH, Robert

The history of motion pictures.

Translated and edited by Iris Barry.

New York, Norton, 1938. 412p. illus.

A lively history of the artistic development of the
motion picture with the emphasis on the silent film era.
Of particular interest are the critical footnotes of the
editor and translator, Iris Barry. Published in
England under title: History of the film.

0002   BLUM, Daniel C

A new pictorial history of the talkies. Revisions by
John Kobal.

New York, Putnam, c1968. 339p. illus.

A revised edition of A pictorial history of the
talkies, first published in 1958. Contains more than
4,000 stills arranged chronologically, from the early
talkies to the late sixties. With index.

0003   BLUM, Daniel C

A pictorial history of the silent screen.

London, Spring Books, 1962. c1953. 334p. illus.

First published in 1953, this illustrated survey
of the cinema's early days includes more than 3,000 photo-
graphs arranged in chronological order, but with minimal
text.

0004   COWIE, Peter, ed.

A concise history of the cinema.

London, Zwemmer, 1971. 2v. illus. *Screen series.*

An outline history of international cinema *consisting of articles written by more than thirty contributors. Volume 1 covers the period up to 1940, volume 2 continuing to 1971. With bibliography.*

0005   COWIE, Peter

Seventy years of cinema.

South Brunswick, N. J., Barnes, 1969. 286p. illus.

An illustrated chronological outline of the major films and events in the development of the cinema from 1895 to 1967. Includes film title index.

0006   DICKINSON, Thorold

A discovery of cinema.

London, Oxford University Press, 1971. 164p. illus.

A personal view of the evolution of the cinema.

0007   FIELDING, Raymond, ed.

A technological history of motion pictures and television; an anthology from the pages of the Journal of the Society of Motion Picture and Television Engineers.

Berkeley, University of California Press, 1967. 255p. illus.

Contents:- Autobiographical reminiscences.- Historical papers: motion pictures.- Historical papers: television. The book is an anthology of reports and studies.

0008   HOUSTON, Penelope

       The contemporary cinema.

       Harmondsworth, Eng., Penguin Books, 1963. 222p. illus.

         A well written survey of film making since World War

       II by the English film critic showing the various trends

       and important developments.

0009   JACOBS, Lewis, 1906-   ed.

       The emergence of film art: the evolution and development of the

       motion picture as an art, from 1900 to the present.

       New York, Hopkinson and Blake, 1969. 453p. illus.

         An anthology of essays on the film medium's artistic

       development, arranged in three parts:- The silent film (1900-

       1930).- The sound and color film (1930-1950).- The creative

       present (1950-   )

0010   KNIGHT, Arthur.

       The liveliest art; a panoramic history of the movies.

       London, Macmillan, 1957. 383p. illus.

         Traces the high-points of the artistic growth of the

       movies, describing the work of the finest directors. Includes

       a useful bibliography.

0011   LENNIG, Arthur.

       The silent voice.

       Albany, Faculty-Student Association of the University

       of New York, 1966. 176p. illus.

         Essays on the silent cinema with emphasis on studies

       of specific films. Arranged in the following sections:-

       Beginnings.- The American film.- The German film.- The

       Soviet film. No index.

0012   LINDGREN, Ernest.

A picture history of the cinema.

London, Vista Books, 1960. 160p. illus.

A pictorial survey of world cinema, arranged chrono-logically from 1895 to 1959. Brief but authoritative text, illustrated by stills from the National Film Archive collection in London.

0013   MAST, Gerald, 1940-

A short history of the movies.

New York, Pegasus, 1971. 463p. illus.

A textbook with bibliographical references and filmo-graphies.

0014   MAYER, Michael F.

Foreign films on American screens.

New York, Arco, c1965. 119p. illus.

Surveys the trends in post-war non-American cinema, and discusses the problems involved in U.S. distribution and censorship. With appendices listing award-winning films, major distributors, exhibitors, etc.

0015   NIVER, Kemp R.

In the beginning: program notes to accompany one hundred early motion pictures.

New York, Brandon Books, 1967. 60p. illus.

0016   O'LEARY, Liam

The silent cinema.

London, Studio Vista, 1965. 160p. illus. *Pictureback series.*

An international survey of the silent film, particularly in the twenties. Brief text with many stills drawn from the collection of the National Film Archive.

0017   PRATT, George C., ed.

Spellbound in darkness; readings in the history and

criticism of the silent film.

Rochester, N.Y., School of Liberal and Applied Studies,

University of Rochester, c1966. 2v. (452p.)

A collection of reviews, articles, and other writings

about the silent film era gleaned from contemporary publications.

The emphasis is on American cinema.

0018   ROTHA, Paul, 1907-

The film till now; a survey of world cinema. With an additional

section by Richard Griffith. Rev. ed.

London, Spring Books, 1967. 831p. illus.

A standard critical survey originally published in 1930,

now greatly revised and enlarged, with additional chapters

by Richard Griffith. Informative and well illustrated.

0019   ROTHA, Paul, 1907-   and MANVELL, Roger, 1909-

Movie parade, 1888-1949; a pictorial survey of world cinema.

London, Studio, 1950. 160p. illus.

A revised edition of the book by Paul Rotha first published

in 1936, which presented the work of three hundred directors.

Principle contents:- Films of fiction.- Films of fact.-

Experimental and animated films. Consists mainly of illustrations,

with a well-written commentary.

0020   SCHICKEL, Richard

Movies: the history of an art and an institution.

New York, Basic Books, 1964. 208p. illus.

A chronological account, well received critically. With

bibliography and index.

0021   SCHICKEL, Richard

The stars. Designed by Allen Hurlburt.

New York, Dial Press, 1962. 287p. illus.

Profusely illustrated survey of "the personalities who made the movies" from the silent era to the stars of the late fifties.

0022   SHIPMAN, David

The great movie stars; the golden years.

London, Hamlyn, c1970. 576p. illus.

Notes on 181 stars who achieved fame before or during World War II and who are still remembered today. Entries are arranged alphabetically, each including mention of feature length films featuring the actor concerned.

0023   SPEED, F. Maurice

Movie cavalcade; the story of the cinema: its stars, studios and producers. 4th ed.

London, Raven Books, 1944. 112p. illus.

Intended as an inexpensive popular history of the cinema, the book concentrates on the early years of film-making up to the introduction of sound.

0024   SWEENEY, Russell C.

The silent idols; a compilation of classic movie ads of the pas

New York, 1969. 60p. illus.

0025   WAGENKNECHT, Edward Charles, 1900-

The movies in the age of innocence.

Norman, University of Oklahoma Press, 1962. 280p. illus.

A personal view of silent films, giving first-hand testimony of the period from the point of view of an enthusiastic film-goer.

0026   WEAVER, John T.

Forty years of screen credits, 1929-1969.

Metuchen, N.J. Scarecrow Press, 1970. 2v. (1458p.) illus.

An alphabetical listing of film titles arranged by

performer. Concentrates on American stars, but includes

many British actors.

0027   WEAVER, John T.

Twenty years of silents, 1908-1928.

Metuchen, N.J., Scarecrow Press, 1971. 514p.

Film title listings arranged in two sequences:-
The players.- The directors and producers. Arrangement
of entries under each name is chronological. Also includes
a list of silent film studio corporations and distributors.

0028   WISEMAN, Thomas

Cinema.

London, Cassell, 1964. 181p. illus.

A well illustrated history of the cinema for the
general reader.

0029   WOOD, Leslie

The miracle of the movies.

London, Burke, 1947. 352p. illus.

A personal history of the cinema, with emphasis on
British studios. Includes sections of the author's earlier
work The romance of the movies. No index.

0030   WOOD, Leslie

The romance of the movies.

London, Heinemann, 1937. 343p. illus.

An account of the past, present, and future of the
film. No chapter headings or index.

0031 ALLISTER, Ray, *pseud.*

    Friese-Greene; close-up of an inventor.

    London, Marsland, 1948. 192p. illus.

    The subject was "the man who first announced, first
    used in public, first patented a commercially practical
    moving picture camera" (author). Includes a list of
    Friese-Greene's British patents. The book was reissued
    in 1951 with the addition of eight pages of photographs
    from the film about Friese-Greene, The magic box.

0032 BARNES, John

    Precursors of the cinema; shadowgraphy, panoramas,
    dioramas and peepshows considered in their relation to
    the history of the cinema.

    St. Ives, Eng., Barnes Museum of Cinematography, 1967.
    68p.

    This is the first part of the catalogue of the
    collection of John and William Barnes, listing 267 items
    from puppets to picture postcards. With bibliography.

0033 CERAM, C.W., *pseud.*

    Archaeology of the cinema.

    London, Thames and Hudson, c1965. 264p. illus.

    A well illustrated history of the early stages of
    development of the cinema up to 1897, from early optical
    toys to the projection of a moving image.

0034   COOK, Olive

Movement in two dimensions: a study of the animated and

projected pictures which preceded the invention of cinema-

tography.

London, Hutchinson, 1963. 142p. illus.

Presents the early history of techniques such as

shadow plays and dioramas that lead to the motion picture.

With bibliography.

0035   DICKSON, Antonia   and   DICKSON, William Kennedy Laurie

Edison's invention of the kinetophonograph.

Los Angeles, Pueblo Press, 1939. 18p. illus.

A reprint of an article originally appearing in

Century magazine in 1894. With an introduction by

Charles G. Clarke.

0036   HENDRICKS, Gordon

Beginnings of the biograph: the story of the invention

of the mutoscope and the biograph and their supplying

camera.

New York, Beginnings of the American Film, 1964. 78p.

illus.

A continuation of the author's investigations into

the beginnings of the American film, first developed in his

book The Edison motion picture myth. This volume covers

the years from 1894 to 1897.

0037   HENDRICKS, Gordon

The Edison motion picture myth.

Berkeley, University of California Press, 1961. 216p.

illus.

This book sets out "1. To be a beginning of the
task of cleaning up the morass of well-embroidered legend
with which the beginning of the American film is permeated,
and 2., to afford some measure of belated credit to the
work done by W.K.L. Dickson." (pref.) A carefully
researched enquiry covering the years from 1888 to 1892.

0038   HENDRICKS, Gordon

The kinetoscope; America's first commercially successful
motion picture exhibitor.
New York, Beginnings of the American Film, 1966. 182p.
illus.

A further volume in the author's series of books on
early American film, concentrating on the story of the
design, production, and exhibition of the kinetoscope, its
camera, and films in the 1890's.

0039   QUIGLEY, Martin, 1917-

Magic shadows; the story of the origin of motion pictures.
New York, Quigley, 1960. 191p. illus.

First published in 1948, the book includes a chronology
tracing the growth of pre-cinema inventions.

0040   THOMAS, David Bowen

The origins of the motion picture; an introductory
booklet on the pre-history of the cinema.
London, H.M.S.O., 1964.

32p. illus. *Science Museum booklets.*

Specialized aspects of screen history

0041   **BALABAN, Abraham Joseph**

Continuous performance; the story of A.J. Balaban, as told to his wife Carrie Balaban.

New York, A.J. Balaban Foundation, 1964. 144p. illus.

First published in 1942, this biography of the founder of the Balaban & Katz cinema chain in the United States is also a history of the development of the American motion picture theatre.

0042   BALL, Robert Hamilton, 1902-

Shakespeare on silent film; a strange eventful history.
New York, Theatre Arts Books, 1968. 403p. illus.

A carefully researched study of the silent film adaptations of Shakespeare's works produced during the silent film era, from 1899. The main work is followed by detailed "Explanations and acknowledgments" a bibliography, and indexes.

0043   CAREY, Gary

Lost films.
New York, Museum of Modern Art, 1970. 91p. illus.

Based on the exhibition "Stills from lost films" prepared by the author for the Museum of Modern Art. The book consists of stills from films thought to be no longer in existence. Credits and synopses for films illustrated are included.

0044   FAY, Arthur

Bioscope shows and their engines.

Lingfield, Eng., Oakwood Press, 1966. 36p. illus. *Locomotion papers series.*

    Published to commemorate the 70th birthday of cinematography.

0045   GREGG, Eugene Stuart, 1892-

The shadow of sound.

New York, Vantage Press, 1968. 174p.

    Discusses many of the problems brought about by the introduction of sound into film-making and film acting.

0046   HALL, Ben M

The best remaining seats; the story of the golden age of the movie palace.

New York, C.N. Potter, 1961. 266p. illus.

    The story of the rise and fall of the giant American movie palaces, well illustrated with photographs, contemporary programmes, advertisements, etc.

0047   HOFMANN, Charles

Sounds for silents.

New York, DBS Publications, 1970. unpaged. illus.

    A history of the use of musical accompaniment for silent films. The illustrations include extracts from scores, and an appendix provides the complete score for an Edison Company short film, Rescued from an eagle's nest. With bibliography, and a sound recording made by the author of extracts from music for five silent films.

0048   MANCHEL, Frank.

When movies began to speak.

Englewood Cliffs, N.J., Prentice-Hall, 1969. 76p. illus.

*An introduction to the development of sound films,
intended for younger readers. Describes some titles in
which audio techniques were perfected.*

0049   SHARP, Dennis

The picture palace, and other buildings for the movies.

London, H. Evelyn, 1969. 224p. illus.

*Traces the development of buildings designed for film
exhibition, with emphasis on British cinemas. Includes
bibliography.*

0050   THOMAS, David Bowen

The first colour motion pictures.

London, H.M.S.O., 1969.

44p. illus. *Science Museum monographs.*

A brief history up to 1917.

0051   THRASHER, Frederick Milton, ed.

Okay for sound; how the screen found its voice.

New York, Duell, Sloan & Pierce, 1946. 303p. illus.

*A non-technical pictorial record of the development
and success of the sound motion picture. Arranged in three
parts:- Finding a voice.- Learning to talk.- Sounding the
future.*

Film history and production surveys of individual countries and regions

Arab countries

0052   ARAB CINEMA AND CULTURE.

        Beirut, 1962-4. 3v.

            *Round-table conferences under the auspices and with
            the participation of UNESCO.*

0053   HOLMES, Winifred, 1903-   comp.

        Orient; a survey of films produced in countries of Arab
        and Asian culture. Prepared by W. Holmes for the British
        Film Institute.

        London, British Film Institute, 1959. unpaged.

0054   LANDAU, Jacob M.

        Studies in the Arab theater and cinema.

        Philadelphia, University of Pennsylvania Press, 1958.

        290p. illus.

            *Part III (p. 155 - 202) deals with the Arab cinema,
            providing an historical outline of the subject, followed
            by notes on production, acting, and themes. With biblio-
            graphical references.*

0055   SADOUL, Georges, 1904-1967, ed.

        The cinema in the Arab countries; anthology prepared for
        UNESCO. Beirut, Interarab Centre of Cinema & Television, 1966
        290p. illus.

            With filmography.

Asia

HOLMES, Winifred, 1903-   comp.

> Orient; a survey of films produced in countries of Arab
>
> and Asian culture. Prepared by W. Holmes for the British
>
> Film Institute.
>
> London, British Film Institute, 1959. unpaged.

Australia

0056   BAXTER, John

> The Australian cinema.
>
> Sydney, Pacific Books, 1970. 118p. illus.
>
> *An introduction to Australian cinema and its*
>
> *problems.*

0057   PORTER, Hal.

> Stars of Australian stage and screen.
>
> Adelaide, Rigby, c1965. 304p. illus.
>
> *A broad survey of "those Australians who have left*
>
> *some mark, vivid or pallid, on the legitimate theatre*
>
> *and the film, and to indicate the fluctuating climate in these*
>
> *two areas from 1789 to the present." Includes a title listing*
>
> *of Australian films, with production dates. Indexed.*

Canada

BUCHANAN, Donald William, 1908-

> Documentary and educational films in Canada, 1935-1950;
>
> a survey of problems and achievements. Revised April 1952.
>
> Ottawa, Canadian Film Institute, 1952. 24p.
>
> *A pamphlet that includes notes on the National Film*
>
> *Board of Canada, Canadian Film Institute, Film Councils,*
>
> *etc.*

0058   MCKAY, Marjorie

History of the National Film Board of Canada.

Montreal, National Film Board of Canada, 1964.

147p.

Issued on the occasion of the 25th anniversary of the
founding of the National Film Board of Canada.

0059   MORRIS, Peter, ed.

Canadian feature films: 1913-1969; part I: 1913-1940.

Ottawa, Canadian Film Institute, 1970. 20p. illus.

Canadian filmography series.

Contents:- Chronological list of feature films:
1913-1940.- Non Canadian films adapted from original
Canadian sources or shot on location in Canada.- Index
to credits of Canadian feature films.- Alphabetical title
index. Main entries include credits, synopses, and
extracts from contemporary reviews. This uncompleted
work is an expanded and revised edition of the index
published in 1965 under the title: Canadian feature
films 1914-1964. Part II will cover the period 1941-1969.

0060   MORRIS, Peter, ed.

The National Film Board of Canada: the war years; a

collection of contemporary articles and a selected index

of productions.

Ottawa, Canadian Film Institute, 1965. 32p. *Canadian*

filmography series.

0061 PAQUET, André, ed.

How to make or not to make a Canadian film.

Montreal, Cinemateque candienne, 1968. unpaged. illus.

A brochure published on the occasion of retrospective of Canadian cinema, presented by La Cinemateque canadienne. Contents:- A chronology of film in Canada, 1898-1967.- The film makers speak.- One hundred essential films of Canadian cinema.

Czechoslovakia

0062 BROZ, Jaroslav, 1907-

The path of fame of the Czechoslovak film; a short outline of its history from the early beginning to the stream of recent international successes.

Prague, Ceskoslovensky Filmexport, 1967. 111p. illus.

A well illustrated booklet concentrating on Czech feature films with mention also of animated and puppet films.

0063 DEWEY, Langdon

Outline of Czechoslovakian cinema.

London, Informatics, 1971. 122p. illus.

A chronological survey of Czechoslovakian feature films from 1898 to 1970.

0064   MODERN CZECHOSLOVAK FILM: 1945-1965. Texts by Jaroslav Bocek
        and others.

        Prague, Artia, c1965. unpaged. illus.

            *Includes an introductory article by Bocek, a survey of
        Czechoslovakian films from 1945 to 1965 consisting of
        brief notes and stills from major films produced in each
        year of review and arranged in reverse chronological order,
        profiles of leading film directors, listings of films
        released between 1945 and 1964, and film periodicals
        published during the same period.*

0065   ZALMAN, Jan, *pseud.*

        Films and film-makers in Czechoslovakia.
        Prague, Orbis, 1968. 99p. illus.

            *A brief survey of contemporary Czech cinema, with
        particular reference to the work of seventeen directors.
        With filmographies.*

Denmark

0066   NEERAARD, Ebbe, 1901-1957.

        Documentary in Denmark; one hundred films of fact in
        war, occupation, liberation, peace, 1940-1948; a cat-
        alogue with synopses.

        Copenhagen, Statens Filmcentral, 1948.   89p.

0067   NEERGAARD, Ebbe, 1901-1957.

        The story of Danish film. With a preface by Carl Th.
        Dreyer, and an appendix, Danish feature films 1956-1962,
        by Erik Ulrichsen.

        Copenhagen, Det Danske Selskab, 1964? 117p.

Egypt

0068   KHAN, Mohamed.

An introduction to the Egyptian cinema.

London, Informatics, 1969. 93p. illus.

A brief survey of Egyptian films and film industry.
With filmographies. No index.

Europe

0069   HIBBIN, Nina

Eastern Europe; an illustrated guide.

London, Zwemmer, 1969. 239p. illus. *Screen series.*

An illustrated guide to directors, actors and others
involved in film-making in Albania, Bulgaria, Czechoslovakia,
East Germany, Hungary, Poland, Romania, U.S.S.R., and
Yugoslavia since the Second World War. A dictionary
arrangement is used for each country, prefaced by notes
about its film industry and production. A general
film title index to all films mentioned in the book is
included.

0070   MANVELL, Roger, 1909-

New cinema in Europe.

London, Studio Vista, c1966. 160p. illus. *Pictureback*
series.

A brief illustrated survey of post-War European feature
film-making, concentrating on Italy, France, Britain, Russia
and Poland, with a chapter devoted to Ingmar Bergman.

France

0071   ARMES, Roy

French cinema since 1946.

London, Zwemmer, 1966. 2v. illus. *International film guide series.*

A concise analysis and guide to twenty years of French cinema. Volume 1, The great tradition, examines the post-war work of 14 directors, from Claude Autant-Lara to Jacques Tati and includes a bibliography, filmography, and biography for each. The second volume, The personal style, considers 15 of the 'New wave' directors, from Alexandre Astruc to Agnes Varda, also including bibliographies, filmographies, and biographies.

0072   ARMES, Roy

French film

London, Studio Vista, 1970. 159p. illus.

A brief illustrated survey of the work of forty French film directors, from Lumiere to the nouvelle vague. With bibliography.

0073   DURGNAT, Raymond, 1932-

Nouvelle vague; the first decade.

Loughton, Eng., Motion Publications, 1963. 90p. illus.

An alphabetical survey, by director, of the French 'New Wave' cinema of the fifties and early sixties. Durgnat offers critical commentary on many of the films mentioned in each filmography. Includes bibliography, but has no title index.

0074   FOWLER, Roy Alexander

The film in France.

London, Pendulum, 1946. 56p. illus.

A brief survey of the French cinema during World War

II.

0075   GRAHAM, Peter John, 1939-   ed.

The new wave: critical landmarks.

London, Thames & Hudson, 1968. 184p. illus. *Cinema one*

series.

A collection of articles, mostly from Cahiers du cinema,

written between 1948 and 1962 by such writers as Bazin,

Chabrol, Godard, Truffaut, etc.

0076   REID, Tony

Innovators of the French cinema.

Ottawa, Canadian Film Institute, 1965. 25p.

A pamphlet intended for use with a film series presented

at the Canadian National Film Theatre and that discusses

directors such as Clair, Bresson, Delluc, Feuillade, Vigo, etc.

0077   SADOUL, Georges, 1904-1967

French film.

London, Falcon Press, 1953. 131p. illus. *National cinema*

series.

A history of the film in France from 1890 to 1950, relating

it to the political and economic conditions of the period.

Written by a leading French critic.

Germany

0078   BUCHER, Felix

Germany, by Felix Bucher in collaboration with Leonhard

H. Gmur.

London, Zwemmer, 1970. 298p. illus. *Screen series.*

An illustrated guide to the German cinema. The 431

main entries, arranged alphabetically, include all major

directors, actors, screenwriters, production companies

and technicians, each entry giving brief biographical

details and filmography. With film title index.

0079   EISNER, Lotte H

The haunted screen: expressionism in the German cinema

and the influence of Max Reinhardt.

London, Thames and Hudson, c1969. 360p. illus.

A new translation of the 1965 revised edition of

L'ecran demoniaque, concentrating on the important period

in the German cinema between 1913 and 1933. Includes

a selective filmography.

0080   HULL, David Stewart

Film in the Third Reich: a study of the German cinema,

1933-1945.

Berkeley, University of California Press, 1969. 291p. illus.

A chronological study of the films of the Nazi era,

with emphasis on the factual background to production

rather than pychological analysis. With bibliography.

0081   KRACAUER, Siegfried, 1889-

From Caligari to Hitler; a psychological history of the German film. Princeton, N.J., Princeton University Press, c1947. 361p. illus.

A standard work on the pre-War German cinema and its psychological implications, relating it to the contemporary social, political and economic conditions in Germany. With a detailed bibliography and an appendix examining the techniques of Nazi propaganda films.

0082   KRACAUER, Siegfried, 1889-

Propaganda and the Nazi war film.

New York, Museum of Modern Art Film Library, 1942. 90p.

0083   MANVELL, Roger, 1909-   and FRAENKEL, Heinrich, 1897-

The German cinema.

London, Dent, 1971. 159p. illus.

Includes bibliography.

0084   WOLLENBERG, Hans H.

Fifty years of German film.

London, Falcon Press, 1948. 48p. illus. *National cinema series.*

An account of German cinema, with emphasis on the period preceeding and during the Second World War, dealing with social implications of German film, as well as the technical and artistic achievements.

Great Britain

0085   BIRD, John H

            Cinema parade; fifty years of film shows.

            Birmingham, Eng., Cornish Brothers, 1947. 106p. illus.

                Largely deals with the life and work of the English

            showman and filmmaker Waller Jeffs, together with other

            subjects concerned with the early years of the cinema,

            particularly in England.

0086   BRITISH FILM AND TELEVISION YEARBOOK. 1946-

            London, British and American Press, etc. v. illus.

            Title varies: 1946-   The British film yearbook.

            Editor: 1946-   P. Noble.

                Early editions included articles on various aspects

            of the British cinema, with a biographical index of actors,

            writers, directors, technicians, etc. This latter feature

            forms the major part of later editions, together with

            information on the British film and television industry.

0087   THE BRITISH FILM ANNUAL. 1948-

            London, Amalgamated Press. v. illus. *annual.*

                Title Varires: 1948, Daily Mail Film award

            annual.

0088   DURGNAT, Raymond, 1932-

            A mirror for England; British movies from austerity to
            affluence.

            London, Faber, 1970. 336p. illus.

                "A survey of some major recurring themes in British

            movies between 1945... and 1958" (introd.) With detailed

            filmography, bibliography and indexes.

0089   FILM REVIEW.

London, Macdonald, 1944-   v. illus. *annual.*

This annual publication has been edited by F. Maurice Speed since its first edition in 1944. Each edition contains a pictorial survey of the year's releases in Britain, giving annotations, brief credits, and distribution information. More recent volumes have included additional notes on awards and festivals as well as articles on various aspects of the cinema.

0090   GIFFORD, Denis

British cinema: an illustrated guide.

London, Zwemmer, 1968. 176p. illus. *International film guide series.*

A reference book with entries for over 500 British film actors and directors, arranged alphabetically with a film title index. Entries include biographical data with chronological filmographies.

0091   HUNTLEY, John, 1921-

British Technicolor films.

London, Skelton Robinson, 1949. 224p. illus.

After a brief introduction to the colour film, the book presents brief essays on 25 British Technicolor films from 1936 to 1948, with notes on art direction, camera work, and colour design for each. An index provides full credits for each film discussed. Other chapters include Technicolor who's who, British Technicolor short films, Colour forum, Profile of Natalie Kalmus, and Technical abstracts.

KINEMATOGRAPH AND TELEVISION YEAR BOOK.

London, Longacre Press, 1914-   v. illus. *annual.*

First published in 1914 by the Kinematograph & Lantern Weekly under the title Kinematograph year book, diary and directory. This British equivalent of the International motion picture almanac provides directory-style information on the British film industry, and since 1961, television industry. provides detailed listings of cinemas in the United Kingdom, lists films released during the preceding year.

0092   LOW, Rachael.

The history of the British film.

London, Allen & Unwin, 1948- v. illus.

An important work covering the following periods:- 1896-1906 (vol.1).- 1906-1914 (vol. 2).- 1914-1918 (vol. 3).- 1918-1929 (vol. 4). Each volume deals with both the industry and the films produced during the period covered. The first volume was written with the collaboration of Roger Manvell. Volume 4 was published in 1971, twenty years after volume 3 was produced.

0093   MANVELL, Roger, 1909-

New cinema in Britain.

London, Studio Vista, 1969. 160p. illus. *Pictureback series.*

A short survey of post-war British cinema, illustrated with numerous stills.

MINNEY, Rubeigh James, 1895–

> Talking of films.

> London, Home & Van Thal, 1947. 80p.

0094   MORGAN, Guy.

> Red roses every night; an account of London cinemas under fire.

> London, Quality Press, 1948. 127p. illus.

> *A factual account of the activities of selected London cinemas during World War II and their difficulties in remaining open. An appendix lists British films shown between the outbreak of war and V.E. Day, arranged by date of release.*

0095   OAKLEY, Charles Allen.

> Where we came in: seventy years of the British film industry.

> London, Allen & Unwin, 1964. 245p. illus.

> *A concise history of the British film industry, written after it became apparent that the Low-Manvell work would not be completed in the form originally intended.*

0096   POWELL, Dilys

> Films since 1939.

> London, Published for the British Council by Longmans, Green, 1947. 40p. illus.

0097   TWENTY YEARS OF BRITISH FILM, 1925-1945, by Michael Balcon,

Ernest Lindgren, Forsyth Hardy and Roger Manvell.

London. Falcon Press, 1947. 96p. illus. *The National*

cinema series.

A survey of British cinema. Contents:- Introduction

by Michael Balcon.- The early feature film, by Ernest

Lindgren.- The British documentary film, by Forsyth Hardy.-

British feature film from 1925 to 1945, by Roger Manvell.

0098   WARREN, Low

The film game.

London, T. Werner Laurie, 1937. 235p. illus.

A personal account of cinema in Britain.

WOOD, Leslie

The miracle of the movies.

London, Burke, 1947. 352p. illus.

A personal history of the cinema, with emphasis on

British studios. Includes sections of the author's earlier

work The romance of the movies. No index.

0099   THE YEAR'S WORK IN THE FILM. 1949-

London, published for the British Council by Longmans, Green

v. illus. *annual.*

0100   NEMESKURTY, Istvan.

Word and image; history of the Hungarian cinema.

Budapest, Corvina Press, 1968. 245p. illus.

A chronological survey of Hungarian cinema from 1896

to the 1960s. An appendix lists Hungarian feature films

made between 1945 and 1966, with the names of the directors

and leading actors and actresses.

India

0101   BARNOUW, Erik, 1908-   <u>and</u>   KRISHNASWAMY, S

Indian film.

New York, Columbia University Press, 1963. 301p. illus.

A history of India's vast film industry. Includes

bibliography.

0102   CHATTERJEA, Bankim Chandra, ed.

Dipali year-book of motion pictures, 1943.

Calcutta, Dipali Granthashala, 1944. 150p. illus.

General information on the Indian film industry and

the films released in India in 1943.

0103   FAZALBHOY, Y. A.

The Indian film; a review.

Bombay, Bombay Radio Press, 1939. 127p. illus.

0104   SHAH, Panna

The Indian film.

Bombay, Motion Picture Society of India, 1950.

290p. illus.

Based on the author's thesis, A social study of the cinema

in Bombay. With bibliography.

30

0105   FIFTY YEARS OF ITALIAN CINEMA. Edited by Luigi Malerba and

Carmine Siniscalco. Editor of the American edition:

Herman G. Weinberg.

Rome, Bestetti, 1955. 75p. illus.

Introduced by Richard Griffith, this well-written

but brief survey of Italian film is arranged in three

parts, covering the periods 1904-1930, 1930-1942, 1942-1954.

With over 200 illustrations, but lacks index.

0106   JARRATT, Vernon.

The Italian cinema.

London, Falcon Press, 1951.

115p. illus. *National cinema series.*

An authoratative review of the Italian cinema, with

emphasis on the pre-war and wartime period. An appendix

lists Italian films directed from 1930-1948 by the leading

directors, while another details casts and credit lists for

some of the more important post-war films.

0107   RONDI, Gian Luigi

Italian cinema today, 1952 - 1965.

New York, Hill and Wang, 1966.

279p. illus.

A retrospective illustrated survey of Italian cinema

from 1952 to 1965. Arrangement is by director, in two sequences

from Antonioni to Zurlini and from Bellocchio to Wertmuller.

Indexed by actors, directors, film titles and producers.

0108   UNITALIA FILM.

          Italian directors.

          Rome, 1958. 203p. illus.

          An alphabetical, non-critical survey of the careers

          of Italian film producers. With filmographies.

0109   UNITALIA FILM

          Italian film production.

          Rome, 1963-   v. illus.   *annual.*

          An annual illustrated non-critical survey of Italian

          feature-length films released in the year prior to publication

          date. Each film receives a synopsis, credits, and stills.

Japan

0110   ANDERSON, Joseph L.   and   RICHIE, Donald, 1924-

          The Japanese film.

          New York, Grove Press, 1960. 456p. illus.

          A valuable work which traces the history and

          development of the Japanese cinema. The book is in two

          parts: Background, and Foreground. Background is

          arranged in chronological order, from 1896 - 1959.

          Foreground discusses content, technique, directors,

          actors, theatres and audiences. First published in 1959.

0111   CINEMA YEARBOOK OF JAPAN. 1936/1937-   By the International

          Cinema Association of Japan.

          Tokyo, Sandeido, 1937- v. illus.   *annual.*

          Annual survey of the Japanese film industry by the

          International Cinema Association of Japan. 1936/37 edition

          edited by Tadasi Iizima and others. 1938 edition published

          by the Society for International Relations. Text in English.

0112   JAPAN MOTION PICTURE ALMANAC, 1957. Compiled by Jiri

Tsushinsha. Tokyo, Promotion Council of Motion Picture

Industry of Japan, 1957. 1v. illus.

An illustrated survey and directory of the Japanese

film industry, with notes on Japanese films produced and

released in the previous year, as well as foreign films shown

in Japan.

0113   JAPANESE FILMS.

Tokyo, Association for the Diffusion of Japanese Films

Abroad.   v. illus.   *annual.*

First published in 1958, this annual consists of

synopses and stills from selected Japanese films produced

in the year of publication, together with listings of films

by production company, and brief industry statistical in-

formation.

0114   RICHIE, Donald, 1924-

The Japanese movie; an illustrated history.

Tokyo, Kodansha International, 1966.

200p. illus.

A pictorial history of Japanese cinema that also shows

how Japanese films reflect the social, philosophical and

artistic background of Japan.

0115   RICHIE, Donald, 1924-

Japanese movies.

Tokyo, Japan Travel Bureau, 1961. 198p. illus.

Concentrates on the qualities peculiar to Japanese films.

In three parts:- The origins of Japanese film style.- Con-

temporary Japanese film.- Form and content in the Japanese film

Fully indexed.

0116   SVENSSON, Arne

Japan.

London, Zwemmer, 1971. 189p. illus. *Screen series.*

A dictionary arrangement of Japanese directors, actors and films. With credits, filmographies, and synopses of plots for important productions. With film title index.

Netherlands

0117   BOOST, C

Dutch art today: film.

Amsterdam, Contact, 1958. 100p. illus.

"Commissioned by the Ministry of Education, Arts and Sciences." A brief history and survey of Dutch cinema, with the emphasis on documentary production. Contents:- Early history.- National film production.- The avant-garde.- Commissioned films.- After the war.- The younger generation. No index.

Pakistan

0118   KABIR, Alamgir, 1938-

The cinema in Pakistan.

Dacca, Sandhani Publications, 1969. 194p. illus.

0119   PAKISTAN. FILM FACT FINDING COMMITTEE.

Report of the Film Fact Finding Committee, Govt. of Pakistan, Ministry of Industries, April 1960-April 1961.

Karachi, Manager of Publications, 1962. 410p.

The report of the Government of Pakistan's enquiry into the film industry of that country. Extremely detailed.

Philippines

0120   SALUMBIDES, Vicente, 1893-

Motion pictures in the Philippines.

Manila, c1952. 144, 31, 62p. illus.

Poland

0121   CONTEMPORARY POLISH CINEMATOGRAPHY

Warsaw, Polonia Publishing House, 1962. 173p. illus.

Polish editor: Jerzy Chocilowski. Text written
by Wladyslaw Banaszkiewicz and others. An overall view
of cinema in Poland. Includes an historical survey of
Polish feature films produced between 1947 and 1961. No
index.

0122   HALLER, Robert

Film against the state: Polish motion pictures from
1956 to 1961.

Cambridge Springs, Pa., Alliance College Polish Club, 1966?
unpaged. illus.

0123   KOWALSKI, Tadeusz, ed.

The Polish film poster.

Warsaw, Filmowa Agencja Wydawnicza, 1957. 142p. illus.

A selection of the best Polish film posters from 1946 to
1956. Introductory text is in English, Russian, Polish, Frenc
and German. The illustrations which comprise the major part
of the book are reproduced in colour and black & white.

Scandinavia

0124   HARDY, Forsyth

Scandinavian film.

London, Falcon Press, 1952. 62p. illus. *National cinema*
series.

A brief survey of the Danish and Swedish cinema, with
mention of Norwegian films. Emphasis is on the early
sound period often neglected by other studies of the
Scandinavian cinema.

0125   COWIE, Peter

         Sweden, by Peter Cowie in collaboration with Arne Svensson.

         London, Zwemmer, 1970.

         2v. illus. *Screen series.*

         The first volume is an alphabetical survey of 170

         directors, actors, screenwriters, technicians, etc. with

         appropriate filmographies, together with synopses of 70

         major films. The index to film titles mentioned in the

         text is in both English and Swedish. The second volume

         consists largely of an expanded version of the author's

         earlier book, Swedish cinema, providing a survey and ass-

         essment of Swedish cinema, with a considerable portion of

         the book being devoted to Ingmar Bergman. Includes biblio-

         graphy.

0126   COWIE, Peter

         Swedish cinema

         London, Zwemmer, 1966. 224p. illus. *International*

         film guide series.

         Historical in approach, with emphasis on the work of

         Ingmar Bergman. With filmographies and bibliography.

         See also the author's Sweden.

0127   HOOD, Robin, pseud.

         Classics of the Swedish cinema; the Stiller & Sjöström

         period. With an introduction by Victor Sjöström.

         Stockholm, Swedish Institute, 1952. 48p. illus.

0128   LAURITZEN, Einar

        Swedish films.

        New York, Museum of Modern Art Film Library, 1962.

        32p. illus.

0129   SUNDGREN, Nils Petter, 1929-

        The new Swedish cinema.

        Stockholm, Swedish Institute for Cultural Relations with
Foreign Countries, 1970. 57p. illus.

           *A brief survey of Swedish cinema in the 1960s. With
bibliography.*

0130   WALDEKRANZ, Rune

        Swedish cinema. English version by Steve Hopkins.

        Stockholm, Swedish Institute, 1959. unpaged. illus.

           *A brief survey of the development of Swedish cinema
with emphasis on the work of Ingmar Bergman. Includes a
selected filmography.*

0131   WINQUIST, Sven G., 1924-   comp.

        Swedish silent pictures, 1896-1931, and their directors;
a checklist.

        Stockholm, Swedish Film Institute, 1967. 182p.

           *Alphabetical listing by Swedish title, with brief
credits and duration for each film, followed by listings
by director and in chronological order by date of production.
Text in Swedish and English but with very few film titles
given in English.*

0132   WINQUIST, Sven G., 1924-

Swedish sound pictures, 1929-66, and their directors;

a checklist.

Stockholm, Swedish Film Institute, 1967. 158p.

Alphabetical listing by Swedish title, noting production

company and director, followed by listing by director.

Introductory notes are in Swedish and English. The major

weakness   for non-Swedish users is the lack of references

from English language titles.

U. S. A.

0133   AMERICAN FILM INSTITUTE

The American Film Institute catalog of motion pictures

produced in the United States. Kenneth W. Munden, executive

editor.

New York, Bowker, 1971 -   v.

A major reference work on the American cinema. The first two

volumes to be published are subtitled Feature films, 1921-

1930. The first volume lists films alphabetically by title,

with identification and physical description, production

credits, cast credits, and description of contents for each.

The second volume provides a complete credit and subject index.

0134   BARBOUR, Alan G

A thousand and one delights.

New York, Collier Books, 1971. 164p. illus.

A nostalgic record of Hollywood films of the forties,

with emphasis on the escapist entertainment of that decade.

The book consists largely of stills with accompanying text.

0135   BAXTER, John

Hollywood in the thirties.

London, Zwemmer, 1968. 160p. illus. *International film guide series.*

Contents:- The fabulous legend.- The studios: Metro-Goldwyn-Mayer.- The studios: Paramount.- The studios: Warners.- Fantasy: universal and elsewhere.- The great originals:1.- The great originals:2.- Powers.- Reputations in eclipse. With index.

0136   THE BEST PICTURES...AND THE YEAR BOOK OF MOTION PICTURES IN AMERICA.

New York, Dodd, Mead, 1940- v. illus. annual.

Contains scenarios of selected films in synopsis form, with plot outlines for many others released in the year of review.

0137   BROWNLOW, Kevin

The parade's gone by.

New York, Knopf, 1968. 577p. illus.

One of the better books dealing with American silent cinema. Largely based on interviews with surviving filmmakers, actors and technicians, and written by a young British film director. Well illustrated.

0138   CROWTHER, Bosley.

The lion's share; the story of an entertainment empire.

New York, Dutton, 1957. 320p. illus.

The history of Metro-Goldwyn-Mayer, written by the former New York Times film critic. The narrative includes the lives not only of Loew, Goldwyn, and Mayer, but also the many stars and directors that contributed to the success of the Hollywood company.

0139   DAY, Beth (Feagles) 1924-

This was Hollywood: an affectionate history of filmland's golden years.

Garden City, N.Y., Doubleday, 1960. 287p. illus.

Reminiscences about the "golden years" of Hollywood.

0140   DE MILLE, William C

Hollywood saga.

New York, Dutton, 1939. 519p. illus.

Written by Cecil B. DeMille's brother, this is a largely autobiographical account of the early days of Hollywood.

DEMING, Barbara, 1917-

Running away from myself; a dream portrait of America drawn from the films of the forties.

New York, Grossman, 1969. 210p. illus.

A look at the way in which Hollywood films of the forties reflected the image of society, not as a mirror, but as in a dream: wish fulfilling and vicarious.

0141   EVERSON, William K

The American movie.

New York, Atheneum, 1963. 149p. illus.

A general introductory chronological survey of American film history.

0142   FERNETT, Gene

Next time drive off the cliff!

Cocoa, Fla., Cinememories, 1968.   205p. illus.

The story of Nat Levine, dubbed 'The king of the
serial makers' and of Mascot Pictures, an independent film
studio typical of many producing serials and 'B' pictures
during the 1930s.   Includes credits and synopses of
representative Mascot films.

0143   FILM DAILY YEAR BOOK OF MOTION PICTURES.

New York, Film and Television Daily, 1918-   v. illus.
annual.

A large annual which is an extremely useful reference wor
The exact title and publisher have changed since the first
edition in 1918.   A cumulative index of feature films released
in the United States since 1915 (33,000 titles in the 1969 ed.
gives sources of distribution and dates of reviews in the Film
daily.   Films produced during the year of review are listed wi
credits, and additional sections list recent work done by
editors, cameramen, directors, etc.   U.S. trade information i
included as well as a bibliography.

0144   FRANKLIN, Joe

Classics of the silent screen; a pictorial treasury.

New York, Citadel Press, c1959.   255p. illus.

Arranged in two parts:- Fifty great films.- Seventy-
five great stars.   Arrangement in the first part is
chronological; in the second part, alphabetical.   Brief
text, and limited in scope to the American cinema.

0145 GOODMAN, Ezra

    The fifty-year decline and fall of Hollywood.

    New York, Simon and Schuster, 1961. 465p.

     A personal account based on the author's twenty years

    in Hollywood.

0146 GOW, Gordon

    Hollywood in the fifties.

    New York, Barnes, 1971. 208p. illus. *International film*

    guide series.

     An account of the successes and failures of Hollywood

    in the 1950s, including the decline of the star system,

    the economic difficulties, new screen processes, etc.

0147 GREEN, Abel, 1900- and LAURIE, Joseph

    Show biz from vaude to video, by Abel Green and Joe Laurie,

    Jr.

    New York, Holt, 1951. 613p.

     A light-hearted survey of the highlights of show

    business from 1905 to 1950. A useful index makes this

    book of interest for its information about the American film

    industry. Contents:- Vaude socko (1905-1913).- War comes

    to show biz (1914-1918).- Big boom (1919-1929).- Big bust

    (1930-1932).- New deal (1933-1940).- Big show (1941-1945).-

    Video era (1946-195-)

0148 GRIFFITH, Richard, 1912-

    The movie stars.

    Garden City, N.Y., Doubleday, 1970. 498p. illus.

     An exploration into the causes of the star system

    and its decline.

0149   GRIFFITH, Richard, 1912-   and MAYER, Arthur, 1886-

The movies. Rev. ed.

New York, Simon and Schuster, 1970. 494p. illus.

The first edition of this large, lavishly illustrated historical survey of the American cinema had a descriptive sub-title:- The sixty-year story of the world of Hollywood and its effect on America, from pre-nickelodeon days to the present. The revised edition extends coverage to the films of the sixties. The general arrangment is chronological.

0150   HIGHAM, Charles, 1931-   and GREENBERG, Joel

Hollywood in the forties.

London, Zwemmer, 1968. 192p. illus. *International film guide series.*

Arrangement is by film genre, eg. melodrama, war propaganda, comedy, etc.

0151   INTERNATIONAL MOTION PICTURE ALMANAC.

New York, Quigley, 1929- v. illus. *annual.*

The first edition of this annual publication under the title The motion picture almanac was compiled and edited by the staff of Exhibitors Herald-World and published in 1929. The largest section was devoted to biographical data about actors, producers, directors, writers, executives, and others in product and distribution. Further sections dealt with various aspects of the American film industry. Films released in 1929 and the preceding few years were listed. The 42nd edition published in 1971 and edited by Richard Gertner contains greatly expanded listings. The film lists cover feature releases from 1955-1970, and emphasis in other sections is placed on directory-style information on the film industry.

0152   JACOBS, Lewis, 1906-

The rise of the American film: a critical history.

Reprinted with an essay: Experimental cinema in

America , 1921-1947.

New York, Teachers College Press, 1968. 631p. illus.

A standard work on the American cinema covering all

aspects of the industry and the films produced. Originally

published in 1939. Contents:- Fade-in (1896-1903).-

Foundations (1903-1908).- Development (1908-1914).- Transition

(1914-1918).- Intensification (1919-1929).- Maturity (1929-1939).

0153   JOBES, Gertrude.

Motion picture empire.

Hamden, Conn., Archon Books, 1966. 398p. illus.

A history of the American film industry. Contents:-

A trust is formed (1,000 B.C. to 1908).- The trust is smashed

(1908 to 1914).- America's fifth industry (1914 to 1918).-

Wall Street invasion (1918 to 1929).- America's fourth industry

(1929 to 1934).- On the heels of financial readjustment (1934

to 1965). With bibliography.

0154   LAHUE, Kalton C.

Dreams for sale; the rise and fall of the Triangle

Film Corporation.

South Brunswick, N.J., Barnes, 1971.

216p. illus.

The story of Harry Aitken and the Triangle Film

Corporation.

0155   LAHUE, Kalton C.   <u>and</u> BREWER, Terry.

Kops and custards; the legend of Keystone Films.

Norman, University of Oklahoma Press, 1968.

177p. illus.

A carefully researched history of the Keystone Film Company and the early work of Mack Sennett, with a valuable appendix which provides a complete listing of the Keystone comedies and their performers from 1912 to 1917.

0156   LEVIN, Martin, comp.

Hollywood and the great fan magazines.

New York, Arbor House, 1970. 224p. illus.

A collection of stories and articles from the American movie magazines of the 1930s, reprinted without commentary or analysis.

0157   MACCANN, Richard Dyer.

Hollywood in transition.

Boston, Houghton Mifflin, 1962. 208p.

Examines the state of the American film industry at the start of the 1960s through analysis and through interviews with producers, directors, writers and stars.

0158   MANVELL, Roger, 1909-

New cinema in the U.S.A.; the feature film since 1946.

London, Studio Vista, 1968. 160p. illus. *Pictureback series.*

The development and changes in the American feature film since 1946, illustrated with many stills. Chapter titles:- American cinema: world cinema.- New realism 1946.- The 1950s: background to the film industry.- The traditionalists The newer man.- The experimenters.- The new generation.

0159   MARLOWE, Don

The Hollywood that was.

Fort Worth, Tex., Branch-Smith, 1969.

189p. illus.

0160   MAYERSBERG, Paul.

Hollywood, the haunted house.

Harmondsworth, Eng., Penguin, 1969, c1967. 171p.

A book about Hollywood written by the British film

critic of 'New Society' and based largely on interviews

with directors such as Hitchcock, Brooks, Sturges, Kramer,

Cukor, and others. Discusses such topics as the economics

of American film production and the star system. Includes

a selective bibliography consisting mainly of fiction about

Hollywood and Los Angeles.

0161   MICHAEL, Paul.

The American movies reference book: the sound era.
Paul Michael, editor in chief; James Robert Parish,
Associate editor.

Englewood Cliffs, N.J., Prentice-Hall, 1969. 629p. illus.

Entries arranged under the following headings:- The

history.- The players.- The films.- The directors.- The

producers.- The awards. The information included is highly

selective and greatly varying in length and detail. With

bibliography.

0162   MORIN, Edgar.

The stars.

New York, Grove Press, 1961. 189p. illus.

An illustrated study of the evolution and significance

of the star system.

0163   MOTION PICTURE PRODUCTION ENCYCLOPEDIA. 1948-

Hollywood, Hollywood Reporter. v. illus.

A directory listing credits for the five years prior to year of publication for American actors, producers, directo writers, etc., followed by credits for films produced in the same period by title and by company. Includes American film industry information.

0164   NIVER, Kemp R., comp.

Biograph bulletins, 1896-1908. Edited by Bebe Bergsten. Los Angeles, Locare Research Group, c1971. 464p. illus.

A collection of handbills and bulletins issued by the American Mutoscope and Biograph Company. This limited edition includes an alphabetical list of films mentioned, with name of cameraman, date of photography, and date of copyright. A further index of cameramen is supplied.

0165   NIVER, Kemp R.

The first twenty years: a segment of film history. Edited by Bebe Bergsten. Los Angeles, Locare Research Group, 1968. 176p. illus.

An illustrated description of over 100 films copyrighted between 1894 and 1922, and selected from the Library of Congress paper print collection.

0166   NIVER, Kemp R.

Motion pictures from the Library of Congress paper
print collection, 1894-1912. Edited by Bebe Bergsten.
University of California Press, 1967. 402p.

*An annotated guide to the three thousand film titles
restored from the Library of Congress paper print collection.
Information given includes producer, copyright date, length,
synopsis, distinguishing features, and, where possible,
director and cast. Film entries are arranged by categories,
with subject and title indexes.*

0167   QUIGLEY, Martin, 1917-   and GERTNER, Richard.

Films in America, 1929-1969.

New York, Golden Press, 1970. 379p. illus.

*Brief notes, with abbreviated credits and stills for
nearly 400 films representative of the development of
cinema in the United States, arranged by year of release.
Includes significant foreign films.*

0168   RIDEOUT, Eric H.

The American film.

London, Mitre Press, 1937.

163p. illus.

With bibliography.

0169   RIVKIN, Allen, 1903-   and KERR, Laura, *comps.*

Hello Hollywood. A book about the movies by the people who
make them.

New York, Doubleday, 1962. 571p.

*An anthology representing one hundred writers concerning
all aspects of Hollywood.*

0170 ROBINSON, David, 1915-

    Hollywood in the twenties.

    London, Zwemmer, 1968.

    176p. illus. *International film guide series.*

    An illustrated survey of the most significant and most representative work of the period. Entries are usually brief.

0171 ROSENBERG, Bernard, 1923- <u>and</u> SILVERSTEIN, Harry

    The real tinsel.

    New York, Macmillan, 1970. 436p. illus.

    Reminiscences of Hollywood pioneers, arranged under the following headings:- The executive.- The publicity director.- The player.- The stuntman.- The voice animator.- The director.- The cameraman.- The sound director.- The music director.- The writ .- The critic.

0172 SARRIS, Andrew

    The American cinema; directors and directions, 1929-1968.

    New York, Dutton, 1968. 383p.

    The author, currently film critic of the Village Voice, discusses in brief the work of 200 directors. A directorial chronology lists the major American films produced between 1915 and 1967. A directorial index compiled by Michael Schwartz and James R. Prickett lists the films mentioned in the book together with numerous others, giving date of production and name of director for each.

0173   SCREEN WORLD. 1949-

New York, Greenberg, etc. v. illus. *annual.*

Publisher varies. Editor: 1949-1965: D. Blum: 1966-

: J. Willis.

The American equivalent to Film review, detailing films

released in the United States during the year covered with

detailed credits and a comprehensive index.

0174   SELDES, Gilbert Vivian, 1893-

Movies for the millions: an account of motion pictures,

principally in America.

London, Batsford, 1937. 120p. illus.

An historical survey of the American cinema - both art

and industry - to the mid-1930s. Includes 130 well-chosen

illustrations. The American edition has the title: The movies

come from America.

0175   SENNETT, Ted

Warner Brothers presents: the most exciting years,

from The jazz singer to White heat.

New Rochelle, N.Y., Arlington House, 1971. 428p. illus.

Memories of Warner Brothers' films of the thirties and

forties. Includes a filmography with brief entries for films

released in the period by Warner Brothers and First National.

0176   SLIDE, Anthony

Early American cinema, by Anthony Slide with the assistance of Paul O'Dell.

New York, Barnes, 1970. 192p. illus. *International film guide series.*

Contents:- The beginnings: Edison and Lubin.- The Vitagraph Company.- The Kalem Company.- The Essanay Company.- The independents.- American Biograph and Griffith.- Comedy and Keystone.- Pearl White and the serial queens.- Conclusion.- Select bibliography.

0177   TAYLOR, Deems, 1885-   <u>and</u> others

A pictorial history of the movies, by Deems Taylor, Marcelene Peterson and Bryant Hale. Rev. and enlarged.

New York, Simon & Schuster, 1950. 376p. illus.

Contents:- Birth and infancy (1893-1914).- Griffith turns a page (1915-1919).- The twenties (1920-1927).- Comes the revolution (1927-1928).- The talking picture (1929-1949). Consists of illustrations with brief textual commentary.

Limited in scope to the American film.

0178   VREELAND, Frank

Foremost films of 1938; a yearbook of the American screen.

New York, Pitman, 1939. 347p. illus.

Includes a survey of the year's film production, awards, etc., and excerpts from the following screenplays:- Wells Fargo.- Snow White and the seven dwarfs.- The buccaneer.- In old Chicago.- Algiers.- Love finds Andy Hardy.- You can't take it with you.- The citadel.- The young in heart.- That certain age.

U. S. S. R.

0179   BASKAKOV, Vladimir

Soviet cinema; a brief essay.

Moscow, Novosti Press Agency Publishing House, n.d. 22p.

with 32p. of photographs.

An essay on the origins and main stages of the

Soviet cinema.

0180   DICKINSON, Thorold and DE LA ROCHE, Catherine

Soviet cinema.

London, Falcon Press, 1948. 136p. illus. *National*

cinema series.

Consists of two essays:- The silent film in Russia,

by Thorold Dickinson, and The Soviet sound film, by

Catherine De La Roche. Appendices include synopses of

Eisenstein's films October, and Old and new. With an

introduction by Roger Manvell.

0181   EISENSTEIN, Sergei Mikhailovich, 1898-1948.

The Soviet screen.

Moscow, Foreign Languages Publishing House, 1939.

39p. illus.

0182   LEYDA, Jay, 1910-

Kino: a history of the Russian and Soviet film.

London, Allen & Unwin, 1960. 493p. illus.

A comprehensive well documented account of the film

in Russia from 1896 to 1947, with a postscript covering

the period from 1948 to 1958. Appendices include 'Fifty years

of Russian and Soviet films, 1908-1958; a select list' and

a detailed list of sources.

0183   MARSHALL, Herbert.

Soviet cinema.

London, Russia Today Society, 1945. 40p. illus.

A booklet surveying the Russian film industry, with emphasis on the war years.

0184   THE SOVIET CINEMATOGRAPHY.

Bombay, People's Publishing House, 1950. 244p.

An anthology, mostly of articles from Soviet sources.

0185   SOVIET FILMS, 1938-1939.

Moscow, State Publishing House for Cinema Literature, 1939. 124p. illus.

Text by V. Fink. Edited by M. Borodin and others. With a foreword by Sergei Eisenstein. A photographic survey of the period covered. Also includes information on the All-Union State Cinema Institute film school.

AESTHETICS AND CRITICISM

Aesthetics of the film

0186   ADLER, Mortimer J.

Art and prudence; a study in practical philosophy.

New York, Longmans, Green, 1937. 686p.

Examines "the problem of the moral and political criticism of the fine arts, occasioned by the conflict in operation of two practical virtues: prudence and art". Arranged in four sections:- Poetry and politics.- The motion picture as popular poetry.- Science and prudence, prudence and art.- Cinematics.

0187   ARNHEIM, Rudolf

Film as art.

London, Faber, 1958. 194p. illus.

A revised and expanded version of Arnheim's earlier book. Film, consisting of essays written between 1933 and 1938. A classic work in film aesthetics.

0188   BALAZS, Bela

Theory of the film; character and growth of a new art.

London, Dobson, 1952. 291p. illus.

A clearly written book on film art and theory by a fine critic and film theorist. Most of his examples are drawn from Soviet silent films.

0189   BAZIN, Andre, 1918-1958

What is cinema?

Berkeley, University of California Press, c1967. 183p.

Ten essays exploring the history, aesthetics, philosophy, and techniques of the film, selected and translated from the original four volume work published in French. Bazin was co-editor of the influential journal Cahiers du cinema.

0190   DURGNAT, Raymond, 1932-

Films and feelings.

Cambridge, Mass., M.I.T. Press, c1967. 288p. illus.

Originally published, in part, in the journal Films and filming. It considers style and content, the connection between cinema entertainment and film realism, aesthetics and popular responses, and cinematic poetry in commercial films. Includes bibliography.

0191   EISENSTEIN, Sergei Mikhailovich, 1898-1948

Film essays, with a lecture. Edited by Jay Leyda.

London, Dobson, 1968. 220p. illus.

Contents:- A personal statement.- The method of making workers' films.- Soviet cinema.- The new language of cinema.- Perspectives.- The dynamic square.- GTK-GIK-VGIK past, present, future.- Lessons from literature.- The embodiment of a myth.- More thoughts on structure.- Charlie The Kid.- Mr. Lincoln by Mr. Ford.- A close-up view.- Problems of composition. The book also includes a list of Eisenstein's published writings (1922-1964) with notes on their English translations.

0192   EISENSTEIN, Sergei Mikhailovich, 1898-1948

Film form; essays in film theory.

New York, Harcourt, Brace, c1949. 279p. illus.

A standard work, edited and translated by Jay Leyda, on a more popular level than the author's The film sense. Consists of essays written between 1928 and 1945 on aesthetics and form, with emphasis on the sound film.

0193   EISENSTEIN, Sergei Mikhailovich, 1898-1948

The film sense.

London, Faber, 1948. New ed. 228p. illus.

A study of film aesthetics on an advanced level, edited and translated by Jay Leyda. First published in 1942, the revised edition includes sequences from Strike, Que viva Mexico, and the projected An American tragedy, Sutter's gold, and Ferghana Canal. An appendix, The work of Eisenstein (1920-1947) and a bibliography add to the importance of this work.

0194   EISENSTEIN, Sergei Mikhailovich, 1898-1948

Notes of a film director.

Moscow, Foreign Languages Publishing House, 1947?

207p. illus.

A collection of articles written between 1932

and 1947, compiled and edited by R. Yurenev. Includes

a final section of Eisenstein's drawings and sketches.

Republished by Dover Press in 1970.

0195   GESSNER, Robert, 1907-

The moving image; a guide to cinematic literacy.

New York, Dutton, 1968. 444p. illus.

"The aim of this book is to discover the unique

patterns and structures that, through the visualization of

ideas and emotions, make cinema art." (pref.) The theme is

illustrated by extracts from film scripts comprising a

cross-section of screen writing. Appendices include a

bibliography and a glossary.

0196   HUGHES, Robert, ed.

Film, book 1: The audience and the filmmaker.

New York, Grove Press, 1959. 158p. illus.

An anthology of articles by critics and film-makers,

and the responses to a questionnaire answered by such names

as Bunuel, Clement, Kazan, Lean, Sidney Meyers and Satyajit

Ray.

0197   HUSS, Roy Gerard, 1927- and SILVERSTEIN, Norman

The film experience; elements of motion picture art.

New York, Harper & Row, 1968. 172p. illus.

An introductory manual on the theory of film art,

production, and direction. With bibliography.

56

0198   JACOBS, Lewis 1906-   ed.

Introduction to the art of the movies; an anthology of ideas

the nature of movie art, selected, arranged and introduced by

Lewis Jacobs.

New York, Noonday Press, c1960. 302p. illus.

A selection of 36 articles from American journals betwee

the years 1910 and 1960, presented chronologically.

0199   JACOBS, Lewis, 1906-   ed.

The movies as medium.

New York, Farrar, Straus and Giroux, 1970. 335p. illus.

Presents directors' aims and attitudes, with essays

on topics such as time and space, colour, sound, image,

movement, etc. With bibliography.

0200   KRACAUER, Siegfried, 1889-

Theory of film: the redemption of physical reality.

New York, Oxford University Press, 1960. 364p.

A complex study of theory and aesthetics of the film.

Includes bibliography. Also published in England under the

title Nature of film.

0201   LAWSON, John Howard, 1895-

Film: the creative process; the search for an audio-visual

language and structure. 2d ed.

New York, Hill and Wang, 1967. 380p. illus.

Divided into five parts: The silent film.- The world

of sound.- Language.- Theory.- Structure. Tends to be

nostalgic about the films between the first and second

World Wars.

0202   LINDEN, George William, 1928-

              Reflections on the screen.

              Belmont, Cal., Wadsworth, 1970. 297p. illus.

                  A book of film theory and aesthetics. With bibliography.

0203   LINDGREN, Ernest.

              The art of the film. 2d ed.

              London, Allen & Unwin, 1963. 258p. illus.

                  A revised enlarged edition of the work first published

              in 1948. In three sections: Mechanics.- Technique.- Criticism.

              An excellent introduction to film aesthetics, appreciation,

              and criticism, the major section dealing with film technique.

0204   MACCANN, Richard Dyer, ed.

              Film; a montage of theories.

              New York, Dutton, 1966. 384p. illus.

                  42 film makers and critics from Eisenstein to Fellini

              discuss the art and theory of film.

0205   MARCUS, Fred Harold, 1921-   ed.

              Film and literature: contrasts in media.

              Scranton, Chandler, 1971. 283p. illus.

                  An anthology in two parts:- The art of the film.-

              From words to visual images. The first part presents

              the language of film and offers historical perspective.

              The second part centers on contrasts between films and

              their literary sources. With filmography.

0206   NILSEN, Vladimir S.

The cinema as a graphic art: on a theory of representation in the cinema. With an appreciation by S.M. Eisenstein. Translation by Stephen Garry, with editorial advice from Ivor Montagu.

London, Newnes, 1936. 227p. illus.

An exposition on the creative uses of the camera and the dynamics of composition.

0207   NIZHNY, Vladimir B.

Lessons with Eisenstein. Translated and edited by Ivor Montagu and Jay Leyda.

London, Allen & Unwin, 1962. 182p. illus.

A full account of Eisenstein's class discussions held at the State Institute of Cinematography in Moscow, written by one of his pupils. Illustrations include blackboard diagrams used in the classes. Principle contents:- Directoria solution.- Mise-en-scene.- Break-up into shots.- Mise-en-shot.

0208   PUDOVKIN, Vsevolod Illarionovich, 1893-1953.

Film technique and Film acting. Memorial ed.

London, Vision Press, 1958. 388p. illus.

Two classic works by the Russian director, translated and edited by Ivor Montagu. Pudovkin on film technique was first published in English in 1937. Both works were developed from lectures delivered at the State Institute of Cinematography in Moscow.

RHODE, Eric, 1934-

Tower of Babel; speculations on the cinema.

London, Weidenfeld & Nicolson, 1966. 214p.

International in scope, this book includes chapters on outstanding directors. It attempts to show how the cinema can become an art by investigating the director's visions and relating their particular insights to some general view of the world. Bresson, Eisenstein, Jennings, Fellini, Resnais, and Wajda are among those discussed.

0209   SPOTTISWOODE, Raymond, 1913-

A grammar of the film; an analysis of film technique.

Berkeley, University of California Press, 1950. 328p. illus.

An attempt to isolate the fundamental principles of film art, that constitutes an advanced theoretical study of film technique. A reprint of the work first published in 1935 with a new preface.

0210   STEPHENSON, Ralph   and DEBRIX, Jean R., 1906-

The cinema as art. Rev. ed.

London, Penguin Books, 1969. 270p. illus.

An introduction to the language of the film, intended as a basis for criticism and a better understanding of film technique.

0211   WHITAKER, Rod

The language of film.

Englewood Cliffs, N. J., Prentice Hall, 1970.

178p. illus.

The book attempts "to trace the linguistic and mech-anical development of the medium; to describe the content implications of image and sound; to suggest the contributions of editing and montage; to examine the cohesive envelopes of plot, theme, narrative organization, and histrionics; to deal with the role of meaning in the modern film; and, finally, to take an overview of the nonlinguistic modes of the avant-garde and the underground." (Appogiatura)

0212   WOLLEN, Peter

Signs and meaning in the cinema.

London, Secker & Warburg in association with the British Film Institute, 1969. 168p. illus. *Cinema one series.*

A scholarly examination of film aesthetics, arranged in three sections:- Eisenstein's aesthetics.- The auteur theory.- The semiology of the cinema.

0213   WOLLEN, Peter, ed.

Working papers on the cinema: sociology and semiology.

London, British Film Institute, 1969. 36p.

Cover title.

0214   ADLER, Renata

A year in the dark; journal of a film critic, 1968-69.

New York, Random House, 1969. 354p.

A collection of reviews and essays written by the author for the New York Times between January 1968 and March 1969. No index.

0215   AGATE, James Evershed, 1877-1947

Around cinemas.

London, Home & Van Thal, 1946. 280p. front.

A collection of articles and essays on the cinema, written by the respected film and drama critic between 1921 and 1945, arranged chronologically and indexed.

0216   AGATE, James Evershed, 1877-1947

Around cinemas, second series.

London, Home & Van Thal, 1948. 284p. front.

A further collection of film essays, written between 1928 and 1946, with indexes.

0217   AGEE, James, 1909-1955

Agee on film.

London, P. Owen, 1963-65. 2 v. illus.

v. 1. Reviews and comments. Includes the articles Agee wrote for The Nation, between 1942 and 1948, together with examples from the Time reviews written between 1941 and 1948, and two essays written for Life. 432p.

v. 2. Five film scripts. Contains Noa Noa, The African Queen, The night of the hunter, The bride comes to Yellow Sky, and The blue hotel. 448p.

0218

ALPERT, Hollis, 1916-

The dreams and the dreamers: adventures of ·a professional
movie goer.

New York, Macmillan, 1962. 258p.

*Critical essays on post-war cinema. Examines the
careers of stars, directors, producers, writers, such as
Bergman, Brando, Fellini, Hitchcock, Monroe, etc.*

0219

ALTSHULER, Thelma C.   and JANARO, Richard Paul

Responses to drama; an introduction to plays and
movies.

Boston, Houghton Mifflin, 1967. 351p. illus.

*Intended to assist a critical approach to drama and
the cinema.*

0220

BELLONE, Julius, ed.

Renaissance of the film.

New York, Collier Books, 1970. 366p. illus.

*A critical anthology with emphasis on the international
cinema as exemplified by such directors as Bergman, Godard,
Fellini, Welles, Truffaut, etc.*

0221

BENNETT, Alfred Gordon

Cinemania; aspects of filmic creation.

London, Jarrolds, 1937. 432p. illus.

*A book of, and about, film criticism. With biblio-
graphy and index.*

0222

BRITISH FILM INSTITUTE, LONDON.

The elements of film criticism.

London, 1944. 27p.

*A simple introduction to film appreciation, with
additional notes by five English film critics.*

0223   CASTY, Alan

The dramatic art of the film.

New York, Harper & Row, 1971. 192p. illus.

"An attempt to place the motion picture among the dramatic arts without in any way diminishing its equally significant distinctions" (pref). The author explains the basic elements of film art.

0224   COOKE, Alistair, ed.

Garbo and the night watchmen; a selection from the writings of British and American film critics.

London, Cape, 1937. 352p.

An anthology of good film criticism, mostly from the mid-thirties. In addition to the editor, the critics include Cecilia Ager, Otis Ferguson, Robert Forsythe, Graham Greene, Don Herold, Robert Herring, Meyer Levin, and John Marks. Different styles and approaches to film criticism are illustrated by the criticisms of Chaplin's Modern times *by all of the above.*

0225   CRIST, Judith

The private eye, the cowboy, and the very naked girl; movies from Cleo to Clyde.

Chicago, Holt, Rinehart & Winston, 1968. 292p.

Collected criticism and reviews written by Miss Crist between 1963 and 1967 for the New York Herald Tribune.

0226   CROWTHER, Bosley

The great films; fifty golden years of motion pictures.
New York, Putnam, 1967. 258p. illus.

Analytical studies of fifty significant films,
ranging from Birth of a Nation (1916) to Ulysses (1967).
Includes credits, together with a supplementary list of
one hundred distinguished films.

0227   DOYLE, George Ralph

Twenty-five years of films: reminiscences and reflections
of a critic.
London, Mitre Press, 1936. 269p. illus.

Reminiscences written in a generally light-
hearted style on many aspects of the cinema. Includes the
writer's comments on a hundred notable films. With a fore-
word by Alexander Korda.

0228   FARBER, Manny

Negative space: Manny Farber on the movies.
New York, Praeger, 1971. 288p.

A collection of Farber's highly personal critical
writings.

0229   FILM. 1967/68-

N. Y., Simon & Schuster.   v. *annual.*

"An anthology by the National Society of Film Critics."
Consists of reviews by members of the National Society of
Film Critics of films released during the year covered.
Often more than one review of a film is included.

0230   FISCHER, Edward

The screen arts; a guide to film and television appreciation. New York, Sheed and Ward, 1960. 184p.

A guide to critical appreciation through the understanding of the techniques and aesthetics of film. The appendix includes hints on forming film study groups.

0231   FRIEDLANDER, Madeline S

Leading film discussions; a handbook for discussion leaders to use films effectively to conduct film discussion workshops.
New York, League of Women Voters of the City of New York, 1963. 59p.

0232   GETLEIN, Frank   <u>and</u> GARDINER, Harold Charles, 1904-
Movies, morals and art.
New York, Sheed and Ward, 1961. 179p.

Contents:- The art of the movie, by F. Getlein.- Moral evaluation of the films, by H.C. Gardiner. The latter part of the book by Father Gardiner offers a Catholic approach to film evaluation.

0233   JONES, George William
Sunday night at the movies.
Richmond, Va., John Knox Press, 1967.
127p. illus.

Discusses the involvement of the church in film criticism. Provides hints on running film discussion groups. With filmography and bibliography.

0234   KAEL, Pauline.

Going steady.

Boston, Little, Brown, 1970. 304p.

A further collection of the author's film criticism originally published in the New Yorker between January 1968 and March 1969.

0235   KAEL, Pauline.

I lost it at the movies.

Boston, Little, Brown, c1965. 365p.

A collection of the author's film reviews and articles on film from the period 1961-1963.

0236   KAEL, Pauline.

Kiss kiss bang bang.

Boston, Little, Brown, c1968. 404p.

A further collection of film articles and reviews, mostly from the period 1965-1967, together with a selection of notes on 280 movies "from Adam's rib to Zazie," selected from the author's writings of the previous 15 years.

0237   KATZ, John Stuart, ed.

Perspectives on the study of film.

Boston, Little, Brown, 1971. 339p. illus.

Brings together articles dealing with the film medium and study, arranged under the following headings:- Film study and education.- The film as art and humanities.- The film as communications, environment and politics.- Curriculum design and evaluation in film study.

KAUFFMANN, Stanley, 1916-

Figures of light; film criticism and comment. New York,

Harper & Row, 1971. 296p.

A collection of Kauffmann's film criticism and reviews

covering the period 1967 to 1970, arranged chronologically.

Most items were written for The New Republic.

0239 KAUFFMANN, Stanley, 1916-

A world on film; criticism and comment.

New York, Dell, 1966. 437p.

A collection of criticism and articles written between

1958 and 1965 for The New Republic. Includes a report on

film-making in Europe and a chapter on the new generation of

film goers and underground film-makers.

0240 KELLER, Hans Heinrich, 1919-

The need for competent film music criticism; a pam-

phlet for those who care for film as art, with a final

section for those who do not.

London, British Film Institute, 1947. 22p.

0241 LEJEUNE, Caroline Alice, 1897-

Chestnuts in her lap, 1936-1946.

London, Phoenix House, 1947. 192p.

An important collection of reviews written by the author

between 1936 and 1946 for The Observer, arranged chronologically.

0242 LIMBACHER, James L.

The movies before 1920; a guide to the study of the

history and appreciation of the motion picture.

Dearborn, Mich., 1965. 57 leaves.

0243   LIMBACHER, James L., ed.

Using films; a handbook for the program planner.

New York, Educational Film Library Association, 1967.

130p.

0244   MACDONALD, Dwight.

Dwight MacDonald on movies.

Englewood Cliffs, Prentice-Hall, 1969. 492p.

Selections from the writings of an outstanding film critic.

0245   McGUIRE, Jeremiah C

Cinema and value philosophy.

New York, Philosophical Library, 1968. 91p.

0246   MINTON, Eric, comp.

Film reviews.

Ottawa, 1969. unpaged. illus.

A collection of reviews of silent films from 1920. "The American material is drawn from a detailed two-volume work on film history... Canadian material is from the files of the Ottawa Journal." (Introd.)

0247   THE NEW YORK TIMES FILM REVIEWS, 1913-

New York, The New York Times, 1970-   v. illus.

The main part of this major reference work is in six volumes and comprises more than 16000 film reviews originally published in The New York Times between 1913 and 1968. Arrangement is chronological, with an index, addenda, lists of awards, and nearly 2000 portraits of film stars included in the sixth volume. A seventh volume covers the period 1969 to 1970, and further volumes are promised.

0248   PECHTER, William S., 1936-

Twenty-four times a second: films and film- makers.

New York, Harper & Row, 1971. 324p.

A collection of the author's film criticism written between 1960 and 1970, arranged under the following headings:- Practice.- Films.- Film-makers.- Spectators.- Theory.

PRATT, George C., ed.

Spellbound in darkness; readings in the history and **criticism of the silent film.**

Rochester, N.Y., School of Liberal and Applied Studies, University of Rochester, c1966. 2v. (452p.)

A collection of reviews, articles, and other writings about the silent film era gleaned from contemporary publications. The emphasis is on American cinema.

0249   PRICE, Ira

A hundred million moviegoers must be right; an aid to movie appreciation. With a chapter on comedy by Charles F. Riesner.

Cleveland, Ohio, Movie Appreciation Press, c1938.

178p. illus.

0250   REED, Rex

Big screen, little screen.

New York, Macmillan, 1971. 433p.

Television and film reviews and commentaries written for Women's wear daily, Holiday, and The New York times between 1968 and 1970.

0251   REED, Stanley

A guide to good viewing.

London, Educational Supply Association, 1961.

122p. illus.

Intended for young readers as an aid to discriminating between good and bad films and television programmes.

0252   SARRIS, Andrew

Confessions of a cultist; on the cinema, 1955-1969.

New York, Simon & Schuster, 1970. 480p.

A selection of Sarris' critical writings, mostly from the Village Voice, arranged chronologically.

0253   SARRIS, Andrew, comp.

The film.

Indianapolis, Bobbs-Merrill, c1968. 64p.

A collection of film criticism intended for discussion. arranged under the following headings:- American directors : Stanley Kubrick, Elia Kazan and Jerry Lewis.- French director Francois Truffaut, Robert Bresson, The new wave.- Italian directors: Michelangelo Antonioni and Federico Fellini.

0254   SHOTS IN THE DARK: A COLLECTION OF REVIEWERS' OPINIONS OF SOME OF THE LEADING FILMS RELEASED BETWEEN JANUARY 1949 AND FEBRUARY 1 Edited by Edgar Anstey, Roger Manvell, Ernest Lindgren, Paul Rotha, assisted by Gitta Blumenthal, for the British branch of The International Federation of Film Critics.

London, A. Wingate, 1951. 268p. illus.

A representative collection of British film criticism cove the work of 27 critics. Reviews of 55 films released in Englar between January 1949 and February 1951 are included. No index.

0255   SIMON, John Ivan

Acid test. Introduction By Dwight Macdonald.

New York, Stein and Day, 1963. 288p.

Discusses films by Billy Wilder, Bergman, Antonioni and Dassin, with other collected articles on the cinema, theatre, and poetry.

0256   SIMON, John Ivan

Movies into film; film criticism 1967-1970.

New York, Dial Press, 1971. 448p.

Collected film criticism mostly written by the author for The new leader. Covers such topics as politics and society, sex, young directors, pseudo-art, etc.

0257   SIMON, John Ivan

Private screenings.

New York, Macmillan, 1967. 316p.

Collected criticism from the author's reviews for The new leader between 1963 and 1966, together with four specially written essays.

0258   SONTAG, Susan, 1933-

Against interpretation, and other essays.

New York, Farrar, Straus & Giroux, 1966. 304p.

Collected critical essays on such topics as Bresson, Godard, Resnais, Jack Smith, science fiction films, and the novel versus the film, among other non-film writings.

0259   SONTAG, Susan, 1933-

Styles of radical will.

New York, Farrar, Straus, & Giroux, 1969, c1968. 274p.

Among non-film essays, this collection includes articles on Godard, theatre and film, and Ingmar Bergman's Persona.

0260   STERNER, Alice P.   and BOWDEN, William Paul, 1907-

Course in motion-picture appreciation. Produced with the co-
operation of the Finer Films Federation of New Jersey.

Newark, N.J., Education and Recreational Guides, c1937 61p.

Topics covered include history, motion-picture vocabulary,
story, acting, direction, sets, sound and music, value of motio
pictures, etc.

0261   TYLER, Parker

Classics of the foreign film; a pictorial treasury.

New York, Citadel Press, 1962. 253p. illus.

Well written commentaries on 75 outstanding films
produced outside the United States, ranging from The Cabinet
of Dr. Caligari (1919) to La Notte (1961). With many stills.

0262   TYLER, Parker

Sex, psyche, etcetera in the film.

New York, Horizon Press, 1969. 239p.

Critical writings arranged in four parts:- Sex ritual
.- The modern psyche.- The artist in crisis.- Film aesthetics,
pro and con.

0263   TYLER, Parker

The three faces of the film: the art, the dream, the cult.

New and revised edition.

South Brunswick, N.J., Barnes, 1967. 141p. illus.

Originally published in 1960, this book tries to
illustrate the abstract meanings, often Freudian, behind
films. Arranged in three sections:- The art: more or less
fine.- The dream: more or less mythical.- The cult: more or
less refined.

0264   TYNAN, Kenneth, 1927-

Tynan right and left: plays, films, people, places and events.
London, Longmans, 1967. 479p.

*A collection of critical writings, featuring a number
of Tynan's film reviews and articles on film-makers, including*

0265   WARSHOW, Robert, 1917-1955.

The immediate experience; movies, comics, theatre &
other aspects of popular culture.
Garden City, N.Y., Doubleday, 1962. 282p.

*The second half of the book contains a collection of
Warshow's major filmic essays under the headings American
popular culture, American movies, Charles Chaplin, and The
art film.*

0266   WEINBERG, Herman G., 1908-

Saint cinema; selected writings, 1929-1970.
New York, DBS Publications, 1970. 354p.

*A collection of film criticism by a distinguished
film writer.*

0267   WINNINGTON, Richard

Drawn and quartered: a selection of weekly film reviews
and drawings.
London, Saturn Press, 1948. 126p. illus.

*A collection of brief reviews written and illustrated
by the author, mostly for the News chronicle, between 1943
and 1948.*

0268   WOLLENBERG, Hans H.

Anatomy of the film; an illustrated guide to film appreciation, based on a course of Cambridge University extension lectures.

London, Marsland, 1947. 104p.

A brief introduction to film history, techniques, economic problems, and appreciation.

0269   ZINSSER, William Knowlton

Seen any good films lately?

London, Hammond, 1960. 188p. illus.

A light-hearted account of Hollywood and the problems of being a film critic. No index. The American edition published in 1958 has title: Seen any good movies lately?

The screen and other media

CASTY, Alan

The dramatic art of the film.

New York, Harper & Row, 1971. 192p. illus.

"An attempt to place the motion picture among the dramatic arts without in any way diminishing its equally significant distinctions" (pref). The author explains the basic elements of film art.

MARCUS, Fred Harold, 1921-   ed.

Film and literature: contrasts in media.

Scranton, Chandler, 1971. 283p. illus.

An anthology in two parts:- The art of the film.- From words to visual images. The first part presents the language of film and offers historical perspective. The second part centers on contrasts between films and their literary sources. With filmography.

0270   NICOLL, Allardyce, 1894-

Film and theatre.

New York, Crowell, 1936. 255p.

Offers "the basic principles underlying artistic

expression in the film... and to relate that form of

expression to the familiar art of the stage. (pref.)

Includes a lengthy bibliography.

0271   RICHARDSON, Robert, 1934-

Literature and film.

Bloomington, Indiana University Press, 1969.

149p.

An examination into the inter-relationships between literature

and cinema. Sample chapter titles include:- Literary origins

and backgrounds of the film.- Griffith and Eisenstein: the uses

of literature in film.- Literary technique and film technique

.- Verbal and visual languages. With bibliography.

0272   ROSS, Theodore J., *comp.*

Film and the liberal arts.

New York, Holt, Rinehart and Winston, 1970.

419p.

Essays arranged under the following headings:- Film and

rhetoric.- Film and literature.- Film and the visual arts.-

Film and music.- Film and society.- Film and esthetics.- Postlude:

film and the liberal arts. Intended as a student text. With

filmography and bibliography.

0273   SHELLEY, Frank

Stage and screen.

London, Pendulum, 1946. 55p. illus.

Discusses Olivier, Portman, Davis, Garbo and others in

a comparison between approaches to theatre and cinema.

0274   VARDAC, A. Nicolas

Stage to screen; theatrical method from Garrick to

Griffith.

Cambridge, Harvard University Press, 1949.

283p. illus.

An unusual and scholarly study of film in the evol-

ution of the theatre, and considered as part of theat-

rical history and development. The book studies the

inter-action and relationships between film and the drama

of the late 19th century and early twentieth century.

With bibliographical references.

0275   WILLIAMS, Raymond   and ORROM, Michael, 1920-

Preface to film.

London, Film Drama, 1954. 129p.

Film and the dramatic tradition; film and its

dramatic techniques; offers an approach to the production

of dramatic films in which all the resources of the arts are us

PERSONALITIES

Collected biographies, studies, reminiscences, portraits, etc.

0276   ABBE, Patience   and others

Of all places! By Patience, Richard, and Johnny Abbe.

New York, F.A. Stokes, 1937. 233p. illus.

Hollywood experiences and anecdotes about the thirties

stars such as Shirley Temple, Our Gang, Laurel & Hardy, etc.

ALPERT, Hollis, 1916-

The dreams and the dreamers: adventures of a professional

movie goer.

New York, Macmillan, 1962. 258p.

Critical essays on post-war cinema. Examines the

careers of stars, directors, producers, writers, such as

Bergman, Brando, Fellini, Hitchcock, Monroe, etc.

0277   ANGER, Kenneth

       Hollywood Babylon.

       Phoenix, Associated Professional Services, 1965. 271p. illus.

   ARMES, Roy

       French cinema since 1946.

       London, Zwemmer, 1966. 2v. illus. *International film guide series.*

       A concise analysis and guide to twenty years of French cinema. Volume 1, The great tradition, examines the post-war work of 14 directors, from Claude Autant-Lara to Jacques Tati and includes a bibliography, filmography, and biography for each. The second volume, The personal style, considers 15 of the 'New wave' directors, from Alexandre Astruc to Agnes Varda, also including biblio-graphies, filmographies, and biographies.

   ARMES, Roy

       French film

       London, Studio Vista, 1970. 159p. illus.

       A brief illustrated survey of the work of forty French film directors, from Lumiere to the nouvelle vague. With bibliography.

0278   BAER, Arthur   <u>and</u> MAJOR, Henry

       Hollywood, with "Bugs" Baer and Henry Major. Lithographed by D. Murphy & Co., 1938.

       Unpaged. illus.

       Caricatures of Hollywood stars, including Chaplin, Bogart, Fairbanks, Lorre, etc.

0279   BAILY, F. E.

Film stars of history.

London, MacDonald, n.d. 167p. illus.

Includes Walter Huston as Abraham Lincoln; Greta
Garbo as Queen Christina; Charles Laughton in The private
life of Henry VIII, and others.

BAXTER, John

The gangster film.

London, **Zwemmer**, 1970. 160p. illus. *Screen series.*

Notes on 225 directors, actors, and other key
figures connected with the gangster film genre. With film
title index.

0280   BOOCH, Harish S   <u>and</u> DOYLE, Karing

Star-portrait; intimate life stories of famous film

stars. New rev. ed.

Bombay, Lakhani Book Depot, 1962. 152p. illus.

Biographical sketches and photographs of India's
leading film stars.

BRITISH FILM AND TELEVISION YEARBOOK. 1946-

London, British and American Press, etc. v. illus.

Title varies: 1946-   The British film yearbook.

Editor: 1946-   P. Noble.

Early editions included articles on various aspects
of the British cinema, with a biographical index of actors,
writers, directors, technicians, etc. This latter feature
forms the major part of later editions, together with
information on the British film and television industry.

BROWNLOW, Kevin

The parade's gone by.

New York, Knopf, 1968. 577p. illus.

One of the better books dealing with American silent cinema. Largely based on interviews with surviving filmmakers, actors and technicians, and written by a young British film director. Well illustrated.

0281   BRUNO, Michael, 1921-

Venus in Hollywood: the continental enchantress from Garbo to Loren.

New York, L. Stuart, 1970. 257p. illus.

BUCHER, Felix

Germany, by Felix Bucher in collaboration with Leonhard H. Gmur.

London, Zwemmer, 1970. 298p. illus. *Screen series.*

An illustrated guide to the German cinema. The 431 main entries, arranged alphabetically, include all major directors, actors, screenwriters, production companies and technicians, each entry giving brief biographical details and filmography. With film title index.

0282   BULL, Clarence Sinclair

The faces of Hollywood, by Clarence Sinclair Bull, with Raymond Lee.

South Brunswick, N.J., Barnes, 1968. 256p. illus.

Consists largely of portraits of Hollywood stars by Clarence Bull, the chief portrait photographer at M.G.M. Studios for over thirty years, preceded by some of the author's reminiscences.

0283   BURROWS, Michael

Charles Laughton and Fredric March.

St. Austell, Eng., Primestyle, 1969. 41p. illus.

Consists of bibliography, filmography, and brief

biographical data for each actor.

0284   CAHN, William. 1912-

A pictorial history of the great comedians.

New York, Grosset and Dunlap, 1970. 221p. illus.

An illustrated survey of American comedy entertainers,

published in an earlier edition as The laugh makers - a

pictorial history of American comedians.

0285   CAIRN, James

The heart of Hollywood.

London, R. Madley; D.S. Smith, 1942-46.

3v. illus.

3 series published. Included biographical notes

on film stars and rising stars of the period covered.

0286   CAMERON, Ian Alexander, 1937-   and CAMERON, Elisabeth

Broads.

London, Studio Vista, 1969. 144p. illus. *Movie paper-*

backs series.

A sequel to The heavies, by the same authors. Consists

of an alphabetical survey of actresses specializing in

'unladylike' roles, each entry including brief biographical

data and a filmography. American edition has title:

Dames.

0287   CAMERON, Ian Alexander, 1937-   and CAMERON, Elisabeth

The heavies.

London, Studio Vista, 1967. 143p. illus. *Movie paper*

backs series.

Brief articles, with biographical notes and film

lists, on more than 80 Hollywood character actors.

The selection is limited to the period after 1940, and

excludes major stars, such as Raft, Bogart, Cagney and

Robinson. Illustrated with photos of all actors included.

0288   CANTOR, Eddie, 1893-

As I remember them.

New York, Duell, Sloan & Pearce, 1963. 144p. illus.

Anecdotes about various show business personalities

including W.C. Fields, Jimmy Cagney, Greta Garbo, Will

Rogers, etc.

0289   CARR, Larry

Four fabulous faces; the evolution and metamorphosis of

Garbo, Swanson, Crawford, Dietrich.

New Rochelle, N. Y., Arlington House, 1970. 492p. illus.

A lavishly illustrated tribute to Gloria Swanson, Greta

Garbo, Joan Crawford, and Marlene Dietrich, consisting of

over one thousand photographs.

CORNEAU, Ernest N

The hall of fame of western film stars.

North Quincy Mass., Christopher Publishing House, 1969.

307p. illus.

A nostalgic survey of the Hollywood western, consist-

ing of biographies and filmographies of most of the western

stars, with additional entries under such topics as The

western serial, The wonder horse, The sidekicks, etc.

0290   COWIE, Peter

Antonioni, Bergman, Resnais.

New York, Barnes, 1964, c1963. 160p. illus.

Concentrates on the early years of the directors discussed and analyzes the films that brought them to the fore. With bibliographies.

COWIE, Peter

Sweden, by Peter Cowie in collaboration with Arne Svensson. London, Zwemmer, 1970.

2v. illus. Screen series.

The first volume is an alphabetical survey of 170 directors, actors, screenwriters, technicians, etc. with appropriate filmographies, together with synopses of 70 major films. The index to film titles mentioned in the text is in both English and Swedish. The second volume consists largely of an expanded version of the author's earlier book, Swedish cinema, providing a survey and assessment of Swedish cinema, with a considerable portion of the book being devoted to Ingmar Bergman. Includes bibliography.

0291   DAVIDSON, William, 1918-

The real and the unreal.

New York, Harper, 1961. 274p.

Basically a collection of reprinted magazine articles purporting to show the 'real' and the 'public' sides of film personalities, such as Gable, Novak, Sinatra, etc.

0292   DIMMITT, Richard Bertrand

An actor guide to the talkies; a comprehensive listing

of 8000 feature-length films from January 1949 until

December 1964.

Metuchen, N.J., Scarecrow Press, 1967-8. 2v. (1555p.)

The first volume is an alphabetical listing of films,

with entries including date and production company followed

by a list of the actors, but often with little or no

indication of the roles played. The second volume is

an actor index. The emphasis of the work is on American

productions.

0293   DIRECTORS AT WORK: INTERVIEWS WITH AMERICAN FILM-MAKERS.

Interviews conducted and edited by Bernard R. Kantor,

Irwin R. Blacker, and Anne Kramer.

New York, Funk & Wagnalls, 1970. 442p.

Detailed interviews with Richard Brooks, George Cukor,

Norman Jewison, Eli Kazan, Stanley Kramer, Richard Lester,

Jerry Lewis, Elliot Silverstein, Robert Wise, and William

Wyler. A filmography for each director is provided.

0294   DUNCAN, Peter, 1915-

In Hollywood tonight.

London, W. Laurie, 1952. 144p. illus.

Interviews with the stars by the English radio re-

porter.

DURGNAT, Raymond, 1932-

Nouvelle vague; the first decade.

Loughton, Eng., Motion Publications, 1963. 90p. illus.

An alphabetical survey, by director, of the French
'New Wave' cinema of the fifties and early sixties.
Durgnat offers critical commentary on many of the films
mentioned in each filmography. Includes bibliography,
but has no title index.

0295   EVERSON, William K.

The bad guys: a pictorial history of the movie villain.
New York, Citadel Press, c1964. 241p. illus.

A well illustrated survey of film villains, arranged
by category, e.g. monsters, social villains, swashbucklers,
etc.

EYLES, Allen

The western: an illustrated guide.
London, Zwemmer, 1967. 183p. illus. International
film guide series.

A reference book consisting of more than 350 entries
for stars, supporting actors, directors, screenwriters,
cameramen, etc. of the Hollywood western, arranged
alphabetically and including brief filmographies. Entries
also appear for famous characters and personalities of the
American west, with details of screen portrayals. There
is a comprehensive index of film titles, and a bibliography.

0296   FAME: ANNUAL AUDIT OF PERSONALITIES OF SCREEN, RADIO AND TELEVIS

New York, Quigley. v. illus. annual.

Title varies. 1933-1935: The box office check-up.
Subtitle also varies slightly.

0297   FILM STAR PARADE; A GLITTERING GALAXY OF YOUR SCREEN FAVOURITIES;
        EMPHASIS ON GLAMOUR.

        London, W.H. Allen, 1944. 60 port.

        *A collection of sixty portaits of film stars in the
        year of publication, with brief text.*

0298   FILMLEXICON DEGLI AUTORI E DELLE OPERE

        Rome, Bianco e nero, 1958-   v. illus.

        *A multi-volume reference work constructed upon
        Francesco Pasinetti's Filmlexicon - piccola enciclopedia
        cinematografica. Although the text is in Italian, film
        titles are given in the language of the country of production.
        The introduction is in Italian, French, English, German
        and Spanish. The first seven volumes so far published
        present entries under names of directors, story and script
        writers, producers, actors, cameramen, composers, art
        directors and costume designers in world cinema, past and
        persent. Entries include biographical information, filmo-
        graphies, and, where relevant, bibliographies.*

0299   FLORA, Paul

        Viva vamp! A book of photographs in praise of vamps, from
        Mae West to Marilyn Monroe, from Marlene Dietrich to Brigitte
        Bardot. Illustrated commentary by Paul Flora, with a
        poetical salute by Ogden Nash.
        New York, D. McKay, 1960. unpaged. illus.

        *A collection of photographs of screen actresses,
        accompanied by satirical drawings.*

0300   FRENCH, Philip

The movie moguls; an informal history of the Hollywood

tycoons.

London, Weidenfeld & Nicholson, 1969. 170p. illus.

An account of the men such as Mayer, Goldwyn, Zukor,

Fox, etc., who controlled the major American film companies.

With bibliography.

GIFFORD, Denis

British cinema: an illustrated guide.

London, Zwemmer, 1968. 176p. illus. *International*

film guide series.

A reference book with entries for over 500 British

film actors and directors, arranged alphabetically with a

film title index. Entries include biographical data with

chronological filmographies.

0301   GRAHAM, Peter John, 1939-

A dictionary of the cinema. Rev. ed.

London, Zwemmer, 1968. 175p. illus. *International film*

guide series.

A useful dictionary with emphasis on directors rather

than on actors, and with the addition of a few subject

entries, such as Avant-garde. Filmographies are usually

reliable, and the film title index includes approximately

20,000 references to the text.

0302   GRAHAM, Sheilah

Confessions of a Hollywood columnist.

New York, Morrow, 1969. 309p.

Based on interviews with various stars. English

edition (Allen) has title: Scratch an actor: confessions

of a Hollywood columnist.

0303   GRUEN, John

Close-up.

New York, Viking Press, 1968. 206p. illus.

Brief interviews with personalities in the arts. The film section includes Fellini, Resnais, Losey, Ruby Keeler, Busby Berkeley, Vivien Leigh, Simone Signoret, Mario Montez, Candice Bergen, Bette Davis, and Judy Garland.

0304   HALLIWELL, Leslie

The filmgoer's companion. 3d ed.

London, Macgibbon & Kee, 1970. 1072p.

An encyclopaedia of film information intended for the general filmgoer, with emphasis on British and American cinema. In addition to biographical entries, information is provided under approximately 200 subject and genre entries, fictional screen characters, and technical terms.

0305   HAMBLETT, Charles

The Hollywood cage.

New York, Hart, 1969. 437p. illus.

A revised and expanded version of the author's Who killed Marilyn Monroe?, published in 1966. Includes an account of the filming of her last film, The misfits, with the addition of essays on Hollywood and interviews with Hollywood's stars.

HIBBIN, Nina

Eastern Europe; an illustrated guide.

London, Zwemmer, 1969. 239p. illus. *Screen series.*

An illustrated guide to directors, actors and others involved in film-making in Albania, Bulgaria, Czechoslovaki East Germany, Hungary, Poland, Romania, U.S.S.R., and Yugoslavia since the Second World War. A dictionary arrangement is used for each country, prefaced by notes about its film industry and production. A general film title index to all films mentioned in the book is included.

0306   HIGHAM, Charles, 1931-   and GREENBERG, Joel

The celluloid muse: Hollywood directors speak.

London, Angus & Robertson, 1969. 268p. illus.

Consists of autobiographical essays by fifteen Hollywood directors, composed from tape interviews compiled by Higham and Greenberg, who also provide brief introductions to each director. Contents:- Robert Aldrich.- Curtis Bernhardt.- George Cukor.- John Frankenheimer.- Alfred Hitchcock.- Fritz Lang.- Rouben Mamoulian.- Lewis Milestone.- Vincente Minnelli.- Jean Negulesco.- Irving Rapper.- Mark Robson.- Jacques Tourneur.- King Vidor.- Billy Wilder. With filmographies.

0307   HIRST, Robert

Three men and a gimmick.

Kingswood, Eng., The World's Work, 1957. 125p.

Biographies of Peter Cushing, Terry Thomas, and Arthur Askey.

0308   HOLLYWOOD ALBUM: THE WONDERFUL CITY AND ITS FAMOUS INHABITANTS.

London, S. Low, Marston, 1947- v. illus.

Editor: I.C. Wilson.

0309   HOLLYWOOD STUDIO BLU-BOOK; MOTION PICTURES, TELEVISION,

RADIO DIRECTORY.

Hollywood.   v.

HOOD, Robin

Classics of the Swedish cinema: the Stiller & Sjostrom

period. With an introduction by Victor Sjostrom.

Stockholm, Swedish Institute, 1952. 48p. illus.

INTERNATIONAL MOTION PICTURE ALMANAC.

New York, Quigley, 1929- v. illus. *annual.*

The first edition of this annual publication under the

title The motion picture almanac was compiled and edited by the

staff of Exhibitors Herald-World and published in 1929. The

largest section was devoted to biographical data about actors,

producers, directors, writers, executives, and others in production

and distribution. Further sections dealt with various aspects

of the American film industry. Films released in 1929 and the

preceding few years were listed. The 42nd edition published

in 1971 and edited by Richard Gertner contains greatly expanded

listings. The film lists cover feature releases from 1955-1970,

and emphasis in other sections is placed on directory-style

information on the film industry.

0310   JESSEL, George Albert, 1898–

Halo over Hollywood.

Van Nuys, Calif., Toastmaster Pub. Co., 1963.

176p. illus.

Biographical sketches in verse, with photographs, of Hollywood stars, in the form of messages from the "world beyond".

KITSES, Jim, *pseud.*

Horizons west: Anthony Mann, Budd Boetticher, Sam Peckinpah; studies of authorship within the western.

London, Thames & Hudson in association with the British Film Institute, 1969. 176p. illus. *Cinema one series.*

A critical analysis of the westerns directed by Mann, Boetticher and Peckinpah. With filmographies.

0311   KNIGHT, Arthur.

The Hollywood style. Photographs by Eliot Elisofon.

New York, Macmillan, 1969. 216p. illus.

A largely pictorial account of the homes and life styles of Hollywood film stars, from Cecil B. DeMille to Steve McQueen.

LAHUE, Kalton C.   and GILL, Samuel, 1946–

Clown princes and court jesters.

South Brunswick, N.J., Barnes, 1970. 406p. illus.

The stories of fifty typical Hollywood silent screen comedy actors, from "Fatty" Arbuckle to Billy West. Well illustrated. No filmographics.

0312   LAHUE, Kalton C.

          Ladies in distress.

          South Brunswick, N.J., Barnes, 1971. 334p. illus.

               Biographical portraits of forty representative silent

          screen heroines, from Mary Astor to Clara Kimball Young.

          No filmographies.

          LAHUE, Kalton C.

          Winners of the west; the sagebrush heroes of the

          silent screen.

          South Brunswick, N.J., Barnes, 1970. 353p. illus.

               Biographical portraits of 38 western stars of the

          silent cinema. No filmographies.

0313   LEVIN, G. Roy

          Documentary explorations; 15 interviews with film-makers.

          Garden City, N.Y., Doubleday, 1971. 420p. illus.

               Interviews with leading documentary filmmakers from

          Bri**tai**n, *France, Belgium, and the United States. With*

          bibliography.

          LEVIN, Martin, comp.

          Hollywood and the great fan magazines.

          New York, Arbor House, 1970. 224p. illus.

               A collection of stories and articles from the American

          movie magazines of the 1930s, reprinted without commentary

          or analysis.

0314   LIKENESS, George C

          The Oscar people: from Wings to My fair lady.

          Mendota, Ill., Wayside Press, 1965. 415p. illus.

               The Oscar winners and the films they appeared in,

          with category appendices and index.

0315   LOVELL, Alan.

Anarchist cinema.

London, Peace News, 1962. 39p. illus.

A pamphlet on the cinema of Bunuel, Vigo, and Franju issued to coincide with a film series at the National Film Theatre in London.

0316   McCAFFREY, Donald W.

4 great comedians: Chaplin, Lloyd, Keaton, Langdon.
London, Zwemmer, 1968. 175p. illus.
International film guide series.

A critical study in the form of a re-evaluation of the major films of the four film-makers mentioned in the title. Includes shot-by-shot analyses and scenario extracts. With bibliography.

0317   MCCRINDLE, Joseph F., comp.

Behind the scenes: theater and film interviews from the Transatlantic review. With an introduction by Jean-Claude van Itallie.

New York, Holt, Rinehart and Winston, 1971. 341p.

The anthology is mostly concerned with the theatre, but also includes interviews with Philippe de Broca, Federico Fellini, Harold Pinter and Clive Donner, and with John Schlesinger.

0318   MALTIN, Leonard.

Movie comedy teams.

New York, New American Library, 1970. 352p. illus.

Of interest for its inclusion of relatively minor screen comedy teams. With filmographies.

0319   MARTIN, Pete

Hollywood without make-up. With a foreword by Nunnally

Johnson and an afterword by Jack Alexander.

Philadelphia, Lippincott, 1948. 255p.

0320   MEYERS, Warren B.

Who is that? The late, late viewers guide to the old,

old movie players.

New York, Personality Posters, 1967. 63p. illus.

A gallery of photographs of American screen character

actors, arranged by type of character portrayed, eg. Other

women, Bad guys, etc.

MICHAEL, Paul.

The American movies reference book: the sound era.

Paul Michael, editor in chief; James Robert Parish,

Associate editor.

Englewood Cliffs, N.J., Prentice-Hall, 1969. 629p. illus.

Entries arranged under the following headings:- The

history.- The players.- The films.- The directors.- The

producers.- The awards. The information included is highly

selective and greatly varying in length and detail. With

bibliography.

0321   MILLER, Edwin, 1921-

Seventeen interviews: film stars and superstars.

New York, Macmillan, 1970. 384p. illus.

58 interviews originally published in Seventeen magazine.

0322   MORELLA, Joe   and EPSTEIN, Edward Z.

Rebels; the rebel hero in films.

New York, Cidael Press, c1971. 210p. illus.

Traces the careers of a group of actors typifying

the concept of rebel heroes. Includes nearly 500 photo-

graphs.

MOTION PICTURE PRODUCTION ENCYCLOPEDIA. 1948-

Hollywood, Hollywood Reporter. v. illus.

A directory listing credits for the five years prior

to year of publication for American actors, producers, direct

writers, etc., followed by credits for films produced in

the same period by title and by company. Includes American

film industry information.

0323   NOBLE, Peter, 1917-

British screen stars.

London, British Yearbooks, 1946. 91p. illus.

0324   PENSEL, Hans

Seastrom and Stiller in Hollywood; two Swedish directors

in silent American films, 1923-1930.

New York, Vantage Press, c1969. 106p. illus.

0325   PLATT, Frank C., ed.

Great stars of Hollywood's golden age.

New York, New American Library, c1966. 214p. illus.

Articles written between 1929 and 1942. Contents:-

Valentino, the life story of The Sheik, by Adela Rogers

St. Johns.- Garbo, the mystery of Hollywood, by Adela

Rogers St. Johns.- The private life of Charlie Chaplin,

by Carlyle K. Robinson.- The loves of John Barrymore, by

Frederick L. Collins.- Why Jean Harlow died, by Edward

Doherty.- Carole Lombard, by Adela Rogers St. Johns.

PORTER, Hal.

Stars of Australian stage and screen.

Adelaide, Rigby, c1965. 304p. illus.

A broad survey of "those Australians who have left some mark, vivid or pallid, on the legitimate theatre and the film, and to indicate the fluctuating climate in these two areas from 1789 to the present." Includes a title listing of Australian films, with production dates. Indexed.

0326   REED, Rex

Conversations in the raw: dialogues, monologues, and selected short subjects.

New York, World Pub. Co., 1969. 312p.

Conversations with stars such as Bette Davis, Ingrid Bergman, Paul Newman and Joanne Woodward, Omar Shariff, and others.

0327   REED, Rex

Do you sleep in the nude?

London, W.H. Allen, 1969, c1968. 276p.

Interviews with such stars as Ava Gardner, Warren Beatty, Marlene Dietrich, Peter Fonda, etc., and directors such as Otto Preminger and Antonioni.

0328   RIGDON, Walter, ed.

The biographical encyclopaedia & who's who of the American theatre.

New York, J.H. Heineman, 1966, c1965. 1101p.

Of interest to the film enthusiast for its "Biographical who's who" (p. 227-939) which features biographical information about the most important names, including foreigners and Americans abroad, connected with the American theatre. Entries include film credits and bibliographies where appropriate.

RONDI, Gian Luigi

Italian cinema today, 1952 - 1965.

New York, Hill and Wang, 1966.

279p. illus.

A retrospective illustrated survey of Italian cinema from 1952 to 1965. Arrangement is by director, in two sequences from Antonioni to Zurlini and from Bellocchio to Wertmuller. Indexed by actors, directors, film titles and producers.

0329   ROSTEN, Leo Colvin, 1908-

Hollywood: the movie colony and the movie makers.

New York, Harcourt, Brace, 1941. 436p.

The results of a three-year research study by the author and a staff of social scientists into all aspects of Hollywood and the people who work there, produced from questionnaires, interviews and research.

SARRIS, Andrew

The American cinema; directors and directions, 1929-1968.

New York, Dutton, 1968. 383p.

The author, currently film critic of the Village Voice, discusses in brief the work of 200 directors. A directorial chronology lists the major American films produced between 1915 and 1967. A directorial index compiled by Michael Schwartz and James R. Prickett lists the films mentioned in the book together with numerous others, giving date of production and name of director for each.

0330   SARRIS, Andrew, ed.

Interviews with film directors.

Indianapolis, Bobbs-Merrill, 1967. 478p. illus.

A collection of interviews taken from various sources with forty film directors, from Antonioni to Orson Welles, arranged alphabetically.

SCHICKEL, Richard

The stars. Designed by Allen Hurlburt.

New York, Dial Press, 1962. 287p. illus.

Profusely illustrated survey of "the personalities who made the movies" from the silent era to the stars of the late fifties.

0331   SCHUSTER, Mel, *comp.*

Motion picture performers; a bibliography of magazine and periodical articles, 1900-1969.

Metuchen, N.J., Scarecrow Press, 1971. 702p.

Brief references without annotations, arranged chronologically under performers.

0332   SECOND WAVE, by Ian Cameron and others.

New York, Praeger, 1970.

144p. illus. *Praeger film library.*

Essays on new directors in world cinems:- Dusan Makavejev.- Jerzy Skolimowski.- Nagasha Oshima.- Ray Guerra.- Glauber Rocha.- Gilles Groulx.- Jean-Pierre Lefebvre.- Jean-Marie Straub. With filmographies.

0333   SHAY, Don

Conversations, volume 1.

Albuquerque, N. M., Kaleidoscope Press, 1969. unpaged

Interviews with eight American film actors:- Buster Crabbe, Peter Falk, Henry Fonda, Charlton Heston, Karl Malden, Gregory Peck, Edward G. Robinson, and Rod Steiger. Each interview is followed by a filmography.

0334   SHERMAN, Eric   <u>and</u> RUBIN, Martin

        The directors event...

        New York, Atheneum, 1970, c1969. 200p. illus.

           Interviews with five American film-makers: Budd

        Boetticher, Peter Bogdanovich, Samuel Fuller, Arthur Penn,

        and Abraham Polonsky.

      SHIPMAN, David

        The great movie stars; the golden years.

        London, Hamlyn, c1970. 576p. illus.

           Notes on 181 stars who achieved fame before or during

        World War II and who are still remembered today. Entries

        are arranged alphabetically, each including mention of featur

        length films featuring the actor concerned.

0335   STUART, Ray, 1899-   ed.

        Immortals of the screen.

        Los Angeles, Sherbourne Press, 1965. 224p. illus.

           Portraits and stills with brief biographical data of

        approximately one hundred Hollywood personalities.

0336   SUMNER, Robert Leslie, 1922-

        Hollywood cesspool; a startling survey of movieland lives

        and morals, pictures and results.

        Wheaton, Ill., Sword of the Lord, 1955. 284p.

           An evangelist's attack on Hollywood stars' lives and mora

      SVENSSON, Arne

        Japan.

        London, Zwemmer, 1971. 189p. illus. *Screen series.*

           A dictionary arrangement of Japanese directors, actors

        and films. With credits, filmographies, and synopses of plot

        for important productions. With film title index.

0337   TAYLOR, John Russell

Cinema eye, cinema ear: some key film-makers of the sixties.

New York, Hill & Wang, 1964. 294p. illus.

*Penetrating and scholarly studies of the work of nine
contemporary film directors: Fellini, Antonioni, Bunuel, Bresson,
Bergman, Hitchcock, Truffaut, Godard, and Resnais. With
filmographies and bibliographies.*

0338   TOWN, Harold Barling, 1924-

Silent stars, sound stars, film stars.

Toronto, McClelland and Stewart, 1971. 127p. illus.

*A collection of 105 full-page drawings of film per-
sonalities, drawn by the Canadian artist.*

0339   TWOMEY, Alfred E.   and McCLURE, Arthur F.

The versatiles; a study of supporting character actors and
actresses in the American motion picture, 1930-1955.

South Brunswick, N.J., Barnes, 1969. 304p. illus.

*Arranged in two alphabetical sequences by name of performer.
The first sequence of 400 supporting players includes photographs, biographical notes, and filmographies. The second
sequence contains photographs and filmographies for a further
200 names.*

UNITALIA FILM.

Italian directors.

Rome, 1958. 203p. illus.

*An alphabetical, non-critical survey of the careers
of Italian film producers. With filmographies.*

VALLANCE, Tom

The American musical.

London, Zwemmer, 1970. 192p. illus. *Screen series.*

Alphabetical arrangements of "artists who gave Hollywood supremacy in the form of the musical. It lists their musical credits with a small amount of biographical material and comment." (Introd.) With film title index.

WALKER, Alexander

The celluloid sacrifice; aspects of sex in the movies.
London, Joseph, 1966. 241p. illus.

An examination of the sexual appeal of the female star personality, with chapters devoted to Pickford, Mae West, Dietrich, Garbo, etc.; also considers film censorship in Britain and the United States. A final section deals with Italian and American sex comedies. Published in United State and in England in a later paperback edition under title:- Sex in the movies: the celluloid sacrifice.

0340   WALKER, Alexander

Stardom: the Hollywood phenomenon.
London, Joseph, 1970. 392p. illus.

"An enquiry into the processes by which some stars are made - and the reasons why the end products turn out as they do" (pref.) The book examines major Hollywood stars and the American star system. With bibliography.

WEAVER, John T.

Forty years of screen credits, 1929-1969.
Metuchen, N.J. Scarecrow Press, 1970. 2v. (1458p.) illus.

An alphabetical listing of film titles arranged by performer. Concentrates on American stars, but includes

WEAVER, John T.

Twenty years of silents, 1908-1928.

Metuchen, N.J., Scarecrow Press, 1971. 514p.

Film title listings arranged in two sequences:- The players.- The directors and producers. Arrangement of entries under each name is chronological. Also includes a list of silent film studio corporations and distributors.

0341   WEISS, Emile

My studio sketchbook.

London, Marsland, 1948.

36 portraits.

Portraits of thirty-six stars of the British screen.

ZALMAN, Jan, *pseud.*

Films and film-makers in Czechoslovakia.

Prague, Orbis, 1968. 99p. illus.

A brief survey of contemporary Czech cinema, with particular reference to the work of seventeen directors. With filmographies.

0342   ZIEROLD, Norman J.

The child stars.

New York, Coward-McCann, 1965. 250p. illus.

A record of the Hollywood child stars of the twenties and thirties. Contents:- The trials of Jackie Coogan.- Baby Leroy.- What was Shirley Temple really like?- Jane Withers: Dixie's dainty dewdrop.- The true Judy.- Little Lord Bartholomew. Edna Mae Durbin, alias Deanna.- The Mick.- Jackie Cooper.- Where are they now?

0343   ZIEROLD, Norman J.

The moguls.

New York, Coward-McCann, 1969. 354p. illus.

Published in England under the title: The Hollywood

tycoons, this book presents reminiscences and anecdotes

under the following chapter headings:- The Selznick

saga.- "Uncle Carl" Laemmle.- "Samuel Goldwyn presents".-

The gentlemen from Paramount.- White Fang.- The films'

forgotten man: William Fox.- The brothers Warner.- The "goy"

studio: Twentieth Century-Fox.- Mayer's-ganz-mispochen.

Individual biographies, studies, reminiscences, portraits, etc.

0344   ACKLAND, Rodney, 1908-   and GRANT, Elspeth

The celluloid mistress; or, The custard pie of Dr. Caligari.

London, A. Wingate, 1954. 264p. illus.

Reminiscences of a playwright and screenwriter.

0345   AHERNE, Brian

A proper job.

Boston, Houghton Mifflin, 1969. 355p. illus.

Autobiographical. With filmography.

LAHUE, Kalton C.

Dreams for sale; the rise and fall of the Triangle

Film Corporation.

South Brunswick, N.J., Barnes, 1971.

216p. illus.

The story of Harry Aitken and the Triangle Film

Corporation.

0346   SUSSEX, Elizabeth   03 wait

Lindsay Anderson.

London, Studio Vista, 1969. 96p. illus. *Movie paperbacks series.*

A critical examination of the director's film work from his early documentaries to If. With filmography and list of theatre productions.

0347   COTTRELL, John

Julie Andrews: the story of a star.

London, Barker, 1969. 222p. illus.

An adulatory biography by "an unabashed Julie Andrews fan." No index.

0348   WINDELER, Robert

Julie Andrews; a biography.

New York, Putnam, 1970. 253p. illus.

A biography, with index.

0349   CAMERON, Ian Alexander, 1937-   and   WOOD, Robin

Antonioni.

New York, Praeger, 1969, c1968. 140p. illus. *Praeger film library.*

Consists mainly of the critical study of Antonioni's films published in 1968 as a Movie monograph and written by Ian Cameron, with the addition of evaluations of Antonioni's later films by Robin Wood. Includes filmography. A further revised edition was published in 1971.

0350   LEPROHON, Pierre.

Michelangelo Antonioni: an introduction.

New York, Simon & Schuster, 1963. 207p. illus.

World of film series.

An account of Antonioni's earlier works, arranged in four parts:- The man and his work.- Antonioni on the cinema.- Antonioni's works.- Criticism and commentary. In addition to quotations from Antonioni's own articles, extra from screenplays of Le amiche, II grido, and La notte are included. Includes filmography and bibliography.

0351   STRICK, Philip

Michelangelo Antonioni.

Loughton, Eng., Motion Publications, 1963.

58p. illus.

A monograph on the films of Antonioni. With filmograph

0352   ARLISS, George, 1868-1946

My ten years in the studios.

Boston, Little, Brown, 1940. 349p. illus.

Reminiscences and anecdotes covering the years from 1928 to 1938. Includes credits for each film made by Arliss during that period. English edition (J. Murray) has title: George Arliss, by himself.

0353   ARNOLD, Edward, 1890- 1956

Lorenzo goes to Hollywood; the autobiography of Edward Arnold, in collaboration with Frances Fisher Dubuc.

New York, Liveright, 1940. 282p. illus.

Autobiography which includes Arnold's first seven years as a screen actor, from 1932 to 1939.

0354   NOBLE, Peter, 1917-

          Anthony Asquith.

          London, British Film Institute, 1952. 44p. illus.

0355   ASTAIRE, Fred, 1899-

          Steps in time.

          New York, Harper, 1959. 338p. illus.

              An autobiography. Includes list of performances
          and index.

0356   HACKL, Alfons

          Fred Astaire and his work.

          Vienna, Schwarcz Erbin, 1970. 120p. illus.

              Half of the book is devoted to Astaire's films, the
          remaining sections covering his Broadway shows, television,
          recordings, etc. Credits are given for each film, together
          with a list of the musical numbers. The entries are
          illustrated with appropriate stills.

0357   THOMPSON, Howard

          Fred Astaire

          New York, Falcon, 1970. 154p. illus. *Hollywood's magic*
          people series.

              A collection of stills with a running commentary at
          the foot of each page, often not matched with the appropriate
          illustration. With filmography.

0358   ASTOR, Mary

          A life on film.

          New York, Delacorte Press, 1971. 288p. illus.

              Recollections of the author's film career. With
          filmography.

BALABAN, Abraham Joseph

Continuous performance; the story of A.J. Balaban, as told to his wife Carrie Balaban.

New York, A.J. Balaban Foundation, 1964. 144p. illus.

First published in 1942, this biography of the founder of the Balaban & Katz cinema chain in the United States is also a history of the development of the American motion picture theatre.

0359   BALCON, *Sir* Michael, 1896-

Michael Balcon presents... a lifetime of films.

London, Hutchinson, 1969. 239p. illus.

The autobiography of a pioneer film-maker since the twenties and one of the most influential producers in the history of British film. Particularly useful for information on the films of Ealing Studios.

0360   DANISCHEWSKY, Monja, 1911-   ed.

Michael Balcon's 25 years in films.

London, World Film Publications, 1947. 112p. illus.

A tribute to the British film producer, with stills from many of Balcon's films, comments by Balcon on various film actors, and biographical contributions by G. Campbell Dixon, Michael Redgrave, Francoise Rosay, and A. de A Calvalcanti, together with the text of a lecture given by Balcon on documentary film.

0361   BALSHOFER, Fred J.   and MILLER, Arthur C.

One reel a week.

Berkeley, University of California Press, 1967. 218p. illus.

The reminiscences of two cameramen in the early days of American cinema.

0362   BANKHEAD, Tallulah

0362   BANKHEAD, Tallulah

Tallulah; my autobiography.

New York, Harper, 1952. 335p. illus.

0363   BEAUVOIR, Simone de., 1908-

Brigitte Bardot and the Lolita syndrome.

New York, Reynal, 1960, c1959. 37p. illus.

An intelligent essay on the film star phenomenon as exemplified by Brigitte Bardot. Includes more than 100 illustrations.

0364   CARPOZI, George

The Brigitte Bardot story.

New York, Belmont Books, 1961. 157p. illus.

0365   LABORDERIE, Renaud de

Brigitte Bardot: Renaud de Laborderie spotlights in words and pictures the career of the remarkable Brigitte Bardot.

Manchester, Eng., World Distributors, 1964. 48p. illus.

0366   REID, Gordon

Brigitte: the story of Brigitte Bardot.

London, Eurap, 1958.

35p. illus. *Film star biographies series.*

0367   BARKAS, Natalie (Webb)

Thirty thousand miles for the films; the story of the filming of Soldiers three, and Rhodes of Africa.

London, Blackie, 1937. 197p. illus.

Non-technical personal notes.

0368   FOWLER, Gene, 1890-1960

Good night, sweet prince; the life and times of John Barrymore.

New York, Viking Press, 1944. 477p. illus.

A personal biography. With index.

0369 ALPERT, Hollis, 1916-

The Barrymores.

New York, Dial Press, 1964. 397p. illus.

A biography   of Ethel, John and Lionel Barrymore.

0370 BARRYMORE, Lionel, 1878-1954

We Barrymores; as told to Cameron Shipp.

London, P. Davies, 1951, c1950. 244p. illus.

Includes many references to the early days of American cinema, including memories of D.W. Griffith and others.

0371 BARTOK, Eva

Worth living for.

London, Putnam, 1959. 181p. front.

A frank and unghosted autobiography, but containing little of film interest.

0372 BENCHLEY, Nathaniel

Robert Benchley; a biography.

New York, McGraw-Hill, c1965. 258p. illus.

A biography, written by Robert Benchley's elder son.

0373 BENCHLEY, Robert Charles, 1889-1945.

The "reel" Benchley; Robert Benchley at his hilarious best in words and pictures.

New York, Wyn, 1950. 96p. illus.

Text and stills from six of Benchley's short films.

0374   COWIE, Peter

Ingmar Bergman; a Motion monograph.

2d ed. London, Motion, 1962. 40p. illus.

A survey of Bergman's work as a film director, with
critical essays on five of his major films. No index.
No mention is made of the often radical title changes
for U.S. release, which may cause confusion for American
readers.

0375   DONNER, Jorn

The personal vision of Ingmar Bergman.

Bloomington, Indiana University Press, 1964. 276p. illus.

A detailed evaluation of Bergman's work, written by
an established Swedish film-maker and critic. An analysis
of each film is included. With bibliography and filmography.

0376   GIBSON, Arthur, 1922-

The silence of God; creative response to the films of
Ingmar Bergman.

New York, Harper & Row, 1969. 171p. illus.

An examination of a continuing theme in Bergman's
films - the silence of God. Seven films are examined:-
The seventh seal.- Wild strawberries.- The magician.-
Through a glass darkly.- Winter light.- The silence.-
Persona.

0377   STEENE, Birgitta

Ingmar Bergman.

New York, Twayne, 1968. 158p.

A critical study concentrating on the literary merits of
Bergman's work. With a thorough bibliography.

0378   WOOD, Robin

        Ingmar Bergman.

        New York, Praeger, 1969. 191p. illus. *Praeger film library.*

        A critical survey of Bergman's films. With filmography and bibliography.

0379   YOUNG, Vernon

        Cinema borealis: Ingmar Bergman and the Swedish ethos.

        New York, D. Lewis, 1971. 331p. illus.

        An analysis of Bergman's films and particularly of the beliefs from which his work is derived. Includes a selective bibliography on Swedish culture and Swedish films, and a Bergman film chronology with principal credits.

0380   QUIRK, Lawrence J.

        The films of Ingrid Bergman.

        New York, Citadel Press, 1970. 224p. illus.

        Following a chapter on Ingrid Bergman's life and career, the book presents an illustrated chronological survey of her films from 1934 to 1970, including those produced in Sweden. Entries include credits, synopsis and contemporary reviews. Further sections also deal with stage and television roles.

0381   STEELE, Joseph Henry

        Ingrid Bergman; an intimate portrait.

        New York, D. McKay, 1959. 365p.

        A biography written by the actress' press agent.

0382   GEHMAN, Richard

        Bogart.

        Greenwich, Conn., Fawcett, 1965. 159p. illus.

        (Humphrey Bogart)

0383   GOODMAN, Ezra

        Bogey: the good-bad guy.

        New York, L. Stuart, 1965. 223p.

        (Humphrey Bogart)

0384   HYAMS, Joe

        Bogie; the biography of Humphrey Bogart.

        New York, New American Library, c1966. 210p. illus.

        An anecdotal portrait of Bogart's life rather than

        a study of his work. No index.

0385   MCCARTY, Clifford, 1929-

        Bogey: the films of Humphrey Bogart.

        New York, Citadel Press, 1965. 187p. illus.

        Consists of cast lists, credits, and synopses of all

        of Bogart's work for the screen arranged chronologically,

        together with numerous illustrations.

0386   MICHAEL, Paul.

        Humphrey Bogart: the man and his films.

        Indianapolis, Bobbs-Merrill, 1965. 190p. illus.

        Following a biographical outline and appreciation,

        each of Bogart's films is listed, together with a synopsis,

        credits, and stills.

0387   RUDDY, Jonah   <u>and</u> HILL, Jonathan

       The Bogey man: portrait of a legend.

       London, Souvenir Press, 1965. 243p. illus.

          Consists largely of quotations from anecdotes and conver-

       sations involving Humphrey <u>Bogart</u>'s life and screen roles. With

       filmography.

0388   <u>BONOMO</u>, Joe, 1901-

       The strongman; a true life autobiography of the Hercules

       of the screen, Joe Bonomo.

       New York, Bonomo Studios, 1968. 352p. illus.

          Reminiscences of a stunt man and star of film serials.

0389   THE FILMS OF ROBERT <u>BRESSON</u>, by Amédée Ayfre and others.

       New York, Praeger, 1970, c1969. 143p. illus. *Praeger*

       film library.

          7 critics analyse Bressson's films and style, each

       offering differing viewpoints. The book also includes

       an interview with Bresson recorded by Ian Cameron at

       Cannes in 1962. With filmography and bibliography.

0390   <u>BROWN</u>, Joe Evan

       Laughter is a wonderful thing, by Joe E. Brown as told to

       Ralph Hancock.

       New York, Barnes, 1956. 312p. illus.

          Autobiography of the American comedy actor, including

       his screen experiences from his first film appearance in

       1927.

0391   <u>BRUNEL</u>, Adrian

       Nice work; the story of thirty years in British film

       production.

       London, Forbes Robertson, 1949. 217p. illus.

          An autobiography of the British film editor and

       director; also interesting as an insight into aspects of

       the British film industry.

0392   DURGNAT, Raymond, 1932-

        Luis Bunuel.

        London, Studio Vista, c1967. 144p. illus. *Movie paper-*

        backs series.

            A discussion of one of the world's most controversial

        film directors, with notes on his films up to Belle de jour.

        Includes bibliography and filmography.

0393   KYROU, Adonis, 1923-

        Luis Bunuel: an introduction by Ado Kyrou.

        New York, Simon & Schuster, 1963. 208p. illus. *World of film*

        series.

            Includes selected critical writings. Contents:- Bunuel:

        the man and his work.- Bunuel on the cinema.- Bunuel's works.-

        Criticism. With chronology/filmography and bibliography.

0394   WATERBURY, Ruth

        Richard Burton.

        New York, Pyramid Books, 1965. 171p. illus.

0395   CAPRA, Frank, 1897-

        The name above the title; an autobiography.

        New York, Macmillan, 1971. 513p. illus.

            An anecdotal autobiography by a leading American

        film director. With index.

0396   GRIFFITH, Richard, 1912-

        Frank Capra.

        London, British Film Institute, n.d. 38p. illus.

            A chronological survey of Frank Capra's films up

        to 1949, with credits, notes, and contemporary reviews.

0397   QUEVAL, Jean.

Marcel Carné.

London, British Film Institute, n.d. 27p. illus.

   A chronological survey of Carné's films up to 1950, with

credits, synopses, comments, and contemporary reviews.

0398   NEMCEK, Paul L.

The films of Nancy Carroll.

New York, Lyle Stuart, 1969. 223p. illus.

   A brief biographical outline, followed by synopses of

Nancy Carroll's 39 films from 1927 to 1938, with credits

and contemporary reviews for each.

0399   WOOD, Robin   and WALKER, Michael

Claude Chabrol.

New York, Praeger, 1870. 144p. illus. *Praeger film library.*

   An illustrated survey of Chabrol's films, with a

chapter devoted to each. With filmography.

0400   CHAPLIN, Charles, 1889-

My autobiography.

London, Bodley Head, 1964. 545p. illus.

   A nostalgic autobiography from Chaplin's childhood

in London and his early life as a music-hall artist to

his Hollywood successes and later life. Includes filmo-

graphy.

0401   CHAPLIN, Charles, 1925-

My father, Charlie Chaplin, by Charles Chaplin Jr., with

N. and M. Rau.

New York, Random House, 1960. 369p. illus.

   A biography. No index.

0402   CHAPLIN, Lita Gray, 1908-

My life with Chaplin; an intimate memoir, by Lita Grey

Chaplin with Morton Cooper.

New York, B. Geis, 1966. 325p. illus.

An extremely personal biography by Chaplin's ex-wife

detailing their marital relationship.

0403   COTES, Peter, 1912-   and NIKLAUS, Thelma

The little fellow; the life and work of Charles Spencer

Chaplin.

New York, Philosophical Library, 1951. 160p. illus.

Divided equally into examinations of Chaplin's

life and work. Appendices include a list of his films from

1914 to 1947, with comments on the more important titles.

With bibliographical references and index.

0404   HUFF, Theodore

Charlie Chaplin.

New York, Schuman, 1951. 354p. illus.

The most detailed and best researched book on Chaplin

and his work. Includes an index to the films of Charles

Chaplin, which lists casts and credits where known, together

with plot summaries of all of Chaplin's films up to

Monsieur Verdoux. A further appendix lists people

professionally associated with Chaplin.

0405   HUFF, Theodore

An index to the films of Charles S. Chaplin.

London, British Film Institute, 1945. 35p.

0406   McCAFFREY, Donald W., ed.

Focus on Chaplin.

Englewood Cliffs, N.Y., Prentice-Hall, 1971.

174p. illus.

Includes bibliography.

0407   MCDONALD, Gerald Doan, 1905-   and others

The films of Charlie Chaplin, by Gerald McDonald, Michael

Conway and Mark Ricci.

New York, Citadel Press, c1965. 222p. illus.

Includes cast, credits, and synopsis for each of Chaplin'

films, together with contemporary reviews and stills.

0408   McDONALD, Gerald Doan, 1905-

The picture history of Charlie Chaplin.

Franklin Square, N.Y., Nostalgia Press, 1965.

unpaged. illus.

0409   MINNEY, Rubeigh James, 1895-

Chaplin: the immortal tramp; the life and work of Charles

Chaplin.

London, Newnes, 1954. 170p. illus.

A personal anecdotal look at Chaplin's art and

personality.

0410   PAYNE, Pierre Stephen Robert, 1911-

The great god Pan; a biography of the tramp played by

Charles Chaplin.

New York, Hermitage House, 1952. 301p. illus.

Concentrates on the screen character created by Charlie

Chaplin. English edition has title The great Charlie. Reissu

as a paperback in 1964 by Ace under title Charlie Chaplin.

No index.

0411   QUIGLY, Isabel.

Charlie Chaplin: early comedies.

London, Studio Vista, 1968. 159p. illus. *Pictureback serie*

Concentrates on Chaplin's work from 1913-1919. Contents

The legend.- Keystone Studios.- The end of Sennett's contract

Essanay.- Mutual Film Corporation.- The First National.- Post

List of films and index. Well illustrated with stills.

0412   TYLER, Parker

Chaplin, last of the clowns.

New York, Vanguard Press, 1948. 180p. illus.

A study of Chaplin's art. Contents:- The caricature of a man.- Foundation of the comic epos.- The clown's triumph and his dream of happiness.- The gestures infront of and behind the screen.- The coronation of the underdog.- Abdication: farewell with flowers.

0413   VON ULM, Gerith, 1905-

Charlie Chaplin, king of tragedy.

Caldwell, Idaho, Caxton, 1940. 403p. illus.

An unauthorized biography based chiefly on information and documents belonging to Toraichi Kono, Chaplin's secretary.

0414   CHAPLIN, Michael, 1946-

I could't smoke the grass on my father's lawn.

London, Frewin, 1966. 173p. illus.

An autobiography by Chaplin's son with the help of ghost writers.

0415   CHERKASOV, Nikolai Konstantinovich, 1903-

Notes of a Soviet actor.

Moscow, Foreign Languages Publishing House, 1957.

227p. illus.

Life and methods of a veteran Soviet stage and screen actor.

0416   CHEVALIER, Maurice, 1889-1972

With love. As told to Eileen and Robert Mason Pollock.

Boston, Little, Brown, 1960. 424p. illus.

An autobiography. No index.

0417   CHRISTIAN, Linda

Linda: my own story.

New York, Crown, 1962. 280p. illus.

0418   CLAIR, Rene, 1898-

Reflections on the cinema.

London, Kimber, 1953. 160p.

Basically a collection of writings from between 1922 and 1935, with the added interest of the author's own comments added prior to publication in this edition interspersed within the text.

0419   DE LA ROCHE, Catherine

Rene Clair: an index.

London, British Film Institute, 1958. 43p. illus.

Filmography and bibliography.

0420   COCTEAU, Jean, 1889-1963.

Cocteau on the film; a conversation recorded by Andre Fraigneau.

London, Dobson, 1954. International theatre and cinema series.

A series of conversations in which Cocteau develops his concepts of film-making and relationships with his audience. With filmography.

0421   COCTEAU, Jean, 1889-1963.

The journals of Jean Cocteau. Edited and translated with an introduction by Wallace Fowlie.

New York, Criterion Books, c1956. 250p. illus.

Includes thirteen pages of Cocteau's writings specifically concerned with film:- On the "fantastic" in films.- From Lettre aux Americains.- Drawings for Orpheus.- Films.

0422   CROSLAND, Margaret

Jean Cocteau.

London, P. Nevill, 1955. 206p. illus.

A critical biography that includes a detailed bibliography.

0423   GILSON, Rene

Jean Cocteau.

New York, Crown, c1969. 192p. illus. *Editions Seghers' Cinema d'aujourd'hui in English.*

An investigation into Cocteau's films and philosophy. Contents:- Jean Cocteau, an essay by R. Gilson.- The cinema according to Jean Cocteau.- Excerpts from screenplays.- Critical spectrum, by Andre Bazin and others.- Witnesses: Cocteau the man, by J.-P. Bastide and others.- Filmography.- Discography.- Phonography.- Chronology of references.

0424   THOMAS, Bob

King Cohn; the life and times of Harry Cohn.

New York, Putnam, 1967. 381p. illus.

A lively biography of the co-founder, president, and head of production of Columbia Pictures.

0425   McCALLUM, John Dennis, 1924-

         Scooper; authorized story of Scoop Conlon's motion
         picture world.

         Seattle, Wood & Reber, 1960. 274p. illus.

0426   GANT, Richard

         Sean Connery: gilt-edged Bond.

         London, Mayflower, 1967. 109p. illus.

0427   CARPOZI, George

         The Gary Cooper story, by George Carpozi Jr.

         New Rochelle, N.Y., Arlington House, 1970. 263p. illus.

         With filmography and index.

0428   DICKENS, Homer

         The films of Gary Cooper.

         New York, Citadel Press, 1970. 278p. illus.

         *Credits, cast and synopsis for each of Cooper's
         films, with additional notes and extracts from contempor-
         ary reviews, preceded by a brief biography.*

0429   GEHMAN, Richard

         The tall American: the story of Gary Cooper.

         New York, Hawthorn Books, 1963. 187p. illus.

         Intended for younger readers.

0430   ROGER CORMAN, by Paul Willemen and others. Edited by

David Will and Paul Willemen.

Cambridge, Eng., Edinburgh Film Festival '70 in association

with Cinema magazine, 1970. 102p. illus.

Contents:- Roger Corman: the millenic vision.-
Corman: genre and grammar.- Roger Corman's descen into the
maelstrom.- 3 gangster films: an introduction.- 2 colour
supplement movies. Includes filmography.

0431   CRAWFORD, Joan, 1908-

A portrait of Joan; the autobiography of Joan Crawford.

With Jane Kesner Ardmore.

Garden City, N.Y., Doubleday, 1962. 239p. illus.

Includes a detailed filmography, from 1925 to 1959.

No index.

0432   QUIRK, Lawrence J.

The films of Joan Crawford.

New York, Citadel Press, 1968. 220p. illus.

Following a brief biographical outline, the book offers
an illustrated chronological survey of each of Joan Crawford's
films from 1925 to 1968, with credits, synopsis, and contemp-
orary reviews.

0433   CAREY, Gary

Cukor & Co.; the films of George Cukor and his collaborators.

New York, Museum of Modern Art, 1971. 167p. illus.

An assessment of Cukor's work and of the writers and
actors participating in his film.

0434   CUSSLER, Margaret

Not by a long shot; adventures of a documentary film

producer.

New York, Exposition Press, 1951. 200p. illus.

A chatty book about the writer's experiences. Of

little technical value. No index.

0435   DANDRIDGE, Dorothy, 1924-1965 and CONRAD, Earl

Everything and nothing: the Dorothy Dandridge tragedy.

New York, Abelard-Schuman, 1970. 215p. illus.

An autobiography prepared for publication by Earl

Conrad from tapes made before Dorothy Dandridge's death.

No index.

0436   DANISCHEWSKY, Monja, 1911-

White Russian - red face.

London, Gollancz. 192p. illus.

Autobiography of the film producer and script writer.

No index.

0437   DAVIS, Bette, 1908-

The lonely life; an autobiography.

New York, Putnam, 1962. 315p. illus.

0438   NOBLE, Peter, 1917-

Bette Davis: a biography.

London, Skelton Robinson, 1948. 231p. illus.

0439   RINGGOLD, Gene

The films of Bette Davis.

New York, Citadel Press, 1966. 191p. illus.

An illustrated chronological survey of Bette Davis' film

from 1931 to 1965, with credits, synopsis, and contemporary

reviews for each.

0440   DAVIS, Sammy

        Yes I can; the story of Sammy Davis, Jr., by Sammy

        Davis, Jr., and Jane and Burt Boyar.

        New York, Farrar, Straus and Giroux, 1965. 612p. illus.

0441   BAST, William, 1931-

        James Dean: a biography.

        New York, Ballantine Books, 1956. 153p. illus.

0442   ELLIS, Royston

        Rebel.

        London, World Distributors, 1962. 157p. illus.

        The story of James Dean, by the English 'beat' poet.

0443   THOMAS, T.T.

        I. James Dean; the real story behind America's most

        popular idol.

        New York, Popular Library, 1957. 128p. illus.

0444   DE MILLE, Cecil Blount, 1881-1959

        Autobiography of Cecil B. DeMille. Edited by Donald Hayne.

        Englewood Cliffs, N.J., Prentice-Hall, 1959. 465p. illus.

        Includes a chronological listing of DeMille's seventy

        feature films. With index.

0445   ESSOE, Gabe   and LEE, Raymond

        DeMille; the man and his pictures.

        South Brunswick, N. J., Barnes, 1970. 319p. illus.

        Biographical outline and anecdotes about DeMille's

        films and stars, illustrated with photographs and stills.

        Includes filmography.

0446   KOURY, Phil A.

    Yes, Mr. DeMille.

    New York, Putnam, 1959. 319p.

An anecdotal biography. The author was personal representative and executive assistant to DeMille for seven years from 1946.

0447   RINGGOLD, Gene   and BODEEN, De Witt

    The films of Cecil B. DeMille.

    New York, Citadel Press, 1969. 377p. illus.

An illustrated chronological survey of DeMille's films from 1914 to 1956, with synopses, credits and contemporary reviews. Includes a biographical outline.

DE MILLE, William C

    Hollywood saga.

    New York, Dutton, 1939. 519p. illus.

Written by Cecil B. DeMille's brother, this is a largely autobiographical account of the early days of Hollywood.

HENDRICKS, Gordon

    The Edison motion picture myth.

    Berkeley, University of California Press, 1961. 216p. illus.

This book sets out "1. To be a beginning of the task of cleaning up the morass of well-embroidered legend with which the beginning of the American film is permeated, and 2., to afford some measure of belated credit to the work done by W.K.L. Dickson." (pref.) A carefully researched enquiry covering the years from 1888 to 1892.

0448   DICKENS, Homer

The films of Marlene Dietrich.

New York, Citadel Press, 1968. 223p. illus.

Brief biographical introduction followed by details of all Dietrich's films, arranged chronologically by release date with credits and synopsis for each.

0449   FREWIN, Leslie Ronald, 1916-

Dietrich: the story of a star.

London, Frewin, 1967. 191p. illus.

An expanded and revised version of the author's earlier biography of Marlene Dietrich, published in 1955 under the title Blond Venus. With filmography.

0450   GRIFFITH, Richard, 1912-

Marlene Dietrich, image and legend.

Garden City, N.Y., Doubleday, 1959. 32p. illus.

0451   KOBAL, John.

Marlene Dietrich.

London, Studio Vista, 1968.

160p. illus. *Pictureback series.*

An illustrated survey of Dietrich's work, including filmography, discography, and bibliography.

0452   FEILD, Robert D

The art of Walt Disney.

London, Collins, 1944, c1942. 290p. illus.

Mainly devoted to an insight into the workings of the Disney Studios in the late 1930s, and an examination of its particular characteristics and qualities.

0453   MILLER, Diane (Disney)

The story of Walt Disney, as told to Pete Martin.

New York, Holt, 1957. 247p. illus.

A first-hand record of Disney's life and work by his daughter

0454   SCHICKEL, Richard

The Disney version; the life, times, art and commerce of Walt
Disney.

New York, Simon & Schuster, 1968. 384p.

A critical survey of the work of Walt Disney, with an
evaluation of his achievements. Includes bibliography. Engli
edition has title: Walt Disney.

0455   THOMAS, Bob

Walt Disney, magician of the movies.

New York, Grosset & Dunlap, 1966. 176p. illus.

Written for children.

0456   THOMAS, Bob

Walt Disney, the art of animation: the story of the Disney
Studio contribution to a new art, by Bob Thomas, with the Walt
Disney staff, with research by Don Graham.

New York, Simon & Schuster, 1958. 181p. illus.

0457   TREWIN, John C., 1908-

Robert Donat; a biography.

London, Heinemann, 1968. 252p. illus.

A biography which includes a list of Donat's roles
on stage and screen.

0458   CARL TH. DREYER, DANISH FILM DIRECTOR, 1889-1968.

        Edited by Søren Dyssegaard.

        Copenhagen, Ministry of Foreign Affairs, n.d. 51p. illus.

           Includes a short biography, a brief article on working with Dreyer, the filmscript of an unmade film, Jesus, and an appreciation by Jean Renoir. Illustrated with stills from Dreyer's films.

0459   MILNE, Tom.

        The cinema of Carl Dreyer.

        New York, Barnes, 1971. 191p. illus. *International film guide series.*

           An illustrated survey of Dreyer's films, with filmography and bibliography.

0460   BOGDANOVICH, Peter, 1939-

        Allan Dwan: the last pioneer.

        New York, Praeger, 1971. 200p. illus. *Praeger film library.*

           Consists mainly of a lengthy interview with the veteran film director, preceded by an introduction, and followed by a detailed filmography.

0461   O'KONOR, Louise, 1931-

        Viking Eggeling, 1880-1925: artist and film-maker, life and work.

        Stockholm, Almqvist & Wiksell, 1971. 299p.

           With bibliography.

0462   MONTAGU, Ivor Goldsmid Samuel, 1904-

        With Eisenstein in Hollywood; a chapter of autobiography.

        New York, International Publishers, 1969, c1967. 356p. illus.

           A personal account, together with the previously unpublished scenarios of Sutter's Gold, and An American Tragedy.

MOUSSINAC, Leon, 1890-1964.

       Sergei Eisenstein.

       New York, Crown, 1970. 226p. illus. *Editions Seghers' Cinema*

       d'aujourd'hui in English.

       A translation of the study first published in 1964.

       Consists of an essay by Moussinac followed by a selection of

       texts and documents.

0464   SETON, Marie

       Sergei M. Eisenstein: a biography.

       New York, Grove Press, 1960. 533p. illus.

       First published in 1952, this 'biography' serves also as

       an analysis of Eisenstein's theories and methods. An important

       study.

0465   COOKE, Alistair

       Douglas Fairbanks: the making of a screen character.

       New York, Museum of Modern Art, 1940. 35p. illus.

       An important monograph which, although brief in format,

       illustrates the process by which a screen character is

       created through tracing the career and work of Douglas

       Fairbanks. With index.

0466   HANCOCK, Ralph, 1903-   and   FAIRBANKS, Letitia

       Douglas Fairbanks: the fourth musketeer.

       New York, Holt, 1953. 276p. illus.

       A personal biography, with many anecdotes. No index.

0467   CONNELL, Brian

       Knight errant; a biography of Douglas Fairbanks, Jr.

       London, Hodder & Stoughton, 1955. 288p. illus.

       A personal biography concentrating on the life rather

       than the work of Fairbanks. With index.

0468   BUDGEN, Suzanne

Fellini.

London, British Film Institute, 1966. 128p. illus.

An evaluation of the Italian film director's work, together with extracts from a television interview and a discussion with Fellini, an excerpt from the script of his
film La strada, and a filmography compiled by John Russell
Taylor.

0469   SALACHAS, Gilbert

Federico Fellini.

New York, Crown, 1969. 224p. illus. *Editions Seghers' Cinema
d'aujourd'hui in English.*

Contents:- Federico Fellini: an essay by G. Salachas.-
The cinema according to Federico Fellini.- The work of
Federico Fellini: excerts from screenplays and film treatments.-
Critical spectrum, by G. Agel and others.- Witnesses.- Selected
bibliography.- Filmography.- Index. The book has a cover
subtitle:- an investigation into his films and philosophy.

0470   SOLMI, Angelo

Fellini.

London, Merlin Press, 1967. 183p. illus.

Arranged in two parts:- Fellini's world of ideas.- A
life in 8½ films. In the first part the author explores
Fellini's recurring themes, and in the second part provides
autobiographical background and an examination of Fellini's
films.

0471   DESCHNER, Donald

The films of W.C. Fields.

New York, Citadel Press, c1966. 192p. illus.

Each film featuring Fields is represented, with casts,

credits, plot summaries, quotes from contemporary reviews,

and stills. Includes an introduction by Arthur Knight,

two essays by Fields, and reviews of Fields as a film

actor and as a stage comedian.

0472   EVERSON, William K

The art of W.C. Fields.

Indianapolis, Bobbs-Merrill, 1967. 232p. illus.

An illustrated survey of the films of W.C. Fields.

No index.

0473   FIELDS, W. C., 1879-1946

Drat! Being the encapsulated view of life by W.C. Fields in

his own words. Edited by Richard J. Anobile.

New York, World Pub. Co., 1968. 128p. illus.

Consists of stills in juxtoposition with quotes

from Fields' films. Sources of both are listed.

0474   MONTI, Carlotta.

W.C. Fields & me, by Carlotta Monti with Cy Rice.

Englewood Cliffs, N.J., Prentice-Hall, 1971. 227p. illus.

Memoirs and anecdotes by Fields' mistress. Very little

of film interest.

0475   TAYLOR, Robert Lewis

W. C. Fields: his follies and fortunes.

Garden City, N.Y., Doubleday, 1949. 340p. illus.

A biography. No index.

0476   LATHAM, Aaron.

Crazy sundays: F. Scott Fitzgerald in Hollywood.

New York, Viking Press, 1971. 308p.

0477   - CALDER-MARSHALL, Arthur, 1908-

The innocent eye: the life of Robert J. Flaherty; based

on research material by Paul Rotha and Basil Wright.

London, W.H. Allen, 1963. 303p. illus.

A detailed and objective study of the work of the

great documentary film maker, based on a manuscript

originally prepared by Rotha and Wright. Includes

filmography and bibliography.

0478   FLAHERTY, Frances (Hubbard)

The odyssey of a film-maker; Robert Flaherty's story.

Urbana, Ill., Beta Phi Mu, 1960. 45p. illus.

A very brief though well illustrated book by

Flaherty's wife. Includes a chronology.

0479   GRIFFITH, Richard, 1912-

The world of Robert Flaherty.

New York, Duell, Sloane and Pearce, c1953. 165p. illus.

A fine biography of the pioneer documentary film-maker.

It includes excerpts from journals, diaries and letters.

0480   FLYNN, Errol Leslie, 1909-1959

My wicked wicked ways.

New York, Putnam, 1959. 438p.

A personal autobiography.

132   0481   HAYMES, Nora (Eddington) Flynn, 1924-

Errol and me, by Nora Eddington Flynn Haymes, as told to
Cy Rice.

New York, New American Library, 1960. 176p. illus.

0482   PARISH, Robert   and others.

Errol Flynn, by Robert Parish, Alan G. Barbour and
Alvin H. Marill.

New York, Cinefax, 1969. unpaged. illus.

*A collection of stills and portraits of Errol Flynn.
With filmography.*

0483   THOMAS, Tony   and others

The films of Errol Flynn, by Tony Thomas, Rudy Behlmer
and Clifford McCarty.

New York, Citadel Press, c1969. 221p. illus.

*An illustrated chronological survey of Flynn's films,
with synopses, credits, and numerous illustrations. Includes a biographical introduction.*

0484   SPRINGER, John Shipman, 1916-

The Fondas: the films and careers of Henry, Jane and Peter
Fonda.

New York, Citadel Press, 1970. 279p. illus.

*Following several introductory sections, the book presen
a chronological illustrated survey of the films in which the
Fonda family have appeared. With credits, synopses, and contemporary reviews.*

0485 BOGDANOVICH, Peter, 1939-

    John Ford.

    London, Studio Vista, c1967. 144p. illus. *Movie paper-*

    backs series.

     Consists largely of interviews with Ford, followed

    by a brief bibliography and filmography.

0486 ALLVINE, Glendon

    The greatest fox of them all.

    New York, Lyle Stuart, 1969. 244p. illus.

     The biography of William Fox, Hollywood tycoon and

    founder of Twentieth Century-Fox.

0487 DURGNAT, Raymond, 1932-

    Franju.

    London, Studio Vista, c1967. 144p. illus. *Movie paper-*

    backs series.

     Following a general consideration of Franju's work,

    Durgnat discusses each of the French director's films, up

    to 1965. Includes filmography and bibliography.

0488 PRATLEY, Gerald

    The cinema of John Frankenheimer.

    London, Zwemmer, 1969. 240p. illus. *International film*

    guide series.

     Based on extensive interviews with Frankenheimer,

    a section of the book being devoted to each of his films,

    each section containing credits, synopsis, comments by

    Pratley and then by Frankenheimer. The book concludes by

    offering more of the director's thoughts on such topics as the

    film-maker's responsibilities and American film critics.

0489 ELWOOD, Muriel

Pauline Frederick, on and off the stage.

Chicago, Kroch, 1940, c1939. 225p. illus.

A biography that concentrates on the actress'

personal life, but with chapters concerning her work in

films. With filmography and index.

ALLISTER, Ray, *pseud.*

Friese-Greene; close-up of an inventor.

London, Marsland, 1948. 192p. illus.

The subject was "the man who first announced, first

used in public, first patented a commercially practical

moving picture camera" (author). Includes a list of

Friese-Greene's British patents. The book was reissued

in 1951 with the addition of eight pages of photographs

from the film about Friese-Greene, The magic box.

0490 FROBOESS, Harry

The reminiscing champ; a world-famous stunt man tells his

story.

New York, Pageant Press, 1953. 141p. illus.

Biographical, mostly consisting of brief reminiscences

about the author's film stunts.

0491 HARDY, Phil

Samuel Fuller.

New York, Praeger, 1970. 144p. illus. *Praeger film library*

An illustrated survey of Fuller's films, arranged

under the following headings:- An American dream.-

Journalism and style.- An American reality.- Asia.- The

violence of love. With filmography.

0492   WILL, David   <u>and</u> WOLLEN, Peter, <u>eds</u>.

Samuel <u>Fuller</u>.

Edinburgh Film Festival '69 in association with Scottish

International Review, 1969. 128p. illus.

"The aim of this book is to provide the first forum of

critical writing on Samuel Fuller to appear in English.

A selection of essays is supplemented by an interview."

(ed.)

0493   CARPOZI, George

Clark <u>Gable</u>.

New York, Pyramid Books, 1961. 160p. illus.

A biography written in journalistic style. No index.

0494   ESSOE, Gabe

The films of Clark <u>Gable</u>.

New York, Citadel Press, 1970. 253p. illus.

Credits, synopses and contemporary reviews for each

of Gable's films, preceded by an introductory essay,

reminiscences by friends and fellow actors, and details of

his major stage appearances prior to his film career.

0495   GABLE, Kathleen (Williams)

Clark <u>Gable</u>: a personal portrait.

Englewood Cliffs, N.J., Prentice-Hall, 1961. 151p. illus.

0496   GARCEAU, Jean

Dear Mr. G---; the biography of Clark <u>Gable</u>, by Jean

Garceau with Inez Cocke.

Boston, Little, Brown, c1961. 297p. illus.

A biography, written by Clark Gable's personal

secretary. No index.

0497   SAMUELS, Charles

The king; a biography of Clark Gable.

New York, Coward-McCann, 1962. 315p.

A biography that concentrates on Gable's private life.

English edition published under title: The king of Hollywood

the story of Clark Gable.

0498   WILLIAMS, Chester

Gable.

New York, Fleet Press Corp., 1968. 154p. illus.

With filmography.

0499   BAINBRIDGE, John

Garbo.

New York, Doubleday, 1955. 256p. illus.

A biography that includes accounts of European and

Hollywood film production during the twenties and thirties.

With filmography.

0500   BILLQUIST, Fritiof

Garbo; a biography.

London, A. Barker, 1960. 180p. illus.

Includes a filmography.

0501   CONWAY, Michael   and others.

The films of Greta Garbo, compiled by Michael Conway,

Dion McGregor, and Mark Ricci. With an introductory essay,

The Garbo image, by Parker Tyler. 155p. illus.

Includes credits, synopsis, stills and contemporary

reviews for each of Garbo's films.

0502   DURGNAT, Raymond, 1932-   <u>and</u> KOBAL, John

Greta <u>Garbo</u>.

London, Studio Vista, 1965. 160p. illus. *Pictureback*
series.

A brief biography illustrated with numerous stills.
Also contains an annotated filmography and a comprehensive
bibliography.

0503   LAING, E. E.

Greta <u>Garbo</u>: the story of a specialist.

London, J. Gifford, 1946. illus.

0504   SJOLANDER, Ture, 1937-

<u>Garbo</u>.

New York, Harper & Row, 1971. 135p. illus.

The story of Garbo's private and public life. Brief
text accompanies nearly two hundred photographs.

0505   ZIEROLD, Norman J.

<u>Garbo</u>.

New York, Stein and Day, 1969.
196p. illus.

A biography. An appendix lists Garbo's films in detail,
with synopses and contemporary criticism as well as credits.
With bibliography.

0506   HANNA, David

Ava, a portrait of a star.

New York, Putnam, 1960. 256p. illus.

(Ava <u>Gardner</u>)

0507   MORELLA, Joe   and EPSTEIN, Edward Z.

Judy: the films and career of Judy Garland.

New York, Citadel Press, 1969. 216p. illus.

A well illustrated survey of the films of Judy

Garland with brief comments, credits, and contemporary

reviews.

0508   GISH, Lillian, 1896-

The movies, Mr. Griffith, and me, by Lillian Gish with

Ann Pinchot.

Englewood Cliffs, N.J., Prentice-Hall, 1969. 388p. illus.

A biography of the screen actress which gives a fascinat

insight into the American silent film period and particularly

the work of D.W. Griffith. Well illustrated and with a

detailed index.

0509   COLLET, Jean

Jean-Luc Godard. Rev. ed.

New York, Crown, 1970. 215p. illus. *Editions Seghers'*

Cinema d'aujourd'hui in English.

A translation of the revised edition of the study

published in French in 1968. Consists of an essay by

Collet, followed by selected texts and documents. With

filmography and bibliography.

0510   THE FILMS OF JEAN-LUC GODARD, by Charles Barr and others. Rev. ed

New York, Praeger, 1970, c1969. 192p. illus. *Praeger film*

library.

Analyses of Godard's films up to One plus one, written

by 16 critics, sometimes offering widely differing critical

approaches to Godard's work. With filmography and bibliograp

0511   MUSSMAN, Toby, ed.

Jean-Luc Godard: a critical anthology.

New York, Dutton, 1968. 319p. illus.

Consists of a selection of critical essays and reviews with the addition of interviews and articles by Godard. The book also includes the scenarios of A woman is a woman, and Vivre sa vie. With chronology and filmography.

0512   ROUD, Richard

Jean-Luc Godard. 2d rev. ed.

London, Thames & Hudson in association with the British Film Institute, 1970. 192p. illus. *Cinema one series.*

A critical study of Godard's controversial career. With detailed filmography.

0513   GODOWSKY, Dagmar

First person plural; the lives of Dagmar Godowsky.

New York, Viking Press, 1958. 249p. illus.

Concerned almost entirely with the author's private life.

0514   GRIFFITH, Richard, 1912-

Samuel Goldwyn: the producer and his films.

New York, Museum of Modern Art Film Library, 1956. 48p. illus.

Introductory remarks evaluate the role of the producer in a motion picture. With filmography.

0515   JOHNSTON, Alva

The great Goldwyn.

New York, Random House, 1937. 99p. illus.

0516   GRANLUND, Nils Thor.

Blondes, brunettes and bullets, by Nils Thor Granlund, with
Sid Feder and Ralph Hancock.

New York, D. McKay, 1957. 300p.

    Autobiography, *written by a cabaret producer who worked*
for the publicity department of Loew's in the early days
of Hollywood. Includes reminiscences of the vaudeville
programmes and the stars, particularly those who started
in chorus lines.

0517   BARRY, Iris, 1895-

D.W. Griffith, American film master.

New York, Museum of Modern Art, 1965. 88p. illus.

    A re-issue of a well documented, informative mono-
graph first published in 1940. The expanded edition
includes an annotated list of Griffith's films compiled
by Eileen Bowser.

0518   CROY, Homer, 1883-

Star maker; the story of D.W. Griffith.

New York, Duell, Sloan & Pearce, c1959. 210p. illus.

    A biography of the American film pioneer that is
personal rather than critical in approach. Includes a
facetious index.

0519   GEDULD, Harry M., ed.

Focus on D.W. Griffith.

Englewood Cliffs, N.J., Prentice-Hall, 1971. 182p. *Film*
focus series.

    A study of Griffith's work that includes extracts
from writings and statements by the director, and a
collection of critical essays. With filmography and
bibliography.

GISH, Lillian, 1896-

The movies, Mr. Griffith, and me, by Lillian Gish with

Ann Pinchot.

Englewood Cliffs, N.J., Prentice-Hall, 1969. 388p. illus.

A biography of the screen actress which gives a fascinating

insight into the American silent film period and particularly

the work of D.W. Griffith. Well illustrated and with a

detailed index.

0520   HENDERSON, Robert M.

D.W. Griffith: the years at Biograph.

New York, Farrar, Straus and Giroux, 1970. 250p. illus.

A well-researched study of Griffith's work between

1908 and 1913. With detailed bibliography, filmography,

and list of players.

0521   O'DELL, Paul.

Griffith and the rise of Hollywood, by Paul O'Dell with

the assistance of Anthony Slide.

New York, Barnes, 1970. 163p. illus. *International*

film guide series.

Contents:- The birth of a nation.- Intolerance.-

Thomas Harper Ince.- The denial of a spectacle: True heart

Susie to Broken blossoms.- Into the twenties: Way down east

and Orphans of the storm.- The star system. With bibliography.

0523   CONWAY, Michael   and   RICCI, Mark

The films of Jean Harlow.

New York, Citadel Press, c1965. 159p. illus.

Includes stills, credits, synopsis, and contemporary
reviews for each of Harlow's films.

0524   DAVIES, Dentner

Jean Harlow, Hollywood comet.

London, Constable, 1937. 153p. illus.

0525   PASCAL, John

The Jean Harlow story.

New York, Popular Library, c1964. 158p. illus.

0526   SHULMAN, Irving

Harlow: an intimate biography.

New York, B. Geis, 1964. 408p. illus.

Based on the memoirs of a publicist close to Harlow.

0527   BOGDANOVICH, Peter, 1939-

The cinema of Howard Hawks.

New York, Museum of Modern Art Film Library, 1962.
38p. illus.

Published in conjunction with the programmes of
Hawks' films presented at the Museum of Modern Art.

0528   WOOD, Robin

Howard Hawks.

London, Secker & Warburg in association with the British
Film Institute, 1968. 200p. illus. Cinema one series.

A study of the American director by one of the youngest
English film critics. With filmography.

HAYAKAWA, Sessue Kintaro, 1889-

Zen showed me the way: to peace, happiness and tranquility.

Edited by Croswell Bowen.

Indianapolis, Bobbs-Merrill, c1960. 256p. illus.

Inspite of the title, this is basically an autobiography

of the Japanese stage and screen actor. No index.

0530   HAYDEN, Stirling, 1916-

Wanderer.

New York, Knopf, 1963. 434p.

0531   HAYS, Will H., 1879-1954.

The memoirs of Will H. Hays.

Garden City, N.Y., Doubleday, 1955. 600p. port.

Part four (p. 323-582) is titled Motion pictures,

1922-1945. Such topics as the Production Code and the

war-time cinema in the United States are dealt with.

0532   HEAD, Edith   and ARDMORE, Jane Kesner (Morris)

The dress doctor.

Boston, Little, Brown, 1959. 249p. illus.

Autobiography by Paramount's fashion chief.

Illustrated with sketches by the author.

0533   BISHOP, James Alonzo, 1907-

The Mark Hellinger story; a biography of Broadway and

Hollywood, by Jim Bishop.

New York, Appleton-Century-Crofts, 1952. 367p.

A biography of the show-business reporter and film

producer.

0534   DICKENS, Homer

The films of Katharine Hepburn.

New York, Citadel Press, 1971. 242p. illus.

A chronological survey of Miss Hepburn's films from 1932 to 1969, with the addition of brief biographical notes and a list of her major stage appearances. The filmography includes credits, synopses and contemporary reviews.

0535   HEPWORTH, Cecil M., 1874-

Came the dawn: memories of a film pioneer.

London, Phoenix House, 1951. 207p. illus.

Autobiography of the English film-maker, covering the period up to the early twenties. With index.

0536   BOGDANOVICH, Peter, 1939-

The cinema of Alfred Hitchcock.

New York, Museum of Modern Art Film Library, 1963. 48p. illus.

"Published in conjunction with the film cycle, The cinema of Alfred Hitchcock... at the Museum of Modern Art, New York".

0537   PERRY, George.

The films of Alfred Hitchcock.

London, Studio Vista, 1965. 160p. illus. *Dutton Vista pictureback series.*

An illustrated guide to Hitchcock's films, arranged chronologically from 1921 to 1964. With filmography.

0538   TRUFFAUT, Francois

Hitchcock, by Francois Truffaut with the collaboration of Helen G. Scott.

New York, Simon & Schuster, 1967. 256p. illus.

A series of incisive interviews between Truffaut and Hitchcock, providing insights into Hitchcock's ideas and approaches to his films. With filmography and bibliography.

0539   WOOD, Robin

Hitchcock's films. 2d enl. ed.

London, Zwemmer, 1969. 204p. illus. *International film guide series.*

An in-depth study of Hitchcock's work from 1950. With filmography and bibliography.

0540   HOLSTIUS, Edward Nils

Hollywood through the back door.

London, Bles, 1937. 419p.

Memoirs of a screen writer.

0541   HOPKINSON, Peter

Split focus: an involvement in two decades.

London, Hart-Davis, 1969. 218p. illus.

Autobiography by a leading documentary film-maker.

0542   COLVIN, Ian Goodhope, 1912-

Flight 777.

London, Evans, 1957. 212p. illus.

An investigation into the circumstances surrounding the death of Leslie Howard.

0543   HOWARD, Leslie Ruth, 1924-

A quite remarkable father.

Toronto, Longmans, Green, c1959. 307p. illus.

A biography of the stage and screen actor, written by his daughter. With index. (Leslie Howard, 1893-1943)

0544   HUDSON, Will E.

Icy hell; experiences of a newsreel cameraman in the

Aleutian islands, eastern Siberia, and the Arctic

fringe of Alaska.

New York, Stokes, 1937. 308p. illus.

0545   GERBER, Albert Benjamin, 1913-

Bashful billionaire: the story of Howard Hughes.

New York, L. Stuart, 1967.

384p.

0546   KEATS, John, 1920-

Howard Hughes.

New York, Random House, c1966. 304p. illus.

A biography of the millionaire film-maker. No index.

0547   NOLAN, Willam F.

John Huston, king rebel.

Los Angeles, Sherbourne Press, c1965. 247p. illus.

A detailed biography, with behind-the-scenes location

stories. Appendices include The projects of John Huston:

films and plays, 1931-1965, and A Huston bibliography. No

index.

0548   TOZZI, Romano

John Huston.

New York, Falcon Enterprises, 1971. 148p. illus.

Hollywood's magic people series.

A largely pictorial survey of Huston's films, both as

a director and actor. With brief text. Includes film-

ography.

0549   IVENS, Joris, 1898–

        The camera and I.

        New York, International Publishers, 1969. 279p. illus.

          An autobiography of a documentary film-maker of interest

        to all students of film history. With filmography.

0550   BRITISH FILM INSTITUTE, LONDON. EDUCATION DEPT.

        Humphrey Jennings.

        London, British Film Institute, 1969. 33p.

          With filmography and bibliography.

0551   BARBOUR, Alan G   and others

        Karloff, by Alan G. Barbour, Alvin H. Marill and James

        Robert Parish.

        Kew Gardens, N.Y., Cinefax, 1969. unpaged. illus.

          "A representative selection of photographs & stills

        covering...[Karloff's] fifty years in films." With

        chronological filmography.

0552   SINGER, Kurt Deutsch

        The Danny Kaye story.

        New York, Nelson, 1958. 241p.

          A biography. No index.

0553   BLESH, Rudi, 1899–

        Keaton.

        New York, Macmillan, c1966. 395p. illus.

          An entertaining biography. Includes a filmography,

        compiled by Raymond Rohauer and Rudi Blesh.

0554   KEATON, Buster, 1895-1966.

My wonderful world of slapstick, by Buster Keaton with

Charles Samuels.

Garden City, N.Y., Doubleday, 1960.   282p.   illus.

An anecdotal autobiography.   No index.

0555   LEBEL, Jean Patrick, 1942-

Buster Keaton.

London, Zwemmer, 1967.   179p.   illus.

International film guide series.

Contents:- The great stone face.- The perfect geom-
etry.- A great director.- A backdrop without values.- The gag
Buster Keaton and the cinema.- Extensions of Keaton's work.-
Provisional conclusion.   With a biographical introduction and
filmography.

0556   ROBINSON, David, 1915-

Buster Keaton.

London, Secker & Warburg in association with the British Film

Institute, 1969.

198p.   illus.   *Cinema one series.*

A study of Keaton as film-maker, actor, and person.
With a filmography of his silent films.

0557   GRIFFITH, Richard, 1912-

The cinema of Gene Kelly.

New York, Museum of Modern Art Film Library, 1962.   16p.   il

With filmography.

0558   GOBEIL, Charlotte, ed.

The film and Ron Kelly.

Ottawa, Canadian Film Institute, 1965. 24p.

Contains an interview with the young Canadian film-maker, his comments on his films, and an excerpt from a magazine article about him.

0559   MARTIN, Bruce.

Allan King; an interview with Bruce Martin, and a filmography. Edited by Alison Reid.

Ottawa, Canadian Film Institute, 1970. 26p. illus.

Canadian filmography series.

An interview with the Canadian film-maker, who discusses his work. With filmography.

0560   KNEF, Hildegard.

The gift horse; report on a life.

New York, McGraw-Hill, 1971. 384p.

Autobiography.

0561   TABORI, Paul, 1908-

Alexander Korda.

London, Oldbourne, 1959. 324p. illus.

A biography of the film director and producer, written by a script-writer and colleague of Korda. With index and a list of Korda's films.

0562   WALKER, Alexander

Stanley Kubrick directs.

New York, Harcourt, Brace, Jovanovich, 1971. 272p. illus.

Contents:- Kubrick: man and outlook from Fear and desire to A clockwork orange.- Kubrick: style and content.- Paths of glory.- Dr. Strangelove, or how I learned to stop worrying and love the bomb.- 2001: a space odyssey.- Filmography. Includ more than 350 illustrations.

0563   RICHIE, Donald, 1924-

The films of Akira Kurosawa.

Berkeley, University of California Press, 1965.
218p. illus.

An illustrated critical study of the famous Japanese director, with filmography and bibliography.

0564   LAHR, John, 1941-

Notes on a cowardly lion; the biography of Bert Lahr.
New York, Knopf, 1969. 394p. illus.

A biography written by the comedy actor's son that places more emphasis on Lahr's stage work, but includes references to his films, particularly his role in The Wizard of Oz referred to in the title.

0565   LAKE, Veronica.

Veronica, by Veronica Lake, with Donald Bain.
London, Allen, 1969. 248p. illus.

A personal autobiography. No index.

0566   LAMARR, Hedy, 1915-

        Ecstasy and me; my life as a woman.

        New York, Bartholomew House, 1966. 318p. illus.

0567   VERMILYE, Jerry

        Burt Lancaster.

        New York, Falcon Enterprises, 1971.

        148p. illus. *Hollywood's magic people series.*

            A largely pictorial survey of Lancaster's films, with

        brief text. Includes filmography.

        LANCHESTER, Elsa.

        Charles Laughton and I.

        London, Faber, 1938. 271p. illus.

            A personal biography of the actor written by his

        actress wife.

0568   BOGDANOVICH, Peter, 1939-

        Fritz Lang in America.

        New York, Praeger, 1969, c1967. 143p. illus. *Praeger*

        film library.

            Consists mainly of an interview with the German film

        director, made in 1965 and dealing with his American work.

        Includes detailed filmography with entries for all of his

        films including those made in Germany.

0569   JENSEN, Paul M.

        The cinema of Fritz Lang. London, Zwemmer, 1969.

        223p. illus. *International film guide series.*

            A monograph on the entire career of Lang, together with

        filmography and bibliography. Includes outlines of all of

        Lang's films. No index.

0570   LASKY, Jessie Louis, 1880-1958.

I blow my own horn, by Jessie L. Lasky with Don Weldon.

London, Gollancz, 1957. 284p.

An anecdotal biography by one of the pioneers of

Hollywood.

0571   BROWN, William

Charles Laughton.

New York, Falcon Enterprises, 1970. 152p. illus. *Hollywood*

magic people series.

An illustrated survey of Laughton's film career, con-

sisting largely of stills with brief accompanying text.

Includes filmography.

0572   LANCHESTER, Elsa.

Charles Laughton and I.

London, Faber, 1938. 271p. illus.

A personal biography of the actor written by his

actress wife.

0573   SINGER, Kurt Deutsch

The Laughton story; an intimate story of Charles Laughton.

Philadelphia, Winston, 1954. 308p. illus.

A biography. With index.

0574   BARR, Charles

Laurel & Hardy.

Berkeley, Calif., University of California Press, 1968,

c1967. 143p. illus. *Movie editions series*

A concise illustrated survey of the film work of

the comedy team. With filmography (from 1927) and

bibliography.

0575 EVERSON, William K

The films of Laurel & Hardy.

New York, Citadel Press, c1967. 223p. illus.

Consists mainly of a complete listing of the films of Laurel and Hardy, each with credits, a synopsis and evaluation.

0576 MCCABE, John.

Mr. Laurel and Mr. Hardy. Rev. ed.

New York, Grosset & Dunlap, 1966. 262p. illus.

A perceptive, affectionate portrait of the comedy team showing insight into their creative processes. (Laurel & Hardy)

0577 LEE, Raymond

M.

Encino, Calif., Defilee, 1958. 64p. illus.

The author's experiences as a child actor in silent films from 1915 to 1927, with reminiscences about early cinema personalities.

BARKER, Felix

The Oliviers; a biography.

Philadelphia, Lippincott, c1953. 371p. illus.

The authorized biography of Sir Laurence Olivier and Vivien Leigh, written by a British drama critic. In five sections: Laurence Olivier; Vivien Leigh; The partnership begins; Marriage; In their own theatre.

0578 DENT, Alan, 1905-

Vivien Leigh: a bouquet.

London, Hamish Hamilton, 1969. 219p. illus.

A biography, with a chapter on Vivien Leigh as a screen actress, and a filmography.

FERNETT, Gene

Next time drive off the cliff!

Cocoa, Fla., Cinememories, 1968. 205p. illus.

The story of Nat Levine, dubbed 'The king of the serial makers' and of Mascot Pictures, an independent film studio typical of many producing serials and 'B' pictures during the 1930s. Includes credits and synopses of representative Mascot films.

0579   GEHMAN, Richard

That kid: the story of Jerry Lewis.

New York, Avon Books, 1964. 192p.

0580   CAHN, William, 1912-

Harold Lloyd's world of comedy.

New York, Duell, Sloan and Pearce, c1964. 208p. illus.

An anecdotal book based on lengthy interviews with Lloyd. With numerous illustrations.

0581   LLOYD, Harold Clayton, 1894-

An American comedy. Written in collaboration with Wesley W. Stout.

New York, Dover, 1971. 138p. illus.

A reprint of the autobiography first published in 1928, with the addition of the text of a 1966 interview with Lloyd on "The serious business of being funny." This reprint also includes a number of additional stills.

0582   LOCKWOOD, Margaret, 1916-

Lucky star; the autobiography of Margaret Lockwood.

London, Odhams Press, 1955. 191p. illus.

0583   LOCKWOOD, Margaret, 1916-

My life and films. Edited by Eric Warman.

London, World Film Publications, 1948. 78p. illus.

0584   **REID, Gordon**

Gina Lollobrigida: her life and films.

London, Eurap, 1956. 64p. illus. *Film star biographies serie.*

0585   LOOS, Anita, 1894-

A girl like I.

New York, Viking Press, 1966. 275p. illus.

Anecdotal autobiography of the Hollywood screenplay writer and socialite.

0586   LABORDERIE, Renaud de

Sophia Loren: Renaud de Laborderie spotlights in words and pictures the career of the remarkable Sophia Loren.

Manchester, Eng., World Distributors, 1964. 48p. illus.

0587   REID, Gordon

The Sophia Loren story.

London, Eurap, 1958.

Film star biographies series.

With filmography.

0588   SNYDER, Robert L

Pare Lorentz and the documentary film.

Norman, University of Oklahoma Press, 1968. 232p. illus.

A detailed examination of the documentary film work of Pare Lorentz and the establishment of the United States Film Service. With bibliography.

0589   LEAHY, James

The cinema of Joseph Losey.

London, Zwemmer, 1967. 175p. illus.

International film guide series.

Consists of interviews with Losey concerning each of his films, followed by the author's critical comments. With filmography and bibliography.

0590   LOSEY, Joseph, 1909-

Losey on Losey. Edited and introduced by Tom Milne.

Garden City, N.Y., Doubleday, 1968.

192p. illus. *Cinema world series.*

A study of an unusual director constructed from taped interviews. With filmography.

0591   WEINBERG, Herman G., 1908-

The Lubitsch touch: a critical study.

New York, Dutton, 1968. 344p. illus.

Following the pattern of the author's earlier work on Von Sternberg, this book includes a critical study of the work of Lubitsch, followed by interviews, excerpts from the screenplay of Ninotchka, and a selection of evaluations and tributes. With filmography and bibliography.

0592   HECHT, Ben, 1893–

Charlie; the improbable life and times of Charles
MacArthur.

New York, Harper, c1957. 242p. illus.

*A biography, the last third of which deals with
MacArthur's life and work in Hollywood. With index.*

0593   GOBEIL, Charlotte, ed.

Terence Macartney-Filgate: the candid eye.

Ottawa, Canadian Film Institute, 1966. 34p. illus. *Canadian
filmography series.*

*An interview with, and articles about the Canadian
documentary filmmaker. Some articles are in French.
With filmography.*

0594   MACLAINE, Shirley

Don't fall off the mountain.

New York, Norton, 1970. 270p.

Autobiographical.

0595   MACPHERSON, Sandy

Sandy presents.

London, Home & Van Thal, 1950. 179p. illus.

*Autobiography of the cinema and radio organist in
Canada and England.*

158   0596   MAMOULIAN, Rouben, 1898-

Style is the man.

Washington, D.C., American Film Institute, 1971.   34p.

illus.

Transcription of a seminar held at the Center for

Advanced Film Studies in which Mamoulian is interviewed

and answers questions about his films. With filmography

and bibliography.

0597   MILNE, Tom.

Rouben Mamoulian.

London, Thames and Hudson in association with the British

Film Institute. 1969.   176p.   illus. Cinema one series.

A critical study of the director's sixteen films,

with filmography.

0598   DWIGGINS, Don

Hollywood pilot; the biography of Paul Mantz.

Garden City, N.Y., Doubleday, 1967.   249p.   illus.

The biography of a Hollywood stunt pilot.

0599   MARX, Arthur, 1921-

Life with Groucho.

New York, Simon & Schuster, 1954.   310p.

Written by Groucho Marx's son.

0600   MARX, Groucho, 1891-

Groucho and me.

New York, B. Geis, 1959.   344p.   illus.

An autobiographical collection of Groucho's thoughts,

opinions, and reminiscences.

MARX, Harpo, 1893-1964

Harpo speaks! By Harpo Marx with Rowland Barber.

New York, B. Geis, 1961. 475p. illus.

A lengthy autobiography by the silent member of the

Marx Brothers.

0602　　CRICHTON, Kyle Samuel, 1896-

The Marx Brothers.

Garden City, N.Y., Doubleday, 1950. 310p. illus.

An entertaining biography of the comedy team's

days in the theatre, but with little mention of their film

career. No index.

0603　　EYLES, Allen

The Marx Brothers: their world of comedy. 2d ed.

New York, Barnes, 1969. 176p. illus. *International*

film guide series.

A much expanded version of the author's The Marx

Brothers: a Motion monograph, published in 1964. Includes

chapters on all of the comedy team's major films, together

with additional notes and filmography.

0604　　ZIMMERMAN, Paul D　　and GOLDBLATT, Burt

The Marx Brothers at the movies.

New York, Putnam, 1968. 224p. illus.

Provides credits for each of the Marx Brothers' films,

together with detailed plot descriptions and dialogue excerpts.

With more than 200 stills.

0605 MONAGHAN, John P

     The authorised biography of James Mason.

     London, World Films Publications, 1947. 78p. illus.

0606 MAYER, Arthur, 1886-

     Merely colossal: the story of the movies from the long

     chase to the chaise longue.

     New York, Simon & Schuster, 1953. 264p. illus.

     An autobiographical account of the experiences of a

     life in the American film industry and with the men involved

     in production, distribution and exhibition of films.

0607 CROWTHER, Bosley

     Hollywood Rajah; the life and times of Louis B. Mayer.

     New York, Holt, Rinehart & Winston, 1960. 339p. illus.

     A biography of the famous Hollywood tycoon and

     producer, written by the former film critic of the New

     York Times.

0608 MENJOU, Adolphe Jean and MUSSELMAN, Morris McNeil
     It took nine tailors.

     New York, Whittlesey House, 1948. 238p. illus.

     Adolphe Menjou's memoirs of his life and experiences

     as a film actor. Includes anecdotes and memories of the

     early days of Hollywood.

0609 MERCOURI, Melina, 1925-

     I was born Greek.

     London, Hodder & Stoughton, 1971. 223p. illus.

     An autobiography.

0610   SHIBUK, Charles

An index to the films of Lewis Milestone.

New York, 1958. 31 leaves.

A research project of the Theodore Huff Memorial Film Society, v.1, #2.

BALSHOFER, Fred J.   and   MILLER, Arthur C.

One reel a week.

Berkeley, University of California Press, 1967.   218p.

illus.

The reminiscences of two cameramen in the early days of American cinema.

0611   MILLER, Virgil E., 1886-

Splinters from Hollywood tripods; memoirs of a camerman.

New York, Exposition Press, 1964.   139p.   illus.

Reminiscences of a veteran Hollywood cameraman.

0612   MIX, Olive (Stokes)

The fabulous Tom Mix, by Olive Stokes Mix, with Eric Heath.

Englewood Cliffs, N.J., Prentice-Hall, 1957.   177p.   illus.

0613   MORRIS, Peter, 1937-

Mizoguchi Kenji.

Ottawa, Canadian Film Institute, 1967.   48p.   illus.

Consists largely of an annotated filmography, preceded by two introductory essays and statements by Mizoguchi.

0614   CARPOZI, George

Marilyn Monroe.

New York, Belmont Books, 1961. 222p. illus.

0615   CONWAY, Michael,   and RICCI, Mark

The films of Marilyn Monroe. With a tribute by Lee

Strasberg and an introductory essay by Mark Harris.

New York, Citadel Press, 1964. 160p. illus.

A chronological survey of Marilyn Monroe's films

from 1948 to her death, each with credits, synopsis, and

contemporary reviews. Well illustrated with stills.

0616   FRANKLIN, Joe   and PALMER, Laurie

The Marilyn Monroe story.

New York, R. Field, 1953. 63p. illus.

0617   GUILES, Fred Lawrence

Norma Jean; the life of Marilyn Monroe.

New York, McGraw-Hill, 1969. 341p. illus.

A serious comprehensive biography. Contents:- In

the time of Cal and Aimee.- Goodbye Norma Jean.- Marilyn.-

An experiment in reality.- The Miller years.- The misfits.

HAMBLETT, Charles

The Hollywood cage.

New York, Hart, 1969. 437p. illus.

A revised and expanded version of the author's Who

killed Marilyn Monroe?, published in 1966. Includes an

account of the filming of her last film, The misfits, with

the addition of essays on Hollywood and interviews with

Hollywood's stars.

0618   HOYT, Edwin Palmer

            Marilyn; the tragic Venus.

            New York, Duell, Sloan & Pearce, 1965. 279p. illus.

            (Marilyn Monroe)

0619   MARTIN, Pete, pseud.

            Will acting spoil Marilyn Monroe?

            Garden City, N.Y., Doubleday, 1956. 128p. illus.

0620   WAGENKNECHT, Edward Charles, 1900-   ed.

            Marilyn Monroe: a composite view.

            Philadelphia, Chilton, 1969. 200p. illus.

                An anthology of memories and reflections about the
            star by such contributors as Hollis Alpert, Edith Sitwell
            Cecil Beaton, Lee Strasberg and others. Also includes
            two interviews with Monroe.

0621   ZOLOTOW, Maurice, 1913-

            Marilyn Monroe.

            New York, Harcourt, Brace, 1960.

            340p. illus.

                A serious, well-written biography.

            MONTAGU, Ivor Goldsmid Samuel, 1904-

            With Eisenstein in Hollywood; a chapter of autobiography.

            New York, International Publishers, 1969, c1967. 356p. illus.

                A personal account, together with the previously
            unpublished scenarios of Sutter's Gold, and An American
            Tragedy.

0622   MOORE, Colleen, 1902-

Silent star.

Garden City, N.Y., Doubleday, 1968. 262p. illus.

An autobiography by the screen actress known as Hollywood's first flapper girl.

0623   MORE, Kenneth, 1914-

Happy go lucky: my life.

London, Hale, 1959. 192p. illus.

An autobiography by the British comedy actor.

0624   MORLEY, Robert   and STOKES, Sewell, 1902-

Robert Morley: 'résponsible gentleman.'

London, Heinemann, 1966. 221p. illus.

Memoirs of the English stage and screen actor.

0625   ARDMORE, Jane Kesner (Morris)

The self-enchanted: Mae Murray, image of an era.

New York, McGraw-Hill, 1959. 262p. illus.

A biography. No index.

0626   NEGRI, Pola, 1897-

Memoirs of a star.

Garden City, N.Y., Doubleday, 1970. 453p. illus.

0627   QUIRK, Lawrence J.

The films of Paul Newman.

New York, Citadel Press, 1971. 224p. illus.

An illustrated chronological survey of Newman's films, with credits, synopses, extracts from contemporary reviews, stills and photographs.

0628   NOBLE, Peter, 1917-

         Reflected glory; an autobiographical sketch.

         London, Jarrolds, 1958. 235p. illus.

0629   NOBLE, Ronald

         Shoot first! Assignments of a newsreel cameraman.

         London, Harrap, 1955. 271p. illus.

0630   BARKER, Felix

         The Oliviers; a biography.

         Philadelphia, Lippincott, c1953. 371p. illus.

         The authorized biography of Sir Laurence Olivier

         and Vivien Leigh, written by a British drama critic.

         In five sections: Laurence Olivier; Vivien Leigh;

         The partnership begins; Marriage; In their own theatre.

0631   DARLINGTON, William Aubrey, 1890-

         Laurence Olivier.

         London, Morgan Grampian Books, 1968. 92p. illus.

         Great comtemporaries series.

         A brief biography and survey of Olivier's work for

         stage and screen. No index.

0632   WHITEHEAD, Peter   and BEAN, Robin.

         Olivier, Shakespeare. Compiled by Peter Whitehead and

         Robin Bean.

         London, Lorrimer Films, 1966. 40p. illus.

         Contains a concise biographical note in English, French,

         and German dealing entirely with Olivier's career as an

         actor, followed by a filmography; the last half of the book

         is composed of stills drawn from his Shakespearean films.

0633   ROUD, Richard

Max Ophuls; an index.

London, British Film Institute, 1958. 43p. illus.

Includes a biographical outline and a critical summary

of the director's work. With bibliography.

0634   BACHMANN, Gideon

Six talks on G.W. Pabst: the man, the director, the artist.

New York, Group for Film Study, 1955.

94p. *Cinemages series.*

With filmography.

0635   STACK, Oswald, *pseud.*

Pasolini on Pasolini; interviews with Oswald Stack.

London, Thames & Hudson in association with the British

Film Institute, 1969.

176p. illus. *Cinema one series.*

Interviews recorded in 1968 dealing with Pasolini's film

and cinema theories. With filmography and bibliography.

0636   PASTERNAK, Joseph, 1901

Easy the hard way, by Joe Pasternak as told to David

Chandler.

New York, Putnam, 1956. 301p. illus.

Autobiography of the Hollywood producer.

0637   PEARSON, George, 1875-

Flashback; the autobiography of a British film-maker.

London, Allen & Unwin, 1957. 236p. illus.

Autobiography of one of the best-known names in British

film production. With filmography.

0638   WOOD, Robin

Arthur <u>Penn</u>. Rev. ed.

New York, Praeger, c1969. 143p. illus. *Praeger film library.*

*Chapters are devoted to all of Penn's films, from The
left-handed gun to Alice's restaurant. Also includes notes
on the filming of Little Big Man, and on Penn's approach to
editing. With filmography.*

0639   COOREY, Philip

The lonely artist: a critical introduction to the films
of Lester James <u>Peries</u>.

Colombo, Lake House Investments, 1970. 118p. illus.

*An introduction to the work of the Ceylonese film-maker.
With bibliography.*

0640   LEE, Raymond.

The films of Mary <u>Pickford</u>.

South Brunswick, N.J., Barnes, c1970. 175p. illus.

*Consists largely of stills and photographs with brief
introductory text and filmography.*

0641   NIVER, Kemp R.

Mary <u>Pickford</u>, comedienne. Edited by Bebe Bersten.

Los Angeles, Locare Research Group, 1969. 156p. illus.

*Concentrating on the films made by Mary Pickford between
1909 and 1912 for the Biograph Company, this book consists
of photographs produced from the Library of Congress paper
print collection, accompanied by reproductions of appropriate
handbills. Production data for each film is supplied.*

0642   PICKFORD, Mary, 1893-

Sunshine and shadow.

Garden City, N.Y., Doubleday, 1955. 382p. illus.

Autobiography. With a foreword by Cecil B. DeMille.
No index.

0643   HOFFMAN, William, 1937-

Sidney.

New York, L. Stuart, 1971. 175p. illus.

An unauthorized "affectionate" biography of Sidney
Poiter.

0644   BUTLER, Ivan

The cinema of Roman Polanski.

New York, Barnes, 1970. 191p. illus. *International*
film guide series.

An illustrated survey of the Polish director's work
with a chapter devoted to each of his films, from Knife
in the water to Rosemary's baby. Also includes synopses
and credits of his short films.

0645   POWDERMAKER, Hortense, 1903-

Stranger and friend: the way of an anthropologist.

London, Secker & Warburg, 1966. 315p.

Of interest for a section dealing with the author's
work in Hollywood. With bibliography.

0646   PREJEAN, Albert

The sky and the stars; the memoirs of Albert Prejean.

London, Harvill Press, 1956.

216p. illus.

0647   PRIESTLEY, John Boynton, 1894-

        Midnight on the desert; a chapter of autobiography.

        London, Heinemann, 1937. 312p.

        Of interest for the inclusion of the author's impressions

        of Hollywood between 1935 and 1936.

0648   WOOD, Alan

        Mr. Rank; a study of J. Arthur Rank and British films.

        London, Hodder & Stoughton, 1952.

        228p. front.

        The story of J. Arthur Rank and the growth of the

        Rank Organization. In five sections:- Background and

        beginnings.- Building an empire.- The best films of our

        lives.- Storm and disaster.- Envoi.

0649   SETON, Marie

        Portrait of a director: Satyajit Ray.

        London, Dobson, 1971. 350p. illus.

        A comprehensive detailed study of the Indian director's

        work, with a biographical introduction. With filmography.

0650   REAGAN, Ronald, 1911-

        Where's the rest of me? By Ronald Reagan with Richard G.

        Hubler.

        New York, Duell, Sloan and Pearce, 1965. 316p. illus.

        A biography mainly concerning Reagan's years as a Hollywood

        film actor and reflecting his political philosophies. With

        index.

0651   FINDLATER, Richard, *pseud.*

Michael <u>Redgrave</u>, actor.

London, Heinemann, 1956.   170p.   illus.

Includes a list of Redgrave's performances in plays

and films.

0652   <u>REDGRAVE</u>, *Sir* Michael

Mask or face: reflections in an actor's mirror.

London, Heinemann, 1958.   188p.   illus.

A book primarily concerned with the·theatre, but includi

the text of a lecture delivered at the British Film Institute

Summer School in 1954 with the title I am not a camera, in

which Redgrave recalls some of his experience as a film actor

0653   ARMES, Roy

The cinema of Alain <u>Resnais</u>.

New York, Barnes, 1968.   175p.   illus.   *International*

film guide series.

An informative survey of the work of the French

director, from his early documentary films to Je t'aime,

je t'aime. With filmography and bibliography.

0654   WARD, John, 1939-

Alain <u>Resnais</u>, or, The theme of time.

London, Secker & Warburg in association with the British

Film Institute, 1968.

167p.   illus.   *Cinema one series.*

An analysis of Resnais' films, concentrating on the

director's continuing themes of memory and time. With

detailed filmography.

0655   EVERSON, William K

The films of Hal Roach.

New York, Museum of Modern Art, 1971. 96p. illus.

A study of the work of the American pioneer comedy

filmaker. With filmography and bibliography.

0656   ROBINSON, Edward, G., 1933-

My father, my son; an autobiography by Edward G. Robinson,

Jr., with William Dufty, based on an idea by N. Peter Dee.

New York, Fell, 1958. 316p. illus.

0657   DUNBAR, Janet

Flora Robson.

London, Harrap, 1960. 276p. illus.

Authorized biography of the English stage and screen

actress. With index.

0658   DAVIS, Elise Miller

The answer is God; the inspiring story of Dale Evans and

Roy Rogers.

New York, McGraw-Hill, 1955. 242p. illus.

A personal biography with a minimal amount of film

information.

0659   RICHARDS, Dick

Ginger: salute to a star.

Brighton, Eng., Clifton Books, 1969. 192p. illus.

With filmography. (Ginger Rogers)

0660   CROY, Homer, 1883-

Our Will Rogers.

New York, Duell, Sloan and Pearce, 1953. 377p.

A biography based partly on interviews with Rogers'
friends and childhood acquaintances. With index and
detailed source notes.

0661   DAY, Donald, 1899-

Will Rogers; a biography.

New York, D. McKay, c1962. 370p. illus.

With index.

0662   ROONEY, Mickey, 1922-

I.E.; an autobiography.

New York, Putnam, 1965. 249p. illus.

0663   GUARNER, Jose Luis

Roberto Rossellini.

New York, Praeger, 1970. 144p. illus. *Preager film*
library.

An illustrated survey with synopses and critical
notes for Rossellini's films. With filmography and
bibliography.

0664   CASTY, Alan

The films of Robert Rossen.

New York, Museum of Modern Art, 1969. 57p. illus.

An essay on the director's work with a detailed
illustrated filmography. With bibliography.

0665   RUSSELL, Geraldine (Jacobi)

        Oh Lord, what next?

        New York, Vantage Press, 1960. 174p. illus.

        A biography of Jane Russell.

0666   FLAHERTY, Frances (Hubbard)

        Sabu, the elephant boy.

        New York, Oxford University Press, 1937. unpaged. illus.

        The story of the Hindu boy chosen to play the lead role in the film Elephant boy.

0667   SAKALL, S. Z.

        The story of Cuddles; my life under the Emperor Francis Joseph, Adolf Hitler, and the Warner Brothers.

        London, Cassell, 1954. 231p. illus.

        An anecdotal autobiography.

0668   SANDERS, George, 1906-

        Memoirs of a professional cad.

        New York, Putnam, 1960. 192p. illus.

        An autobiography. No index.

0669   SCHARY, Dore

        For special occasions.

        New York, Random House, 1962. 200p.

        Autobiographical.

0670   SCOTT, Audrey

        I was a Hollywood stunt girl.

        Philadelphia, Dorrance, 1969. 119p.

0671   EVANS, Peter

Peter Sellers: the mask behind the mask.

Englewood Cliffs, N. J., Prentice-Hall, 1968.

249p. illus.

An intimate story of the life and work of the

English comedy actor.

0672   THOMAS, Bob

Selznick.

Garden City, N.Y., Doubleday, 1970. 381p. illus.

An illustrated biography of the Hollywood producer

with filmography and bibliography.

LAHUE, Kalton C.   **and** BREWER, Terry.

Kops and custards; the legend of Keystone Films.

Norman, University of Oklahoma Press, 1968.

177p. illus.

A carefully researched history of the Keystone Film

Company and the early work of Mack Sennett, with a

valuable appendix which provides a complete listing of

the Keystone comedies and their performers from 1912 to

1917.

0673   SENNETT, Mack, 1880-1960

King of comedy. As told to Cameron Shipp.

Garden City, N.J., Doubleday, 1954. 284p. illus.

An anecdotal autobiography recalling the early days of f

making and Sennett's individual methods.

0674   COSTELLO, David Paul, 1909-

The serpent's eye: Shaw and the cinema.

Notre Dame, University of Notre Dame Press, c1965. 209p.

illus.

A study of Shaw's theories on the cinema, together

with criticism and discussion of the film versions of

Pygmalion, Major Barbara, and Caesar and Cleopatra.

Includes a listing of motion pictures made from Shaw's

works.

0675   RINGGOLD, Gene   and MCCARTY, Clifford

The films of Frank Sinatra.

New York, Citadel Press, 1971. 249p. illus.

An illustrated survey of Sinatra's films with critical

quotes and filmography.

0676   SHAW, Arnold

Sinatra: twentieth-century romantic.

New York, Holt, Rinehart & Winston, 1968. 371p. illus.

A biography. No index but includes filmography. The

English edition (W.H. Allen) has title Sinatra: retreat of the

romantic.

0677   CURTI, Carlo

Skouras, king of Fox Studios.

Los Angeles, Holloway House, 1967. 311p.

0678   SMITH, Albert E.

Two reels and a crank, by Albert E. Seth, in collaboration with
Phil A. Koury.

Garden City, N.Y., Doubleday, 1952. 285p. illus.

*Recollections of the early days of American film-making,
written by one of the founders of the pioneer Vitagraph Company.
No index.*

0679   BURROWS, Michael

John Steinbeck and his films.

St. Austell, Eng., Primestyle, 1970. 36p. illus. *Formative
films series.*

Illustrated notes, with filmography and bibliography.

0680   RICHIE, Donald, 1924-

George Stevens: an American romantic.

New York, Museum of Modern Art, 1970. 104p. illus.

*An illustrated monograph on Stevens' career, with a
detailed filmography.*

0681   JONES, Ken D.   and others.

The films of James Stewart, by Ken D. Jones, Arthur F.
McClure, and Alfred E. Twomey.

South Brunswick, N. J., Barnes, 1970. 256p. illus.

*An illustrated chronological survey of Stewart's
films, with credits, synopses, and extracts from contemporary reviews. With bibliography.*

0682   HUDSON, Richard M   and LEE, Raymond

Gloria Swanson.

South Brunswick, N.J., Barnes, 1970. 269p. illus.

*Contains synopses of Gloria Swanson's 66 films,
with biographical outline. Numerous illustrations.*

0683   ALLAN, John B.

Elizabeth <u>Taylor</u>: a fascinating story of America's most

talented actress and the world's most beautiful woman.

Derby, Conn., Monarch Books, 1961. 131p.

The subtitle is a suitable revelation of the author's

attitude to his subject.

0684   LEVY, Alan

The Elizabeth <u>Taylor</u> story.

New York, Hillman Books, 1961. 176p. illus.

0685   RICE, Cy

Cleopatra in mink.

New York, Paperback Library, 1962.

160p.

(Elizabeth <u>Taylor</u>)

0686   <u>TAYLOR</u>, Elizabeth Rosemond, 1932-

Elizabeth Taylor; an informal memoir. With photos.

by Roddy McDowell, plus a collection from Elizabeth Taylor's

family album.

New York, Harper & Row, 1965. 177p. illus.

0687   WATERBURY, Ruth

Elizabeth <u>Taylor</u>.

New York, Appleton-Century, 1964. 310p. illus.

A biography.

0688 TEMPLE, Shirley, 1928- <u>and</u> the editors of Look.

My young life.

Garden City, N.Y., Garden City Pub. Co., 1945. 253p. illus.

An illustrated 'autobiography' published by the child

star at the age of 17.

0689 THOMAS, Bob

<u>Thalberg</u>: life and legend.

Garden City, N.Y., Doubleday, 1969.

415p. illus.

A biography of the M.G.M. tycoon, illustrated through-

out. With filmography and bibliography.

0690 <u>THOMAS</u>, Terry, *pseud.*

Filling the gap; perpetual freeman of the deckchairs,

Margate. London, Parrish, 1959. 168p. illus.

0691 TREWIN, John C., 1908-

Sybil <u>Thorndike</u>: an illustrated study of Dame Sybil's work,

with a list of her appearances on stage and screen.

London, Rockliff, 1955. 123p. illus.

Contents:- A study of her work for stage and screen.-

Chronological list of appearances on the stage.- Chronologica

list of appearances in films.

0692 <u>TIOMKIN</u>, Dimitri <u>and</u> Buranelli, Prosper, 1890-

Please don't hate me.

Garden City, N.Y., Doubleday, 1959. 261p. illus.

Reminiscences of the film composer.

0693   COHN, Art, 1909-1958.

The nine lives of Michael Todd.

New York, Random House, 1958. 396p. illus.

A biography of the producer and showman, written by

a friend and associate who died in the same airplane crash

that killed Mike Todd.

0694   DESCHNER, Donald

The films of Spencer Tracy.

New York, Citadel Press, 1968. 253p. illus.

Consists mainly of a chronological survey of Tracy's

films, each with credits, synopsis, and extracts from con-

temporary reviews. The book also contains brief tributes

and biographical notes.

0695   SWINDELL, Larry

Spencer Tracy: a biography.

New York, World Pub. Co., 1969. 319p. illus.

A general biography spanning Tracy's life and career

on stage and in film. With filmography.

0696   BOCEK, Jaroslav

Jiri Trnka: artist and puppet master.

Prague, Artia, 1965, c1963. 272p. illus.

A well illustrated study of the Czech filmmaker

famous for his puppet films. Includes a filmography

and a list of books illustrated by Trnka.

0697   PETRIE, Graham.

         The cinema of Francois Truffaut.

         New York, Barnes, 1970. 240p. illus. *International film guide series.*

         Not so much a systematic evaluation of Truffaut's films, but rather a study of the ways in which the director uses the cinematic tools. One film, Mississipi mermaid, is used to illustrate Truffaut's style. With filmography and bibliograph

0698   ARNOLD, Alan, 1922-

         Valentino.

         New York, Library Publishers, 1954. 165p. illus.

         A reasonably straight-forward account of the actor and the legend that surrounded him. No index.

0699   OBERFIRST, Robert.

         Rudolph Valentino: the man behind the myth.

         New York, Citadel Press, 1962. 320p. illus.

         A personal biography. No index.

0700   PETERSON, Roger C., 1903-

         Valentino, the unforgotten.

         Los Angeles, Wetzel, c1937. 256p. illus.

0701   SHULMAN, Irving

         Valentino.

         New York, Trident Press, 1967. 499p. illus.

         A biography. No index.

0702   STEIGER, Brad   and MANK, Charles, 1902-

         Valentino, by Brad Steiger and Chaw Mank.

         New York, MacFadden-Bartell, 1966. 192p. illus.

0703   CANNOM, Robert C

Van Dyke and the mythical city, Hollywood.

Culver City, Calif., Murray & Gee, 1948. 424p. illus.

A biography of Woody Van Dyke that also provides

background to the Hollywood of the thirties. With filmo-

graphy but no index.

0704   VIDOR, King Wallis, 1895-

A tree is a tree.

New York, Harcourt, Brace, 1953. 315p. illus.

An autobiography arranged in four parts:- Early films

: the open-air stage.- Silent films: mastering a form.-

Sound and color.- Little screen, big screen. With detailed

filmography.

0705   VIERTEL, Salka

The kindness of strangers.

New York, Holt, Rinehart & Winston, 1969.

338p. port.

Autobiography of the actress and screen-writer. No

index.

0706   FELDMAN, Joseph   and FELDMAN, Harry

Jean Vigo.

British Film Institute, n.d. 28p. illus.

Credits and notes for each of Vigo's four films, with

additional articles by James Agee, George Barbarow,

Gyula Zilzer, and Siegfried Kracauer.

0707   NOWELL-SMITH, Geoffrey.

Luchino Visconti.

London, Secker & Warburg in association with the British

Film Institute, 1967. 192p. illus. *Cinema one series.*

A well-written analysis of the work of the Italian

director, with a chapter devoted to each of his films.

With filmography.

0708   VIZZARD, Jack

See no evil; life inside a Hollywood censor.

New York, Simon & Schuster, 1970. 381p.

Offers an insight into film censorship in the United

States.

0709   SARRIS, Andrew

The films of Josef von Sternberg.

New York, Museum of Modern Art, 1966.

54p. illus.

A chronological survey of von Sternberg's films from 192

to 1953.

0710   VON STERNBERG, Josef, 1894-1969

Fun in a Chinese laundry.

New York, Macmillan, 1965. 348p. illus.

Forthright, immodest autobiography by the director

of The Blue Angel. Includes his ideas on film aesthetics

and techniques, and on the roles of actors and the director.

0711   WEINBERG, Herman G., 1908-

Josef von Sternberg; a critical study.

New York, Dutton, 1967. 254p. illus.

In addition to a critical study of the director's work,
the book includes extracts from two scenarios, an interview,
excerpts from correspondence, and a selection of critical
reviews. With filmography and bibliography.

0712   CURTISS, Thomas Quinn

Von Stroheim.

New York, Farrar, Straus and Giroux, 1971. 357p. illus.

A bibliography with considerable emphasis on Von Stroheim's
film work. With bibliography and filmography.

0713   FINLER, Joel Waldo

Stroheim.

London, Studio Vista, 1967. 143p. illus. *Movie paper-*
backs series.

Includes a detailed study of Stroheim's film Greed,
and notes of varying length on his other works. With
filmography and bibliography. (Von Stroheim)

0714   GOBEIL, Charlotte, ed.

Hommage a Erich von Stroheim: a tribute; a compilation
of selected articles and a filmography.

Ottawa, Canadian Film Institute, 1966. 54p. illus.

Articles written by Iris Barry, Gloria Swanson,
Karel Reisz, and others, with full filmography.

0715   NOBLE, Peter, 1917-

          Hollywood scapegoat: the biography of Erich <u>von Stroheim</u>.

          London, Fortune Press, 1950. 246p. illus.

          A detailed survey of Stroheim's work as director,

      actor, and writer. Includes contributions from thirteen

      other writers. With filmography and bibliography.

0716   McARTHUR, Colin, ed.

          Andrzej <u>Wajda</u>: Polish cinema; a B.F.I. Education Department

          dossier.

          London, British Film Institute Education Department, 1970.

          60p.

          Includes essays on Wajda's films, with an interview and

      filmography.

0717   GIDAL, Peter

          Andy <u>Warhol</u>: films and paintings.

          London, Studio Vista, 1971. 160p. illus. *Pictureback*

      series.

          Warhol's films are examined (p. 80-149) and a film-

      ography is incorporated in the opening chronology.

0718   <u>WARNER</u>, Jack Leonard, 1892-

          My first hundred years in Hollywood, by Jack L. Warner

          with Dean Jennings.

          New York, Random House, 1965. 331p. illus.

          An autobiography.

0720   FERNETT, Gene

            Starring John <u>Wayne</u>.

            Cocoa, Fla., Cinememories, 1969. 191p. illus.

                A chronological listing of John Wayne's films, with

            cast lists and illustrated by stills. Very little editorial

            or critical commentary.

0721   RICCI, Mark   <u>and others.</u>

            The films of John <u>Wayne</u>, by Mark Ricci, Boris Zmijewsky and

            Steve Zmijewsky.

            New York, Citadel Press, 1970. 288p. illus.

                An illustrated chronological survey of Wayne's films,

            with credits, synopses, and numerous stills & photographs.

            With a biographical introduction.

0722   TOMKIES, Mike

            Duke; the story of John <u>Wayne</u>.

            Chicago, Regnery, 1971. 149p. illus.

                A biography, with filmography. English edition

            (Barker, 1971) has title: The big man; the John Wayne

            story.

0723   ONYX, Narda

            Water, world and <u>Weissmuller</u>; a biography.

            Los Angeles, VION Pub. Co., 1964. 330p. illus.

0724   COWIE, Peter

            The cinema of Orson <u>Welles</u>.

            London, Zwemmer, 1965. 208p. illus. *International*

            film guide series.

                An informative study of Welles' work. Appendices

            list his major work on the stage and in television.

            Includes bibliography and filmography.

0725   FOWLER, Roy Alexander

Orson Welles; a first biography.

London, Pendulum, 1946. 100p. illus.

0726   HIGHAM, Charles, 1931-

The films of Orson Welles.

Berkeley, University of California Press, 1970. 210p. ill

A descriptive and critical study of Welles' films,

with a chapter devoted to each. With filmography and

bibliography.

0727   NOBLE, Peter, 1917-

The fabulous Orson Welles.

London, Hutchinson, 1956. 276p. illus.

A biography, with additional indexes to roles and

works of Orson Welles.

0728   WEST, Mae, 1892-

Goodness had nothing to do with it; autobiography of
Mae West.

Englewood Cliffs, N.J., Prentice-Hall, 1959. 271p. illus.

Reminiscences. No index.

0729   WEST, Mae, 1892-

The wit and wisdom of Mae West. Edited by Joseph Weintraub.
New York, Putnam, 1967. 92p. illus.

Consists largely of brief dialogue excerpts from Mae

West's films, illustrated with stills, followed by a collecti

of remarks attributed to her.

0730   WELTMAN, Manuel, 1931-   <u>and</u> LEE, Raymond

           Pearl <u>White</u>: the peerless fearless girl.

           South Brunswick, N.J., Barnes, 1969. 266p. illus.

               An illustrated biography, written in the form of a

           film serial scenario. With filmography.

0731   <u>WILCOX</u>, Herbert Sydney, 1892-

           Twenty-five thousand sunsets; the autobiography of Herbert

           Wilcox.

           London, Bodley Head, 1967. 233p. illus.

               An entertaining autobiography by the British producer-

           director.

0732   MADSEN, Axel.

           Billy <u>Wilder</u>.

           London, Secker & Warburg in association with the British

           Film Institute. c1968. 167p. illus. *Cinema one series.*

               Provides a general introduction to Wilder's work, with

           a detailed filmography and many illustrations.

0733   WOOD, Tom

           The bright side of Billy <u>Wilder</u>, primarily.

           Garden City, N. Y., Doubleday, 1970. 257p. illus.

               Anecdotal biography and profile of the director and

           his films. With filmography.

0734   SHIBUK, Charles

           An index to the films of William <u>Wyler</u>.

           New York, 1957. 21 leaves.

               A research project of the Theodore Huff Memorial Film

           Society, v.1, #1

0735   YOUNG, Loretta, 1913-

  The things I had to learn; as told to Helen Ferguson.

  Indianapolis, Bobbs-Merrill, 1961. 256p. illus.

  An autobiography. Includes screen credit list.

0736   GUSSOW, Mel

  Don't say yes until I finish talking; a biography of

  Darryl F. Zanuck.

  Garden City, N.Y., Doubleday, 1971. 318p. illus.

  A biography of the head of production at 20th Century

Fox. With filmography.

0737   ZAVATTINI, Cesare, 1902-

  Zavattini: sequences from a cinematic life.

  Englewood Cliffs, N.J., Prentice-Hall, 1970. 297p. illus.

  Contents:- Diary of cinema and of life.- Going back.-

Little journey along the Po.- Letter from Cuba to an unfait

ful woman. Zavattini is an Italian screenwriter.

0738   ZIMMER, Jill (Schary)

  With a cast of thousands; a Hollywood childhood.

  New York, Stein and Day, 1963. 252p.

  Written by the daughter of Dore Schary.

0739   GRIFFITH, Richard, 1912-

  Fred Zinnemann.

  New York, Museum of Modern Art Film Library, 1958. 20p.

  illus.

  With filmography.

0740   ZUKOR, Adolph, 1873-

  The public is never wrong; the autobiography of Adolph

  Zukor, with Dale Kramer.

  New York, Putnam, 1953. 309p. illus.

  Autobiography of the producer and former head

of Paramount Studios.

<u>SCREENPLAYS AND FILM STUDIES</u>

<u>Collected screenplays</u>

AGEE, James, 1909-1955

Agee on film.

London, P. Owen, 1963-65. 2 v. illus.

v. 1. Reviews and comments. Includes the articles
Agee wrote for The Nation, between 1942 and 1948, together
with examples from the Time reviews written between 1941
and 1948, and two essays written for Life. 432p.

v. 2. Five film scripts. Contains Noa Noa, The Africai
Queen, The night of the hunter, The bride comes to Yellow
Sky, and The blue hotel. 448p.

0741   ANTONIONI, Michelangelo

Screenplays of Michelangelo Antonioni.

New York, Orion Press, 1963. 361p. illus.

Screenplays, with credits, of Il grido; L'avventura;
La notte. Illustrated with stills and photographs of the
director at work. Includes a brief introduction by
Antonioni.

BENCHLEY, Robert Charles, 1889-1945.

The "reel" Benchley; Robert Benchley at his hilarious
best in words and pictures.

New York, Wyn, 1950. 96p. illus.

Text and stills from six of Benchley's short films.

190   0742   BERGMAN, Ingmar, 1918-

A film trilogy: Through a glass darkly; The communicants
(Winter light); The silence. Translated by Paul Britten
Austin.

London, Calder and Boyars, 1967. 143p. illus.

*The scripts of three films directed by Ingmar Bergman
between 1960 and 1962.*

0743   BERGMAN, Ingmar, 1918-

Four screenplays of Ingmar Bergman.

New York, Simon & Schuster, 1960. 329p. illus.

*Contains the screenplays of Smiles of a summer night
(1955); The seventh seal (1956); Wild strawberries (1957);
The magician [The face] (1958). Also includes a chronology
of films directed by Ingmar Bergman.*

THE BEST PICTURES...AND THE YEAR BOOK OF MOTION PICTURES IN
AMERICA.

New York, Dodd, Mead, 1940-   v. illus. annual.

*Contains scenarios of selected films in synopsis form,
with plot outlines for many others released in the year
of review.*

0744   BUNUEL, Luis, 1900-

L'age d'or, and, Un chien andalou: films by Luis Bunuel.

New York, Simon and Schuster, 1968. 120p. illus. *Classic
film scripts series.*

*Scripts by Luis Bunuel and Salvador Dali, each preceded
by notes and commentary, with credits. Includes filmography of Bunuel's work from 1928 to 1966.*

0745   BUNUEL, Luis, 1900-

Three screenplays.

New York, Orion Press, c1969. 245p. illus.

Screenplays for three films by Bunuel:- Viridiana,-
The exterminating angel.- Simon of the desert.

0746   CLAIR, René, 1898-

A nous la liberté, and Entr'acte; films by René Clair.

English translation and description of the action by

Richard Jacques and Nicola Hayden. New York, Simon and

Schuster, 1970. 140p. illus. *Classic film scripts.*

Scripts based on viewings of the films. Each shot
is numbered.

0747   CLAIR, René, 1898-

Four screenplays. Translated from the French by Piergiuseppe

Bozzetti.

New York, Orion Press, 1970. 439p. illus.

Contents:- Le silence est d'or.- La beauté du diable.-
Les belles-de-nuit.- Les grandes manoeuvres.

0748   COCTEAU, Jean, 1889-1963.

Two screenplays: The blood of the poet; The testament

of Orpheus.

New York, Orion Press, 1968. 144p. illus.

Screenplays, each with credits and a preface by
Cocteau. Illustrated with stills from the films.

0749   DREYER, Carl Theodor, 1889-1968

Four screenplays.

London, Thames & Hudson, 1970. 312p. illus.

Contents:- The passion of Joan of Arc.- Vampire.-
Day of wrath.- The word. Includes an introductory essay by
Ole Storm, and a detailed filmography.

0750   DURAS, Marguerite

Hiroshima mon amour. Translated by Richard Seaver. Une
aussi longue absence. Translated by Barbara Wright.
London, Calder and Boyars, 1966. 191p. illus.

Two contrasting screenplays, the first directed by
Alain Resnais, the second directed by Henri Colpi.

0751   FELLINI, Federico

Early screenplays: Variety lights; The white sheik;
Translated from the Italian by Judith Green.
New York, Grossman, 1971. 198p. illus.

The first two screenplays which Fellini both wrote
and directed. With credits.

0752   FELLINI, Federico

Three screenplays: I vitelloni; Il bidone; The temptations
of Doctor Antonio.
New York, Orion Press, 1970. 288p. illus.

3 screenplays representative of different stages of
Fellini's development as a director.

753   GARRETT, George P., 1929-   and others.

Film scripts. Edited by George P. Garrett, O.B. Hardison,

Jr., Jane R. Gelfman.

New York, Appleton-Century-Crofts, 1971. 2v.

An anthology containing the following scripts:- Henry

V.- The big sleep.- A streetcar named Desire.- High noon.-

Twelve angry men.- The defiant ones. With glossary of film

terms and a general bibliography.

754   GASSNER, John, 1903-1967   and NICHOLS, Dudley, 1895-   eds.

Best film plays, 1943-44; 1945.

New York, Crown, 1945-46. 2v. illus.

Contents:- 1943-44: Wilson.- The purple heart.- Going

my way.- Miracle of Morgan's Creek.- Watch on the Rhine.-

Dragon seed.- The more the merrier.- The Ox-Bow incident.-

Hail the conquering hero.- Casablanca. 1945: The lost weekend.-

Spellbound.- Double indemnity.- A tree grows in Brooklyn.-

None but the lonely heart.- The southerner.- Ernie Pyle's

story of G.I. Joe.- 30 seconds over Tokyo.- Over 21.- A

medal for Benny.

755   GASSNER, John, 1903-1967   and NICHOLS, Dudley, 1895-   eds.

Great film plays, being volume 1 of a new edition of Twenty

best film plays.

New York, Crown, c1959. 334p.

Screenplays with casts and credits for:- It happened

one night.- Rebecca.- The life of Emile Zola.- The good

earth.- All that money can buy.- Stagecoach.

0756   GASSNER, John, 1903-1967   _and_ NICHOLS, Dudley, 1895-   eds

Twenty best film plays.

New York, Crown, 1943. 1112p.

Contents:- It happened one night.- The women.- My man Godfrey.- Here comes Mr. Jordan.- Rebecca.- Wuthering Heights.- The grapes of wrath.- How green was my valley.- Make way for tomorrow.- Little Caesar.- Fury.- Mr. Smith goes to Washington.- The life of Emile Zola.- Juarez.- Mrs. Miniver.- This land is mine.- The good earth.- All that money can buy.- Stagecoach.- Yellow Jack.- The fight for life. The 21 screenplays are preceded by The screenplay as literature, by John Gassner, and The writer and the film, by Dudley Nichols.

HUGHES, Robert, ed.

Film, book 2: Films of peace and war.

New York, Grove Press, c1962. 255p. illus.

A discussion by leading filmmakers on war and anti-war films, together with the scripts for two films: Let there be light, and Night and fog.

0757   JOHN, Errol

Force majeure, The dispossessed, Hasta Luego: three screen-plays. London, Faber, 1967.

194p.

Three screenplays, as yet unfilmed.

0758   MACALL, Martin

Four star feature...Warner Bros.' Mildred Pierce, Saratoga trunk, The time, the place and the girl, The big sleep.

London, World Film Publications, 1947. 112p. illus.

MCCARTY, Clifford, 1929-

Published screenplays; a checklist.

Kent; Ohio, Kent State University Press, 1971.

127p.

A bibliography of screenplays published in English and issued commercially, arranged alphabetically. Information includes production company and date, director, writer and source of work if not original, and the bibliographical details of the screenplay.

0759   MANVELL, Roger, 1909-   ed.

Three British screen plays: Brief encounter, Odd man out, Scott of the Antarctic.

London, Methuen, 1950. 299p. illus.

Screenplays of the films directed by David Lean, Carol Reed, and Charles Frend.

0760   NOBLE, Lorraine, ed.

Four-star scripts: actual shooting scripts and how they are written.

New York, Doubleday, Doran, 1936. 392p.

Following a brief introduction to film-script technique, the book provides the screenplays for Lady for a day, It happened one night, Little women, and The story of Louis Pasteur.

0761   PINTER, Harold.

Five screenplays: The servant; The pumpkin eater; The Quiller memorandum; Accident; The go-between.

London, Methuen, 1971. 367p.

0762   THOMAS, Dylan, 1914-1953.

The doctor and the devils, and other scripts.

New York, New Directions, 1966.   229p.

Contents:- The doctor and the devils, from the story by Donald Taylor.- Twenty years a-growing, from the story by Maurice O'Sullivan.- A dream of winter.- The London model for Dylan Thomas's Under Milk Wood, by R. Maud.- The Londoner.

0763   VISCONTI, Luchino, 1906-

Three screenplays.

New York, Orion Press, 1970.   313p.   illus.

Contents:- White nights.- Rocco and his brothers.- The job (an episode from Boccaccio '70)

0764   VISCONTI, Luchino, 1906-

Two screenplays.

New York, Orion Press, 1970.   186p.   illus.

Contents:- La terra trema.- Senso.

VREELAND, Frank

Foremost films of 1938; a yearbook of the American screen.

New York, Pitman, 1939.   347p.   illus.

Includes a survey of the year's film production, awards, etc., and excerpts from the following screen-plays:- Wells Fargo.- Snow White and the seven dwarfs.- The buccaneer.- In old Chicago.- Algiers.- Love finds Andy Hardy.- You can't take it with you.- The citadel.- The young in heart.- That certain age.

0765 WILDER, Billy, 1906- <u>and</u> DIAMOND, I.A.L.

  The apartment, and The fortune cookie; two screenplays

  London, Studio Vista, 1970.

  191p. illus. *Movie paperbacks series.*

   Two original screenplays of the films directed by

  Billy Wilder. With credits.

Individual screenplays and film studies

0766 WOLFE, Maynard Frank

  The making of <u>The adventurers</u>; plus an exclusive interview

  with Lewis Gilbert, producer/director of the Paramount

  picture.

  New York, Paperback Library, 1970. 239p. illus.

   Consists mainly of stills from the film, but also

  includes a 29 page interview with the director.

0767 COHEN, John

  <u>Africa addio.</u>

  New York, Ballantine Books, 1966. 320p. illus.

   From the film by Gualtiero Jacopetti and Franco

  Prosperi.

0768 HERNDON, Venable <u>and</u> PENN, Arthur

  <u>Alice's restaurant</u>; a screenplay...based on Arlo Guthrie's

  The Alice's restaurant massacree.

  Garden City, N.Y., Doubleday, 1970. 141p. illus.

   The original screenplay of the film directed by

  Arthur Penn.

0769   MANKIEWICZ, Joseph L.

    All about Eve; a screenplay based upon a short story by

    Mary Orr.

    New York, Random House, 1951. 245p. illus.

0770   GODARD, Jean Luc, 1930-

    Alphaville; a film by Jean-Luc Godard. English trans-

    lation and description of action by Peter Whitehead.

    New York, Simon and Schuster, c1966. 100p. illus.

    Modern film scripts series.

        Includes an introduction by Richard Roud, cast, credits,

    stills, scenario, and filmography.

0771   GRIFFITH, Richard, 1912-

    Anatomy of a motion picture.

    New York, St. Martin's Press, c1959. 113p. illus.

        The story of the filming of Otto Preminger's film

    Anatomy of a murder, from inception to its release.

0772   COHN, Art, 1909-1958, ed.

    Michael Todd's Around the world in 80 days almanac.

    New York, Random House, c1965. 71p. illus.

        Includes notes on Mike Todd, the actors and principle

    technicians in the film, and the Todd-AO process, together

    with stills, and a synopsis of S.J. Perelman's adaptation

    of Jules Verne's Around the world in eighty days.

0773   ANTONIONI, Michelangelo

L'avventura; a film by Michelangelo Antonioni. From the
filmscript by Michelangelo Antonioni, with Elio Bartolini
and Tonino Guerra.

New York, Grove Press, 1969. 288p. illus.

*Includes scenario, with omitted and variant scenes,
credits and filmography, together with an introductory
essay, interviews with Antonioni, and a collection of
criticism.*

0774   WILLIAMS, Tennessee, 1914-

Baby Doll; the script for the film, incorporating the
two one-act plays which suggested it: 27 wagons full of
cotton (and) The long stay cut short; or, The unsatisfactory
supper.

New York, New Directions, 1956. 208p.

0775   CHAYEFSKY, Paddy, 1923-

The bachelor party; a screenplay.
New York, New American Library, 1957. 127p. illus.

0776   ELSE, Eric

The back of beyond; a compilation for use in studying
John Heyer's film of inland Australia.
London, Longmans, 1968. 176p. illus.

0777   JONES, Lon, ed.

Barabbas; the story of a motion picture. Produced by
Dino de Laurentis. Directed by Richard Fleischer.
Bologna, Cappelli, 1962. 189p. *From story to screen series.*

0778   MOSLEY, Leonard, 1913-

The Battle of Britain: the making of a film.

New York, Stein and Day, 1969. 207p. illus.

The story of the production of the film The Battle

of Britain, directed by Guy Hamilton.

0779   THOMAS, Dylan, 1914-1953.

The beach of Falesa.

New York, Stein & Day, 1963. 126p.

A screenplay based on a story by Robert Louis

Stevenson.

0780   COCTEAU, Jean 1889 - 1963.

Beauty and the beast. Scenario and dialogs by Jean

Cocteau. Edited and annotated by Robert M. Hammond.

New York, New York University Press, 1970. 441p. illus

Text of the shooting script in English and in French.

0781   COCTEAU, Jean, 1889-1963.

Diary of a film. (La belle et la bête)

London, D.Dobson, 1950. 216p. illus.

A diary of the production of La belle et la bête,

forming a highly personal account which reveals the

creative processes of a great director. (Beauty and the bea

0782   BUNUEL, Luis, 1900-

Belle de jour.

New York, Simon and Schuster, 1971.

168p. illus. *Modern film scripts series.*

The shooting script with brief critical introduction,

and credits.

0783   FREIMAN, Ray, ed.

The story of the making of <u>Ben-Hur</u>, a tale of the Christ,
from Metro-Goldwyn-Mayer.

New York, Random House, 1959. unpaged. illus.

A souvenir book which contains stills, credits, and
production notes.

0784   FRY, Christopher, 1907-

<u>The Bible</u>; original screenplay by Christopher Fry, assisted
by Jonathan Griffin.

New York, Pocket Books, 1966. 175p. illus.

Screenplay of the film directed by John Huston.

0785   SICA, Vittorio de, 1901-

<u>The bicycle thief</u>; a film by Vittorio de Sica.

New York, Simon & Schuster, 1968.

96p. illus. *Modern film scripts series.*

Script by Oreste Biancoli and others. English edition
(Lorrimer) has title: Bicycle thieves.

0786   AITKEN, Roy E.

<u>The Birth of a nation</u> story, by Roy E. Aitken, as told
to Al P. Nelson.

Middleburg, Va., Denlinger, 1965. 96p. illus.

A book dealing mainly with the financing and distri-
bution of D.W. Griffith's film. Written by one of the
owners of the production company and present-day holder
of the copyright to Birth of a nation.

0787   COCTEAU, Jean, 1889-1963.

The blood of a poet; a film by Jean Cocteau.

New York, Bodley Press, 1949. 53p. illus.

Includes the film scenario together with the text

of an address given by Cocteau in 1932 when the film was

shown.

0788   HUSS, Roy Gerard, 1927-   ed.

Focus on Blow-up.

Englewood Cliffs, N.J., Prentice-Hall, 1971. 171p. illus.
Film focus series.

Reviews, essays, interpretations and criticism of

Antonioni's film. Contributors include Sarris, Knight

and Kauffmann.

0789   LIEBMANN, Robert

The blue angel; a film by Josef von Sternberg. An authorized
translation of the German continuity.
New York, Simon & Schuster, 1968. 111p. illus.
Classic film scripts series.

Script of the motion picture Der Blaue Engel, directed

by Josef von Sternberg after a free adaptation of the novel

Professor Unrath, by Heinrich Mann.

0790   WARHOL, Andy, 1930-

Blue movie; a film by Andy Warhol.

New York, Grove Press, 1970. 126p. illus.

0791   FOREMAN, Carl

A cast of lions: the story of the filming of Born free.

London, Collins, 1966. 128p. illus.

Written by the film's director.

0792   JAY, John Mark, 1920-

Any old lion. London, Frewin, 1966.

138p. illus.

The story of the filming of Born free, written by the

production's stills cameraman.

0793   MCKENNA, Virginia, 1931-   and TRAVERS, Bill

On playing with lions.

London, Collins, 1966. 124p. illus.

A written and photographic record of the filming

of Born free. Prologue and epilogue by Virginia McKenna.

Photographs and text by Bill Travers.

0794   MCCLELLAND, C. Kirk.

On making a movie: Brewster McCloud; a day-by-day journal of the

on-location shooting of the film in Houston ... Edited by Nancy

Hardin. New York, New American Library, 1971. 359p. illus.

The record of the time spent by the author as a camera

student present on the set of the filming of Brewster McCloud.

Also includes the shooting script and the original screenplay by

Doran William Cannon. Illustrated with production shots and stills

from the film.

0795   GOLDMAN, William, 1931-

Butch Cassidy and the Sundance Kid.

Toronto, Bantam Books, 1969. 184p. illus.

The screenplay of the film directed by George Roy

Hill.

0796   DEANS, Marjorie

Meeting at the sphinx: Gabriel Pascal's production of
Bernard Shaw's <u>Caesar and Cleopatra</u>.

London, Macdonald, 1946. 146p. illus.

*Background to the production of the film, with
additional material on Bernard Shaw as a screen-writer
and the partnership between Shaw and the director,
Gabriel Pascal.*

0797   FEIFFER, Jules

<u>Carnal knowledge</u>; a screenplay.

New York, Farrar, Straus & Giroux, 1971. 117p. illus.

*Screenplay of the film produced and directed by
Mike Nichols.*

0798   DOWNEY, Robert

<u>Chafed elbows</u>.

New York, Lancer Books, 1967. 144p. illus.

Screenplay.

0799   PRÉVERT, Jacques, 1900-

<u>Children of paradise</u>; a film by Marcel Carné.

New York, Simon & Schuster, 1968. 218p. illus. *Classic
film scripts.*

*Prévert's final shooting script, preceded by brief
interviews with Carné and Prévert in 1944-5, together
with credits for the film. English edition (Lorrimer,
1968) has title: Les enfants du paradis.*

0804   BELLOCCHIO, Marco, 1939-

China is near.

New York, Orion Press, 1969. 160p. illus.

Screenplay illustrated with stills. Includes an

introduction to the film by Tommaso Chiaretti, and the

transcript of a tape-recorded conversation with Bellocchio.

0805   NORTON, Bill L.

Cisco Pike; original screenplay by Bill L. Norton, plus

four articles about the making of the movie and sixteen

pages of photographs. Edited by Norma M. Whittaker and

Bob Silverstein.

New York, Bantam Books, 1971. 165p. illus.

0806   THE CITIZEN KANE BOOK.

Boston, Little, Brown, 1971. 440p. illus.

Includes the complete shooting script of Orson Welles'

film, written by Herman J. Mankiewicz and Welles, the cutting

continuity of the finished film, and Pauline Kael's Raising

Kane.

0807   GOTTESMAN, Ronald, ed.

Focus on Citizen Kane.

Englewood Cliffs, N.J., Prentice-Hall, 1971. 178p. illus.

Film focus series.

Includes reviews of Welles' film by John O'Hara,

Bosley Crowther, Otis Ferguson, Cedric Belfrage, and

Tangye Lean. Also features essays and commentaries by such

names as Peter Cowie, Arthur Knight, Andre Bazin, Francois

Truffaut and Welles himself. With plot synopsis, script

extract, filmography and bibliography.

0804   BRODSKY, Jack   <u>and</u>   Weiss, Nathan

The <u>Cleopatra</u> papers: a private correspondence.

New York, Simon & Schuster, 1963. 175p.

The correspondence between the publicity manager

of 20th Century-Fox and the assistant publicity manager

during the making of the film Cleopatra, starring

Richard Burton and Elizabeth Taylor.

0805   WANGER, Walter   <u>and</u> HYAMS, Joe

My life with <u>Cleopatra</u>.

New York, Bantam Books, 1963. 182p.

The behind-the-scenes story of the production of

Cleopatra - by the producer.

0806   GINSBERG, Milton Moses

<u>Coming apart</u>.

New York, Lancer, 1969. 205p. illus.

0807   LEE, Laurie   <u>and</u>   KEENE, Ralph

We made a film in Cyprus.

London, Longmans, Green, 1947. 92p. illus.

A sourvenir of a documentary, <u>Cyprus is an island</u>,

made during the last days of the European War. With photos

by Ralph Keene and stills from the film.

0808   AXEL, Gabriel

<u>Danish blue</u>; a film by Gabriel Axel.

New York, Grove Press, 1970. 126p. illus.

Illustrated scenario of the Danish semi-documentary

about pornographic films.

0809   CURRY, George

Copperfield '70: the story of the making of the Omnibus-20th

Century-Fox film of <u>David Copperfield</u>.

New York, Ballantine Books, 1970. 210p. illus.

Includes "A performance version of the Frederick Brogger - Jack

Pulman screenplay" (p. 107-210) The story of the production

of the film directed by Delbert Mann.

0810   CARSON, L. M. Kit

<u>David Holzman's diary</u>; a screenplay by L.M. Kit Carson

from a film by Jim McBride.

New York, Farrar, Straus and Giroux, 1970. 125p. illus. *Noon-*

day original screenplays series.

0811   CAMERON, Evan

An analysis of <u>A diary for Timothy</u>: a film by

Humphrey Jennings.

Bridgewater, Mass., The Experiment Press, 1967. 68p.

Cinema studies series.

0812   THOMAS, Dylan, 1914-1953.

<u>The doctor and the devils</u>. From the story by Donald

Taylor. London, Dent, 1953.

138p.

A pre-production film scenario.

0813   BOLT, Robert

<u>Doctor Zhivago</u>: the screenplay by Robert Bolt, based on

the novel by Boris Pasternak.

New York, Random House, c1965. 224p. illus.

The screenplay of the film directed by David Lean,

with credits and brief introductory notes.

0814   FELLINI, Federico

La dolce vita.

New York, Ballantine Books, 1961. 274p. illus.

The screenplay, with many illustrations and stills.

0815   PENNEBAKER, D. A.

Bob Dylan; Don't look back.

New York, Ballantine Books, 1968. 152p. illus.

0816   SONTAG, Susan, 1933-

Duet for cannibals; a screenplay.

New York, Farrar, Straus and Giroux, 1970.

129p. illus. *Noonday original screenplays series.*

Screenplay of the film by the author.

0817   FONDA, Peter, 1940-   and others.

Easy rider; original screenplay by Peter Fonda, Dennis

Hopper, Terry Southern, plus stills, interviews and

articles. Edited by Nancy Hardin and Marilyn Schlossberg.

New York, New American Library, 1969. 191p. illus.

Includes articles by Dennis Hopper, Robert Christgau

and others, in addition to the screenplay.

0818   POWELL, Michael

200,000 feet on Foula.

London, Faber, 1938. 334p. illus.

American edition published under title: 200,000 feet,

the edge of the world. The book is the story of the

production of the film The edge of the world, a documentary

made in 1936 on the Shetland Island of Foula.

0819   BOYER, Deena

The two hundred days of 8-1/2.

New York, Macmillan, 1964. 218p. illus.

A day-to-day account, written in the form of a diary, of Federico Fellini's film 8-1/2.

0820   FLAHERTY, Frances (Hubbard)

Elephant dance.

New York, Scribner, 1937. 136p. illus.

Letters written by Robert Flaherty's wife to her family during the filming of Elephant boy.

0821   MAUGHAM, William Somerset, 1874-1965.

Encore.

London, Heinemann, 1951. 165p. illus.

Includes the original short stories by Maugham that were included in the film Encore, together with the screen plays written by T.E.B. Clarke, Arthur Macrae, and Eric Ambler.

0822   SCHULBERG, Budd

A face in the crowd; a play for the screen.

New York, Random House, 1957. 172p. illus.

Based upon the author's short story Your Arkansas traveler, from the book Some faces in the crowd.

0823   CASSAVETES, John

Faces. Book compiled by Al Ruban.

New York, New American Library, 1970. 319p. illus.

Parallel-page original and final versions of the screenplay of the film written and directed by Cassavetes, together with notes, credits and essays by Cassavetes and the director of photography, Al Ruban.

0824   TAYLOR, Deems, 1885-

Walt Disney's _Fantasia_.

New York, Simon & Schuster, 1940. 157p. illus.

Includes anecdotes as well as a summary of the film.
With a foreword by Leopold Stokowski.

0825   BECKETT, Samuel, 1906-

Film. Complete scenario, illustrations, production

shots. With an essay, On directing Film, by Alan

Schneider.

New York, Grove Press, 1969. 95p. illus.

The original scenario of the film written in his
highly individual way by Beckett, and starring Buster
Keaton. With an illuminating essay by the director.

0826   STEINBECK, John, 1902- 1968.

The forgotten village; with 136 photographs from the film of

the same name by Rosa Harvan Kline and Alexander Hackensmid.

New York, Viking Press, 1941. 143p. illus.

Screenplay of the documentary directed by Herbert Kline.

0827   TRUFFAUT, Francois,   and MOUSSY, Marcel

The 400 blows; a film by Francois Truffaut and Marcel

Moussy. Edited by David Denby.

New York, Grove Press, 1969. 255p. illus.

A translation of the dialogue of the completed film

directed by Francois Truffaut, with descriptions of the action

and camera positions and also notes, criticisms and stills.

0828   WEST, Jessamyn

To see the dream.

New York, Harcourt, Brace, 1957. 314p.

Developed from the author's journal kept during the time that she was a script writer and technical advisor to William Wyler who was filming her book, Friendly persuasion.

0829   MARGRAVE, Seton

Successful film writing: as illustrated by The ghost goes west.

London, Methuen, 1936. 216p. illus.

Following an essay on the principles of film writing, this volume presents the short story by Eric Keown of Sir Tristram goes west, a short article by Rene Clair on the story's cinematic qualities, a first treatment of the screen adaptation now titled The ghost goes west, and the final scenario of Clair's film, with detailed times and measurements.

0830   CHAYEFSKY, Paddy, 1923-

The goddess; a screenplay.

New York, Simon and Schuster, 1958. 167p.

0831   THE FILM STORY OF GONE WITH THE WIND.

London, Hollywood Publications, 1948. 88p. illus. *Famous film series.*

A summary of Margaret Mitchell's book, illustrated by stills from the film. With profiles of the leading characters, the producer, and the director.

0832   RENOIR, Jean, 1894-

<u>Grand illusion</u>; a film by Jean Renoir.

New York, Simon & Schuster, 1968.

104p. illus. *Classic film scripts series.*

Screenplay by Charles Spaak and Jean Renoir, with an introductory note by Erich von Stroheim.

0833   SEMPRUN, Jorge

<u>La guerre est finie</u>.

New York, Grove Press, 1967. 192p. illus.

Scenario for the film directed by Alain Resnais.

0834   NEWQUIST, Roy.

A special kind of magic.

Chicago, Rand McNally, 1967. 156p. illus.

Consists of interviews made on the set of the film <u>Guess who's coming to dinner</u>. *Subjects include the director Stanley Kramer, the stars, Katharine Hepburn, Spencer Tracy, Sidney Poiter, and Katharine Houghton, in which they discuss their careers.*

0835   CROSS, Brenda, ed.

The film <u>Hamlet</u>: a record of its production.

London, Saturn Press, 1948. 76p. illus.

Essays by those concerned with the Olivier production, including executives, technicians and actors, as well as Olivier himself.

0836   DENT, Alan, 1905-   ed.

Hamlet: the film and the play.

London, World Film Publications, 1948. unpaged. illus.

Consists of foreward by Sir Laurence Olivier, a chapter by Alan Dent on text-editing Shakespeare with particular reference to Hamlet, and a chapter by Roger Furse on designing the film of Hamlet. The main body of the book is devoted to the text of the play, with film directions and text cuts indicated.

0837   KOZINTSEV, Grigorii Mikhailovich

Shakespeare: time and conscience.

New York, Hill and Wang, 1966. 276p. illus.

Written by the director of the Russian film version of Hamlet. The book, mainly a study of King Lear and Hamlet, contains considerable information on the writer's approach to filming Shakespeare. Partial contents:- Hamlet, Prince of Denmark (p. 105-174).- Ten years with Hamlet, from the director's diary (p. 211-276).

0838   HUTTON, Clayton

The making of Henry V.

London, Eagle Lion Film Distributors, 1944. 72p. illus.

Background but little detailed information on the production of the Olivier film.

0839   FAST, Howard Melvin, 1914-

The hill; an original screenplay.

Garden City, N. Y., Doubleday, 1964. 123p.

A modern version of the cruxifixion, set in New York City.

0840   DURAS, Marguerite

        <u>Hiroshima mon amour</u>. Text by Marguerite Duras for
the film by Alain Resnais. Translated by Richard Seaver.
Picture editor: Robert Hughes.

        New York, Grove Press, c1961. 112p. illus.

        *Text and illustrations from one of the most important
of the French "New Wave" films.*

0841   JHABVALA, Ruth Prawer, 1927-

        <u>The householder.</u>

        Delhi, Ramlochan Books, 1965? 168p. illus.

        A screenplay based on the author's novel.

0842   SJOMAN, Vilgot

        <u>I am curious (blue)</u>; a film.

        New York, Grove Press, 1970. 219p. illus.

        *Translation of the screenplay of the sequel to I am
curious (yellow).*

0843   SJOMAN, Vilgot

        <u>I am curious (yellow)</u>; a film by Vilgot Sjoman.

        New York, Grove Press, 1968. 254p. illus.

        *Scenario, with stills, of the controversial Swedish film
that raised censorship problems in its distribution. Include
"Excerts from the transcript of the trial" in the United Stat
following the seizure of the film.*

0844   SJOMAN, Vilgot

        I was curious; diary of the making of a film.

        New York, Grove Press, c1968. 217p. illus.

        *A personal account of the making of <u>I am curious (Yellow</u>
written by its Swedish director.*

0845   ANDERSON, Lindsay, 1923-   and SHERWIN, David

If...; a film by Lindsay Anderson and David Sherwin.

New York, Simon and Schuster, 1969. 167p. illus. *Modern*

filmscripts series.

Screenplay with credits and stills. Includes a

preface by Anderson.

0846   KUROSAWA, Akira, 1910-

Ikiru: a film by Akira Kurosawa. Edited and with an introduction

by Donald Richie.

New York, Simon & Schuster, 1968. 84p. illus. *Modern film*

scripts.

Scenario written by Akira Kurosawa, Shinobu Hashimoto and

Hideo Oguni of the film released in English-speaking countries

under the title Living. Includes credits and a filmography of

the work of Kurosawa.

0847   TROTTI, Lamar, 1900-   and LEVIEN, Sonya, 1894-

In old Chicago. Written for the screen by Lamar Trotti

and Sonya Levien; based on the story, We the O'Leary's,

by Niven Busch...

Beverly Hills, Twentieth Century-Fox Film Corp., 1937.

263p.

Screenplay of the film directed by Henry King. One

of the few examples of a screenplay being published by a

film company for general distribution.

0848   SARTRE, Jean Paul, 1905-

In the mesh; a scenario.

London, A. Dakers, 1954. 128p.

Scenario of the projected film that was never

produced.

0849   HUFF, Theodore

Intolerance; the film by David Wark Griffith; shot by
shot analysis.

New York, Museum of Modern Art, 1966. 155p.

*An extremely detailed analysis of the classic film,
including footage of each shot as existing in the print
viewed.*

0850   WILDER, Billy, 1906-   and DIAMOND, I.A.L.

Irma la douce; a screenplay.

New York, Tower Publications, 1963. 127p. illus.

0851   COLLIER, John W

A film in the making, featuring It always rains on
Sunday, from the novel by Arthur J. La Bern.

London, World Film Publications, 1947. 93p. illus.

0852   BROWNLOW, Kevin

How it happened here.

London, Secker and Warburg in association with the British
Film Institute, c1968. 184p. illus. *Cinema one series.*

*Relates the story of eight years in which the film
It happened here was filmed, and the problems that
ensued. Written by the director.*

0853   EISENSTEIN, Sergei Mikhailovich, 1898-1948

Ivan the Terrible.

New York, Simon & Schuster, 1970. 264p. illus. *Classic film scripts series.*

Includes the scenario for the uncompleted third part of the monumental film project. The script of the first two parts is based on a copy of the shooting script, and all shots are numbered.

0854   EISENSTEIN, Sergei Mikhailovich, 1898-1948

Ivan the Terrible: a screenplay. Translated by Ivor Montagu and Herbert Marshall. Edited by Ivor Montagu. New York, Simon and Schuster, 1962. 319p. illus.

The complete screenplay, with an introduction, notes and appendices. Includes a selection of Eisenstein's drawings for the film.

0855   KRATOCHVIL, Miles V., 1904-   and VAVRA, Otakar.

Jan Huss; a screen play.

Prague, Artia, 1957? 173p. illus.

0856   ANDERSON, Maxwell, 1888-   and SOLT, Andrew P., 1916-

Joan of Arc. Text and pictures from the screen play by Maxwell Anderson and Andrew Solt.

New York, Sloane, 1948. 170p. illus.

Includes excerpts from the screenplay of the film directed by Victor Fleming and adapted from Anderson's stage play Joan of Lorraine.

0857   PRÉVERT, Jacques, 1900-

      Le jour se lève; a film by Marcel Carné and Jacques Prévert.

      English translation and description of action by Dinah Brooke an

      Nicola Hayden.

      London, Lorrimer, 1970. 128p. illus. *Classic film scripts*

      series.

        An adaptation from Prévert's shooting script to conform

      with the final version of the film directed by Marcel Carné.

0858   MANN, Abby.

      Judgment at Nuremberg: the script of the film.

      London, Cassell, 1961. 182p. illus.

        The illustrated film script of Stanley Kramer's

      production.

0859   TRUFFAUT, Francois

      Jules and Jim; a film by Francois Truffaut.

      New York, Simon & Schuster, 1968. 100p. illus. *Modern film*

      scripts series.

        Scenario together with credits and stills. Adaptation

      and dialogue by Francois Truffaut and Jean Gruault after

      the novel by Henri-Pierre Roche.

0860   FELLINI, Federico

      Juliet of the spirits. Edited by Tullio Kezich.

      New York, Ballantine Books, 1966. 318p. illus.

        In addition to a preliminary version of the screenplay

      and a transcription of the final film, an extensive

      interview with Fellini is included.

0861   ROBBE-GRILLET, Alain, 1922-

   Last year at Marienbad. Text by Alain Robbe-Grillet for the
   film by Alain Resnais.

   New York, Grove Press, 1962. 168p. illus.

0862   KENT, Howard.

   Single bed for three: a Lawrence of Arabia notebook.

   London, Hutchinson, 1963. 208p. illus.

      An account of the production of the David Lean film by

      the picture editor.

0863   VAILLARD, Roger   and others

   Roger Vadim's Les liasons dangereuses; screenplay by Roger

   Vaillard, Roger Vadim and Claude Brule.

   New York, Ballantine Books, 1962. 256p. illus.

      "Inspired by the novel by Choderios Laclos"

0864   FIELDING, Hubert

   The life of Emile Zola; the authorized story of the film.

   London, Joseph, 1938. 128p. illus.

      The story of the film starring Paul Muni.

0865   GOLDMAN, James

   The lion in winter.

   New York, Dell, 1968. 139p. illus.

      Screenplay of the film directed by Anthony Harvey.

0866   EASTMAN, Charles

   Little Fauss and big Halsey; a screenplay.

   New York, Farrar, Straus, and Giroux, 1970, c1969.

   163 p. illus.

0867   SOUTHERN, Terry

The journal of <u>The loved one</u>; the production log of a motion

picture. Photographs by William Claxton.

New York, Random House, 1965. unpaged. illus.

Consists largely of photographs taken on the set of

The loved one, with a light-hearted commentary by Southern.

Includes full credits.

0868   HARBOU, Thea von, 1888-

<u>M</u>; a film by Fritz Lang. English translation and

description of action by Nicholas Garnham.

New York, Simon and Schuster, 1968. 108p. illus.

Scenario of the film classic directed by Fritz Lang.

0869   HUTTON, Clayton

<u>Macbeth</u>: the making of the film.

London, Parrish, 1960. 48p. illus.

Very brief, non-technical notes on the background to

the play and to the production of the film, followed by

32 pages of stills and photographs.

0870   GODARD, Jean Luc, 1930-

<u>Made in U.S.A.</u>; screenplay.

London, Lorrimer, 1967. 87p. illus.

Contents:- Synopsis, by Jean-Luc Godard.- The left

and Made in U.S.A., by Jean-Luc Godard.- Who kidnapped

Ben Barka, by Henry Bagehot.- The Ben Barka fiasco, by

K.S. Karol.- Introduction, by Michael Kustow.- Screen-

play.- Filmography.

0871   SHAW, George Bernard, 1856-1950.

        <u>Major Barbara; a</u> screen version.

        New York, Penguin Books, 1946. 154p.

        Screenplay of the film by Gabriel Pascal.

0872   WELLS, Herbert George, 1886-1946.

        <u>Man who could work miracles</u>; a film by H.C. Wells based

        on the short story entitled The man who could work miracles.

        London, Macmillan, 1936. 109p.

        In script form.

0873   MARION, Frances, 1890-

        How to write and sell film stories; with a complete

        shooting script for <u>Marco Polo</u> by Robert E. Sherwood.

        New York, Covici, Friede, 1937. 375p.

        Contents:- The motion picture story.- Characterization.-
Plot.- Motivation.- Theme.- Dialogue.- Dramaturgy.- Emotion.-
Common errors.- Story ideas.- Censorship.- How stories are
sold.- Author's rights and plagiarism.- Adaptation.-
Continuity.- Marco Polo: a shooting script. (p. 231-364).-
Glossary.

0874   GODARD, Jean Luc, 1930-

        <u>The married woman</u>: a Jean-Luc Godard film.

        New York, Berkley, 1965. unpaged. illus.

        A twelve page introduction by Tom Milne is followed
by a text based on the film's English subtitles by Ursule
Molinaro. Illustrated by stills on nearly every page.

0875   GODARD, Jean Luc, 1930-

Masculine feminine; a film by Jean-Luc Godard.

New York, Grove Press, 1969. 288p. illus.

A translation of the film dialogue with description of the action. Illustrated by frame enlargements. The supplementary material includes two short stories by Maupassant which formed the source of the film, extracts from Godard's working script, interviews and collected criticism of the film.

0876   THOMAS, Dylan, 1914-1953.

Me and my bike.

New York, McGraw-Hill, 1965. 53p. illus.

First of five sequences of an unfinished film script written by Dylan Thomas in 1948.

0877   SICA, Vittorio de, 1901-

Miracle in Milan.

New York, Orion Press, 1968. 120p. illus.

The screenplay, with an introduction by De Sica and an essay by the author on his methods of film direction. With filmography.

0878   GOODE, James

The story of The misfits.

Indianapolis, Bobbs-Merrill, 1963. 331p. illus.

A diary of the production of the film written by Arthur Miller, directed by John Huston and starring Marilyn Monroe and Clark Gable.

0879   ELIOT, Thomas Stearns, 1888-1965

The film of <u>Murder in the cathedral</u>.

New York, Harcourt, Brace, 1952. 110p. illus.

The screenplay by T. S. Eliot of the film produced

and directed by George Hoellering, with prefaces by Eliot

and Hoellering.

0880   BEATON, Cecil Walter Hardy, 1904-

Cecil Beaton's fair lady.

London, Weidenfeld & Nicolson, 1964. 128p. illus.

A diary recording the events before and during the

production of the film version of <u>My fair lady</u>, written

by the designer of the costumes and sets.

0881   FLAHERTY, Robert Joseph, 1884-1951

<u>Nanook of the north</u>. Edited from the film by Robert

Kraus.

New York, Windmill Books, c1971. unpaged. illus.

Consists solely of selected frame enlargements and

titles from Flaherty's film classic.

0882   SCHARY, Dore

Case history of a movie, by Dore Schary as told to Charles

Palmer.

New York, Random House, 1950. 242p. illus.

Written by the former vice-president in charge of production

at M-G-M, this book follows the step-by-step production of the film

<u>The next voice you hear</u>. General contents:- The story and the

script.- Preparation for production.- Shooting the picture.-

Finishing the picture.

0883 OWEN, Don.

    <u>Nobody waved good-bye</u>. Edited by Hermon Voaden

    Toronto, Macmillan, 1971. 120p. illus.

     The script of the award-winning Canadian film, with

    extracts from reviews and production notes.

0884 HELLMAN, Lillian

    <u>The north star</u>; a motion picture about some Russian people.

    New York, Viking Press, 1943. 118p.

     The master script of the film directed by Lewis

    Milestone.

0885 SOLZHENITSYN, Aleksandr Isaevich, 1918-

    The making of <u>One day in the life of Ivan Denisovich</u>, by

    Alexander Solzhenitsyn. Translated by Gillon Aitken. Introduct

    and screenplay by Ronald Harwood.

    New York, Ballantine Books, 1971. 271p. illus.

     Consists of a brief introduction outlining the problems

    of filming the production, followed by the text of the original

    novel, and the screenplay. With credits.

0886 MACLIAMMHOIR, Micheal, 1899-

    Put money in thy purse; the diary of the film of <u>Othello</u>

    by Michael MacLiammoir.

    London, Methuen, 1952. 258p. illus.

     Follows the day-to-day activities of the filming of

    Orson Welles' version of Othello in which MacLiammoir

    played Iago.

0887 KIMBROUGH, Emily, 1899- and SKINNER, Cornelia Otis, 1901-

We followed our hearts to Hollywood. Drawings by Helen E. Hokinson.

New York, Dodd, Mead, 1943. 210p. illus.

The authors' experiences in Hollywood working for Paramount in connection with the production of the film based on their book Our Hearts were young and gay.

0888 VAJDA, Ladislaus, 1906-

Pandora's box (Lulu); a film by G.W. Pabst.

New York, Simon & Schuster, 1971. 136p. illus. *Classic film scripts series.*

Screenplay of the film directed by G.W. Pabst.

0889 PARDON ME SIR, BUT IS MY EYE HURTING YOUR ELBOW? Written by Gregory Corso and others. Produced by Bob Booker and George Foster.

New York, B. Geis, c1968. 170p. illus.

12 sequences, written by American humourists forming a film script for an intended motion picture.

0890 GODARD, Jean Luc, 1930-

Le petit soldat; screenplay. English translation and screenplay by Nicholas Garnham.

London, Lorrimer, 1967. 95p. illus.

With an introduction by Nicholas Garnham, and a filmography.

0891 GODARD, Jean Luc, 1930-

Pierrot le fou; a film by Jean-Luc Godard. English translation and description of action by Peter Whitehead.

New York, Simon & Schuster, 1969. 104p. illus. *Modern film scripts series.*

0892   DE ANTONIO, Emile   <u>and</u> TALBOT, Daniel

<u>Point of order</u>! A documentary of the Army - McCarthy

hearings. Produced by Emile de Antonio and Daniel Talbot.

New York, Norton, 1964. 108p. illus.

The text of the film produced from the Army - McCarthy

hearings of 1954.

0893   EISENSTEIN, Sergei Mikhailovich, 1898-1948

<u>Potemkin</u>; a film by Sergei Eisenstein.

New York, Simon & Schuster, 1968. 100p. illus. *Classic*

film scripts series.

Includes an introduction written by Eisenstein in

1939. English edition has title: The battleship Potemkin

0894   RATTIGAN, Terence.

<u>The prince and the showgirl</u>: the script for the film.

New York, New American Library, 1957. 127p. illus.

0895   KEROUAC, Jack.

<u>Pull my daisy</u>; text ad-libbed by Jack Kerouac for the film

by Robert Frank and Alfred Leslie.

New York, Grove Press, 1961. 38p. illus.

0896   MAUGHAM, William Somerset, 1874-1965.

<u>Quartet</u>; stories by W. Somerset Maugham, screen-plays

by R.C. Sherriff.

London, Heinemann, 1948. 243p. illus.

Includes The facts of life; The alien corn; The kite

The colonel's lady.

0897   EISENSTEIN, Sergei Mikhailovich, 1898-1948

Que viva Mexico! With an introduction by Ernest

Lindgren.

London, Vision Press, 1951. 89p. illus.

Scenario of Eisenstein's uncompleted film, illustrated

with 36 stills, together with an introduction that relates

the circumstances surrounding the production.

0898   GEDULD, Harry M.   and GOTTESMAN, Ronald, comps.

Sergei Eisenstein and Upton Sinclair: the making and un-

making of Que viva Mexico!

Bloomington, Indiana University Press, 1970. 449p. illus.

A documented objective account of the conception,

development, and abortive end of Eisenstein's film financed

by Upton Sinclair. With detailed bibliography.

0899   KUROSAWA, Akira, 1910-

Rashomon; a film by Akira Kurosawa from the filmscript by

Akira Kurosawa and Shinobu Hashimoto.

New York, Grove Press, 1969. 255p. illus.

A translation of the dialogue from the film Rashomon; a

scenario based on Ryunosuke Akutagawa's Rashamon, and In a grove.

Both are included in this volume together with an extract from

the screenplay of the American re-make called The Outrage.

Illustrated largely by frame enlargements.

0900   ROSS, Lillian

Picture. London, Gollancz, 1953.

240p.

A cynical day-to-day account of the making of John Huston's

film The Red Badge of Courage, that gives an insight into Hollywood

of the early 50s. Amusing as well as informative.

0901   GIBBON, Monk, 1896-

The Red shoes ballet; a critical study.

London, Saturn Press, 1948. 95p. illus.

Although concentrating on the ballet itself, the

direction and art direction of the film by Michael Powell

are also considered.

0902   SHAKESPEARE, William, 1564-1616.

Romeo and Juliet; a motion picture edition illustrated with

photographs. Produced for Metro-Goldwyn-Mayer by Irving G.

Thalberg. Directed by George Cukor. Arranged for the scree

by Talbot Jennings.

New York, Random House, 1936. 290p. illus.

Contents:- Picturizing Romeo and Juliet, by I. Thalberg

Foreword to Romeo and Juliet, by W. Strunk, Jr.- Romeo and

Juliet, by W. Shakespeare.- Romeo and Juliet scenario versic

Juliet, by N. Shearer.- Romeo, by L. Howard.- Mercutio, by

J. Barrymore.-Directing Romeo and Juliet, by G. Cukor.- Rome

and Juliet script, by T. Jennings.- Design of settings for

Romeo and Juliet, by C. Gibbons.- Romeo and Juliet costumes,

by Adrian.- Romeo and Juliet costumes, by Oliver Messel.- A

preliminary guide, by M.J. Herzberg.

0903   MOISEIWITSCH, Maurice, ed.   and   WARMAN, Eric, 1904-   ed.

The Royal Ballet on stage and screen: the book of the

Royal Ballet film.

London, Heinemann, c1960. 56p. illus.

A companion to the Paul Czinner film, The Royal

Ballet, with a chapter by the director on the film's

production, and other chapters about the ballet company

and the ballets staged for the film.

0904   RENOIR, Jean, 1894-

The rules of the game; a film by Jean Renoir.

London, Lorrimer, 1970.

168p. illus. *Classic film scripts series.*

Screenplay, preceded by interviews with Renoir and

brief notes.

0905   SHAW, George Bernard, 1856-1950

Saint Joan; a screenplay. Edited and with an introduction

by Bernard F. Dukore.

Seattle, University of Washington Press, 1968.

162p. illus.

The introduction by Dukore surveys all of Shaw's filmed

work. Appendices include a Shaw filmography, Censor's proposed

deletions and changes for Saint Joan, and Shaw's alternative

endings for the screenplay.

0906   MAYSLES, Albert   and MAYSLES, David

Salesman; a film by the Maysles brothers and Charlotte

Zwerin.

New York, New American Library, 1969. 128p. illus.

The screenplay of the Maysles brothers documentary,

with production notes.

0907   BIBERMAN, Herbert J

Salt of the earth; the story of a film.

Boston, Beacon Press, c1965. 373p. illus.

The story of the making of the film Salt of the

earth, and the problems encountered, together with

subsequent events, written by the director. Includes

the screenplay of the film by Michael Wilson.

0908   FELLINI, Federico

Fellini's Satyricon. Edited by Dario Zanelli.

New York, Ballantine Books, 1970. 280p. illus.

*Contents:- From the planet Rome.- Documentary of a dream
a dialogue between Alberto Moravia and Federico Fellini.- Th*
*strange journey.- The treatment.- Preface by F. Fellini.- The
screenplay.- Titles.*

0909   JAMES, David, 1919-

Scott of the Antarctic: the film and its production.

London, Convoy, 1948. 151p. illus.

*Description and production notes of the film starring
John Mills, Derek Bond, and James Robertson Justice.*

0910   ANDERSON, Lindsay, 1923-   ed.

Making a film; the story of Secret people, chronicled
and edited by Linday Anderson, together with the shooting
script of the film by Thorold Dickinson and Wolfgang
Wilhelm.

London, Allen & Unwin, 1952. 223p. illus.

*The book by a well-known English film director
follows the production in the Ealing studios of Secret
people.*

0911   MARKOPOULOS, Gregory J.

Quest for Serenity; journal of a film-maker.

New York, Film-Makers' Cinemateque, 1965? 80p. illus.

0912   KUROSAWA, Akira, 1910-

The seven samurai. English translation and introduction by

Donald Richie.

New York, Simon & Schuster, 1970. 224p. illus. *Modern film*

scripts.

Shots are numbered throughout and are based on the Toho

Company script of the 160 minute version of the film.

0913   BERGMAN, Ingmar, 1918-

The seventh seal; a film by Ingmar Bergman.

New York, Simon & Schuster, 1968. 82p. illus. *Modern*

film scripts series.

The screen play, with credits, stills, and a brief

introduction by Bergman.

0914   WILDER, Billy, 1906-   and DIAMOND, I.A.L.

Some like it hot; a screenplay.

New York, New American Library, 1959. 144p. illus.

0915   DUNN, Maxwell

How they made Sons of Matthew.

Sydney, Angus and Robertson, 1949. 209p. illus.

A detailed book about the shooting of the Australian

film Sons of Matthew, produced and directed by Charles

Chauvel.

0916   SKOURAS, Thana, ed.

The tale of Rogers and Hammerstein's South Pacific.

Edited and produced by Thana Skouras; designed by John de

Cuir and Dale Henessy.

New York, Lehmann, 1958. 63p. illus.

A souvenir book with very brief production notes and

information on the story and music.

0917   INGE, William Mather

Splendor in the grass; a screenplay.

New York, Bantam Books, 1961. 121p.

0918   NICHOLS, Dudley, 1895–

Stagecoach; a film by John Ford and Dudley Nichols.

New York, Simon & Schuster, 1971. 152p. illus. *Classic film scripts series.*

Screenplay by Dudley Nichols of the film directed by John Ford, and based on 'Stage to Lordsburg' by Ernest Haycox.

0919   LEWIS, Sinclair, 1885–1961   and SCHARY, Dore.

Storm in the west.

New York, Stein & Day, 1963. 192p. illus.

'The screenplay... as it was written except that technical terms have been translated into narrative story telling.'

0920   PERRY, Eleanor.

The swimmer. Based on the story by John Cheever.

New York, Stein and Day, 1967. 127p.

A screenplay, with no technical directions.

0921   TAKING OFF by Milos Forman, John Guare, Jean-Claude Carriere, John Klein. With screenplay scene settings written for the bo[ok] by Milos Forman and Nancy Hardin.

New York, New American Library, 1971. 220p. illus.

The screenplay, together with an interview and an articl[e] by Milos Forman, the film's director.

0922   GIBBON, Monk, 1896-

The tales of Hoffman; a study of the film.

London, Saturn Press, 1951. 96p. illus.

Background to the production of the film directed by

Michael Powell.

0923   NOEDLINGER, Henry S.

Moses and Egypt; the documentation to the motion picture

The Ten Commandments. With an introduction by Cecil B.

DeMille.

Los Angeles, University of Southern California Press, 1956.

202p. illus.

A summary of the research conducted for the film

The Ten Commandments, covering all facets required for

the authenticity of the production. Annotated throughout.

0924   MCCOY, Horace, 1897-1955   and THOMPSON, Robert E.

They shoot horses, don't they?

New York, Avon, 1969. 319p.

Includes the novel by McCoy, and the text of the screen-

play (p. 131-319) by Robert E. Thompson.

0925   WELLS, Herbert George, 1866-1946.

Things to come; a film by H. G. Wells; a new story

based on the material contained in his book The shape of

things to come.

New York, Macmillan, 1935. 155p.

Scenario of the film directed by Alexander Korda.

0926   GREENE, Graham, 1904-

The third man; a film by Graham Greene and Carol Reed.

New York, Simon and Schuster, c1968. 134p. illus. *Modern film scripts series.*

The complete script by Graham Greene of the film directed by Carol Reed, with additions and omissions made by the director indicated.

0927   REID, Alastair, 1926-

To be alive. From the film produced by Francis Thompson, Inc. for Johnson Wax. Text by Alastair Reid.

New York, Macmillan, 1966. unpaged. illus.

Devoted to the award-winning documentary. Consists large of stills.

0928   FOOTE, Horton

The screenplay of To kill a mockingbird.

New York, Harcourt, Brace & World, 1964. 117p.

Screenplay of the film directed by Robert Mulligan, and based on Harper Lee's novel.

0929   OSBORNE, John, 1929-

Tom Jones: a film script. Rev. ed.

New York, Grove Press, 1965, c1964. 192p. illus.

Script of the completed film directed by Tony Richardson.

0930   WELLES, Orson, 1915-

The trial; a film. English translation and description of acti by Nicholas Fry.

New York, Simon & Schuster, 1970.

176p. illus. *Modern film scripts series.*

0931   CAPOTE, Truman, 1924-   and others.

Trilogy; an experiment in multimedia, by Truman Capote,

Eleanor Perry, and Frank Perry.

New York, Macmillan, 1969. 276p. illus.

The original stories and the screen plays for the

film Trilogy, together with notes and production data

by Capote with Frank and Eleanor Perry. Illustrated with

stills and location shots.

0932   MAUGHAM, William Somerset, 1874-1965.

Trio; original stories by W. Somerset Maugham, screenplays

by R.C. Sherriff and Noel Langley.

Garden City, N.Y., Doubleday, 1950. 156p.

Contents:- The verger.- Mr. Know-All.- Sanatorium.

0933   THOMAS, Dylan, 1914-1953.

Twenty years a-growing; a film script from the story

by Maurice O'Sullivan.

London, Dent, 1964. 91p.

The unfinished film script, with a synopsis of the

uncompleted second half.

0934   RAPHAEL, Frederic, 1931-

Two for the road.

London, Cape, 1967. 141p.

A screenplay, prefaced by an illuminating thirty page essay

on writing for the cinema, and on the future of the film

medium generally. Written by the novelist and scriptwriter

of Darling, and Far from the madding crowd.

0935   AGEL, Jerome, ed.

The making of Kubrick's 2001.

New York, New American Library, 1970. 367p. illus.

An anthology of essays, criticism, interviews, and production notes on the filming of 2001: a space odyssey. The text of Arthur C. Clarke's short story, The sentinel, which was the source of the screenplay is included.

0936   FICTION INTO FILM: A WALK IN THE SPRING RAIN, by Rachel Maddux, Stirling Silliphant, and Neil D. Isaacs.

Knoxville, University of Tennessee Press, 1970.

239p. illus.

Contents:- Fiction: A walk in the spring rain, by R. Maddux.- Screenplay: A walk in the spring rain, by S. Silliphant.- Fiction into film...by N.D. Isaacs.

0937   WATKINS, Peter

The war game.

London, Sphere Books, 1967. unpaged. illus.

An illustrated adaptation of the BBC documentary film that was banned from television showing in Britain and eventually released theatrically.

0938   WHOLLY COMMUNION; THE FILM BY PETER WHITEHEAD. New ed.

London, Lorrimer Films, 1966. 72p. illus.

Poems featured in the film of the international poetry reading at the Royal Albert Hall, London, June 11th, 1965. Illustrated with stills.

0939   BERGMAN, Ingmar, 1918-

Wild strawberries; a film by Ingmar Bergman.

London, Lorrimer, 1970. 120p. illus. *Modern film*

scripts series.

Screenplay with credits, together with an essay by

Bergman and a tribute to Victor Sjostrom who played the

lead role. Includes cutting continuity and stills.

0940   SCHULBERG, Budd

Across the Everglades; a play for the screen.

New York, Random House, 1958. 126p. illus.

Screenplay of the film directed by Nicholas Ray and

released under the title: Wind across the Everglades.

0941   BASS, Ulrich

Young Aphrodites. Based on the film by Nikos Koundourous.

London, Rodney Books, 1966. unpaged. illus.

TECHNIQUE

General works

0942   BADDELEY, Walter Hugh

The technique of documentary film production. 2nd rev. ed.

London, Focal Press, 1969. 268p. illus.

A manual dealing with all aspects of the production of

documentary films, discussed in a technical manner. Includes

all stages, from scripting to distribution.

0943   BENDICK, Jeanne

Making the movies. Directed by Robert Bendick.

London, Elek, 1946. 190p. illus.

A pictorial account of film production for children.

0944   BLAKESTON, Oswell, ed.

Working for the films; articles by 19 studio technicians.

London, Focal Press, 1947. 207p. illus.

Filmmakers such as David Lean and John Halas describe
their particular areas of responsibility in film production
in relation to the whole. Style is non-technical.

0945   BRODBECK, Emil E.

Handbook of basic motion picture techniques.

Philadelphia, Chilton, 1966.

224p. illus.

Covers mechanics and techniques of film-making
without becoming too technical for the layman.

0946   BRUNEL, Adrian

Film production.

London, Newnes, 1936. 184p. front.

A continuation of the author's earlier work, Film-
craft. Chapters cover such topics as Inspiration, Treat-
ment, Editing, Casting, Acting, Set economy, etc. With
appendices written by specialists in areas such as casting,
continuity, dialogue, make-up, etc.

0947 BUCHANAN, Andrew, 1897-

The art of film production. With an appreciation by

John Grierson.

London, Pitman, 1936. 99p. illus.

A collection of the author's articles and essays

covering both technical and non-technical aspects of film

production. Contents:- Introductory.- Behind the screens.-

What is screen art.- Choosing a subject.- Creative

direction.- Dramatizing industry.- Newsreels or real

news.- The camera goes to see.- Screen magazine production.

0948 BUCHANAN, Andrew, 1897-

Film-making from script to screen. Rev. ed.

London, Faber, 1951. 159p.

Revised edition of the book first published in 1937.

Covers all fundamental processes of film production.

0949 BUTLER, Ivan

The making of feature films; a guide.

Harmondsworth, Eng., Penguin Books, 1971. 191p. illus.

The author states the purpose of the book as being

"to describe systematically the inner workings of the

film industry in the words of its workers." Contributions

are made by producers, directors, scriptwriters, sound-

men, distributors, and others.

0950 CAMERON, James Ross, 1886- and CIFRE, Joseph S

Cameron's encyclopedia: sound motion pictures. 6th ed.

Coral Gables, Fla., Cameron Pub. Co., 1959.

unpaged. illus.

A largely technical encyclopaedia.

0951   COOKE, David Coxe, 1917-

Behind the scenes in motion pictures.

New York, Dodd, Mead, 1960. 64p. illus.

A brief introduction to film production, written for children.

0952   CURRAN, Charles W., 1899-

Screen writing and production techniques; the nontechnical handbook for TV, film and tape.

New York, Hastings House, 1958. 240p. illus.

Arranged in three parts:- The pre-production phase.- Putting the subject into production.- Screen production cost Previously published in 1953 as The handbook of TV and film technique, and in 1952 as The handbook of motion picture techniques for businessmen.

0953   FELDMAN, Joseph   and   FELDMAN, Harry

Dynamics of the film.

New York, Hermitage House, 1952. 255p. illus.

Contents:- The film and the older arts.- The basis of film technique.- The composition of a shot.- Acting in the film.- More about the composition of a shot.- The rhythm of the film.- The film and sound. Also includes bibliography.

0954   FIELD, Alice Evans

Hollywood, U.S.A.; from script to screen.

New York, Vantage Press, 1952. 256p. illus.

Explores all phases of film production. With a foreword by Will Hays.

0955   THE FOCAL ENCYCLOPEDIA OF FILM & TELEVISION TECHNIQUES.

New York, Hastings House, 1969. 1100p. illus.

A comprehensive encyclopaedia of over 1600 entries,
written by more than one hundred named contributors. A
valuable reference work, technical in nature, but with
many articles also of general interest to the student of
the cinema.

0956   GREY, Elizabeth, *pseud.*

Behind the scenes in a film studio.

New York, Roy, 1968,c1966. 102p. illus.

An introductory guide for young people, with particular
reference to film-making in Britain.

0957   HOADLEY, Ray

How they make a motion picture.

New York, Crowell, 1939. 119p. illus.

0958   HUMFREY, Robert

Careers in the films.

London, Pitman, 1938. 104p. illus.

"... the various special crafts which go to make up
the industry." (p. 5) With bibliography.

HUSS, Roy Gerard, 1927- *and* SILVERSTEIN, Norman

The film experience; elements of motion picture art.

New York, Harper & Row, 1968. 172p. illus.

An introductory manual on the theory of film art,
production, and direction. With bibliography.

0959   KIESLING, Barrett C.

Talking pictures: how they are made, how to appreciate them.
Richmond, N.Y., Johnson Pub. Co., 1937. 332p. illus.

Covers all aspects of film production as it was done at the time of publication, from story selection to editing.

0960   LEGG, Stuart   <u>and</u> FAIRTHORNE, Robert

The cinema and television.

London, Longmans, Green, 1939. 78p.

March of time series.

An introduction intended for younger readers that explains the basic technical processes of the cinema industry, with brief reference to television.

0961   LEROY, Mervyn, 1900-

It takes more than talent. As told to Alyce Canfield.
New York, Knopf, 1953. 300p.

An introduction to occupations in motion pictures, from acting to writing.

0962   LEWIS, Jerry, 1926-

The total film-maker.

New York, Random House, 1971. 208p. illus.

Edited from lectures given by Jerry Lewis at the University of Southern California, arranged under the following headings:- Production.- Post-production.- Comedy.

Four aspects of the film.

New York, Brussel & Brussel, 1968.   386p.   illus.

Concentrates on technical advancements of film art:
sound, colour, 3-D, widescreen, and others. Appendices include
lists of natural colour and tinted films, widescreen films,
third-dimensional films, and pioneer sound films. Chronological
arrangement within each group is followed, with distributor
and technical processes noted. Includes bibliography.

LINDGREN, Ernest.

The art of the film. 2d ed.

London, Allen & Unwin, 1963.   258p.   illus.

A revised enlarged edition of the work first published
in 1948. In three sections: Mechanics.- Technique.- Criticism.
An excellent introduction to film aesthetics, appreciation,
and criticism, the major section dealing with film technique.

0964   MANOOGIAN, Haig P.

The film-maker's art.

New York, Basic Books, 1966.   340p.   illus.

A handbook on film production that emphasises the
artistic processes as well as the practical details
involved in the creation of a film from the initial outline
to the finished product.

0965   MANVELL, Roger, 1909-

The living screen: background to the film and television.

London, Harrap, 1961.   192p.   illus.

0966   MASCELLI, Joseph V.

The five C's of cinematography; motion picture filming
techniques simplified.

Hollywood, Cine/Grafic Publications, 1965. 251p. illus.

*An easy-to-read introduction to the film-maker's
techniques of interest to film enthusiasts as well as
to students. The five C's represent camera angles,
continuity, cutting, close-ups, and composition.*

0967   NAUMBERG, Nancy, 1911-   ed.

We make the movies.

New York, Norton, 1937. 284p. illus.

*A collection of articles about Hollywood studio
production, contributed by leading personalities and technic
of the 1930s, such as Jesse Lasky, Sidney Howard, Bette
Davis, Paul Muni and Walt Disney.*

0968   PRYOR, William Clayton   and   PRYOR, Helen Sloman.

Let's go to the movies.

New York, Harcourt, Brace, 1939. 183p. illus.

*A general introduction to film production, intended for
teenagers.*

PUDOVKIN, Vsevolod Illarionovich, 1893-1953.

Film technique and Film acting. Memorial ed.

London, Vision Press, 1958. 388p. illus.

*Two classic works by the Russian director, translated
and edited by Ivor Montagu. Pudovkin on film technique
was first published in English in 1937. Both works were
developed from lectures delivered at the State Institute
of Cinematography in Moscow.*

0969   QUIGLEY, Martin, 1917-   ed.

New screen techniques.

New York, Quigley, 1953. 208p. illus.

An anthology of 26 articles, explaining such techniques

as widescreen and 3-D.

0970   REED, Stanley   and HUNTLEY, John, 1921-

How films are made. 2d ed.

London, Educational Supply Association, 1959.

90p. illus.

Intended for younger readers; explains the role of

technicians in film making.

SCHARY, Dore

Case history of a movie, by Dore Schary as told to Charles
Palmer.

New York, Random House, 1950. 242p. illus.

Written by the former vice-president in charge of production

at M-G-M, this book follows the step-by-step production of the film

The next voice you hear. General contents:- The story and the

script.- Preparation for production.- Shooting the picture.-

Finishing the picture.

0971   SHAPIRO, Clarence M.

I scout for movie talent; a guide to the requirements for

an artist's entry into motion pictures, with practical suggestions

applicable to any line of dramatic endeavour.

Chicago, Kroch, 1940. 84p.

0972 SPENCER, Douglas Arthur, 1901-   and WALEY, Hubert D.

The cinema today. 2d ed.

London, Oxford University Press, 1956. 202p.

A text on cinema techniques, covering all aspects from cameras, projection, sound, animation, 3-D & wide-screen, etc.

0973 SPOTTISWOODE, Raymond, 1913-

Basic film techniques.

Berkeley, University of California Press, 1948.

185p. illus.

0974 SPOTTISWOODE, Raymond, 1913-

Film and its techniques. Illustrated by Jean-Paul Ladouceur.

Berkeley, University of California Press, 1951.

516p. illus.

A basic reference, bearing in mind its date of publicatic Covers camera techniques, editing and laboratory processes, film storage and film libraries etc. Well illustrated and wit glossary and bibliography.

SPOTTISWOODE, Raymond, 1913-

A grammar of the film; an analysis of film technique.

Berkeley, University of California Press, 1950. 328p. illus.

An attempt to isolate the fundamental principles of film art, that constitutes an advanced theoretical study of film technique. A reprint of the work first published in 1935 with a new preface.

0975   TAYLOR, Theodore, 1922-

People who make movies.

Garden City, N.Y., Doubleday, 1967. 158p. illus.

Informative; an anecdotal behind-the-scenes look at the film industry, and the types of occupations involved in film production.

0976   WATTS, Stephen, ed.

Behind the screen: how films are made.

London, Barker, 1938. 176p. illus.

A collection of essays by experts in the field of film production, ranging from George Cukor on directing to Leslie Howard and Lionel Barrymore on acting.

WILLIAMS, Raymond **and** ORROM, Michael, 1920-

Preface to film.

London, Film Drama, 1954. 129p.

Film and the dramatic tradition; film and its dramatic techniques; offers an approach to the production of dramatic films in which all the resources of the arts are used.

0977   WOODHOUSE, Bruce

From script to screen.

London, Winchester, 1948. 192p. illus.

Follows the steps in film production from the acceptance of the script to the final press-showing. Includes a brief extract from the shooting script by Nigel Balchin for Mine own executioner.

0978   YOUNGBLOOD, Gene, 1942-

    Expanded cinema.

    New York, Dutton, 1970. 432p. illus.

       Examines new developments such as laser and computer-generated films, and multi-screen environments. Includes interviews with the people involved, and has an introduction by R. Buckminister Fuller.

Acting

0979   ALBERTSON, Lillian, 1881-

    Motion picture acting.

    New York, Funk & Wagnalls, 1947. 135p.

       Written by RKO's talent coach. Covers different approaches in acting in films or for the stage, and gives practical hints and exercises.

0980   ANDREWS, Cyril Bruyn

    The theatre, the cinema and ourselves.

    London, Clarence House Press, 1947. 52p. illus.

       A brief study of the ways in which acting techniques have changed, particularly in the cinema.

0981   BENNER, Ralph   and CLEMENTS, Mary Jo

    The young actors' guide to Hollywood.

    New York, Coward-McCann, 1964. 185p. illus.

       With an introduction by Richard Chamberlain.

CHERKASOV, Nikolai Konstantinovich, 1903-

    Notes of a Soviet actor.

    Moscow, Foreign Languages Publishing House, 1957. 227p. illus.

       Life and methods of a veteran Soviet stage and screen actor.

0982   PATE, Michael

The film actor; acting for motion pictures and television.
South Brunswick, N.J., Barnes, 1970. 245p. illus.

*Of interest to a wider audience than its title would
suggest because of a lengthy glossary of film terms: The
terminology of the film medium (p.29-150) Other sections
deal with exercises and the staging of a scene from a
screen play.*

PUDOVKIN, Vsevolod Illarionovich, 1893-1953.

Film technique and Film acting. Memorial ed.
London, Vision Press, 1958. 388p. illus.

*Two classic works by the Russian director, translated
and edited by Ivor Montagu. Pudovkin on film technique
was first published in English in 1937. Both works were
developed from lectures delivered at the State Institute
of Cinematography in Moscow.*

0983   ROSS, Lillian   and ROSS, Helen

The player: a profile of an art.
New York, Simon & Schuster, 1962. 459p. illus.

*In autobiographical form, based on edited interviews
with 55 actors.*

SHELLEY, Frank

Stage and screen.
London, Pendulum, 1946. 55p. illus.

*Discusses Olivier, Portman, Davis, Garbo and others in
a comparison between approaches to theatre and cinema.*

250

Animation and allied techniques

0984   BRYNE-DANIEL, J

Grafilm: an approach to a new medium.

London, Studio Vista, 1970. 96p. illus.

Deals with graphic (i.e. non-photographic) film

processes and techniques.

0985   FALK, Nat

How to make animated cartoons; the history and technique.

Illustrated by the author and the cartoon studios.

New York, Foundation Books, 1941. 79p. illus.

0986   HALAS, John   and MANVELL, Roger, 1909-

The technique of film animation. 2d ed.

New York, Hastings House, c1958. 360p. illus.

Discusses forms, techniques, and uses of animation.

With bibliography.

0987   LEVITAN, Eli L.

Animation art in the commercial film.

New York, Reinhold, 1960. 128p. illus.

0988   MADSEN, Roy

Animated film: concepts, methods, uses.

New York, Interland, 1969. 234p. illus.

0989   MANVELL, Roger, 1909-

The animated film. With pictures from the film Animal

farm, by Halas & Batchelor.

London, Sylvan Press, 1954. 63p. illus.

A non-technical introduction to the processes involved

in the creation of an animated film. Includes a brief

history.

0990   REINIGER, Lotte

Shadow theatres and shadow films.

London, Batsford, 1970. 120p. illus.

Shadow films are dealt with from page 82, discussing such topics as animation, story-board, and other aspects of shadow film-making.

Directing

0991   BARE, Richard L

The film director; a practical guide to motion picture and television techniques.

New York, Macmillan, 1971. 243p. illus.

Inspite of its subtitle this book is of interest to the film enthusiast as well as to the film student for its insight into a director's viewpoints and experiences. With glossary and bibliography.

DIRECTORS AT WORK: INTERVIEWS WITH AMERICAN FILM-MAKERS.

Interviews conducted and edited by Bernard R. Kantor, Irwin R. Blacker, and Anne Kramer.

New York, Funk & Wagnalls, 1970. 442p.

Detailed interviews with Richard Brooks, George Cukor, Norman Jewison, Eli Kazan, Stanley Kramer, Richard Lester, Jerry Lewis, Elliot Silverstein, Robert Wise, and William Wyler. A filmography for each director is provided.

0992   GEDULD, Harry M., ed.

Film makers on film making; statements on their art by thirty directors.

Bloomington, Indiana University Press, 1967. 302p.

Divided into two parts: Pioneers and prophets, and Film masters and film makers. Presents "an intimate view of the art and craft of the film as conceived by its most distinguished practitioners." No index.

0993   GELMIS, Joseph, 1935-

The film director as superstar.

Garden City, N.Y., Doubleday, 1970. 316p. illus.

Interviews with sixteen filmmakers who represent the importance of film as a medium of the director. Each expresses his personal views.

JACOBS, Lewis, 1906-   ed.

The movies as medium.

New York, Farrar, Straus and Giroux, 1970. 335p. illus.

Presents directors' aims and attitudes, with essays on topics such as time and space, colour, sound, image, movement, etc. With bibliography.

0994   LIVINGSTON, Don.

Film and the director.

New York, Capricorn Books, 1969.

A reprint of the book first published in 1953. Explains basic principles of film direction intended for film-makers and technicians, but also of general interest.

0995   REYNERTSON, A. J.

The work of the film director.

New York, Hastings House, 1970. 259p. illus.

Contents:- Directing today.- Time and design.- Realizing the time design.- Film sound.- The object in space.- Internal composition.- External composition.- Ideas in physical form.- The actor.- Directors and their public. With filmography, bibliography, and glossary.

0996   RHODE, Eric, 1934-

Tower of Babel; speculations on the cinema.

London, Weidenfeld & Nicolson, 1966. 214p.

International in scope, this book includes chapters on

outstanding directors. It attempts to show how the cinema can

become an art by investigating the director's visions and relating

their particular insights to some general view of the world.

Bresson, Eisenstein, Jennings, Fellini, Resnais, and Wajda are

among those discussed.

Editing

0997   REISZ, Karel

The technique of film editing, by Karel Reisz with Gavin Millar,

2d ed.

New York, Hastings House, 1968. 411p. illus.

An enlarged edition of a now standard work originally

published in 1953. Despite the title, this is a lucid account of

the art rather than the mechanics of film editing, written by a

respected English director.

Lighting

0998   ALTON, John

Painting with light.

New York, Macmillan, 1949.

191p. illus.

An introduction to studio and exterior motion picture

lighting techniques, illustrated with 295 photographs

and line cuts. Chapters include Hollywood photography;

Mystery lighting; The Hollywood close-up; Visual music;

The portrait studio; The laboratory, etc.

Make-up

0999   KEHOE, Vincent J.R.

         The technique of film and television make-up.

         New York, Hastings House, 1958. 263p. illus.

         A general introduction to the subject.

Music

1000   EISLER, Hanns, 1898-1962.

         Composing for the films.

         New York, Oxford University Press, 1947. 165p.

         A report for the Rockefeller Foundation Film Music
         Project in which the composer presents his own theories
         on the use of music in films, and offers strong criticism
         of the traditional Hollywood approach.

         HOFMANN, Charles

         Sounds for silents.

         New York, DBS Publications, 1970. unpaged. illus.

         A history of the use of musical accompaniment for
         silent films. The illustrations include extracts from
         scores, and an appendix provides the complete score for
         an Edison Company short film, Rescued from an eagle's
         nest. With bibliography, and a sound recording made by
         the author of extracts from music for five silent films.

1001   HUNTLEY, John, 1921-

         British film music.

         London, Skelton-Robinson, 1947. 247p. illus.

         Partial contents:- Film music: its composers,
         orchestras and functions.- The story of British film
         music.- Music for the documentary film.- The industrial,
         cartoon and newsreel film.- Recording film music.- Film
         music forum.- Biographical index. With bibliography and
         discography.

KELLER, Hans Heinrich, 1919-

> The need for competent film music criticism; a pamphlet
>
> for those who care for film as art, with a final section
>
> for those who do not.
>
> London, British Film Institute, 1947. 22p.

1002   LONDON, Kurt, 1899-

> Film music: a summary of the characteristic features of
>
> its history, aesthetics, technique and possible development.
>
> London, Faber, 1936. 280p. illus.
>
> *A wide-ranging introduction to the subject.*

1003   MANVELL, Roger, 1909-   and   HUNTLEY, John, 1921-

> The technique of film music. 2d ed.
>
> London, Focal Press, 1967. 299p. illus.
>
> *Sponsored by the British Film Academy, this book*
>
> *serves as an introduction to musical techniques in the*
>
> *cinema. Includes an index of film music recordings,*
>
> *and a biography.*

<u>Photography and screen processes</u>

1004   HIGHAM, Charles, 1931-

> Hollywood cameramen: sources of light.
>
> London, Thames and Hudson in association with the British
>
> Film Insitute, 1970. 176p. illus. *Cinema one series.*
>
> *Interviews with seven cameramen:- Leon Shamroy.- Lee*
>
> *Garmes.- William Daniels.- James Wong Howe.- Stanley*
>
> *Cortez.- Karl Struss.- Arthur Miller. With filmographies.*

HUNTLEY, John, 1921-

British Technicolor films.

London, Skelton Robinson, 1949. 224p. illus.

After a brief introduction to the colour film, the book presents brief essays on 25 British Technicolor films from 1936 to 1948, with notes on art direction, camera work, and colour design for each. An index provides full credits for each film discussed. Other chapters include Technicolor who's who, British Technicolor short films, Colour forum, Profile of Natalie Kalmus, and Technical abstracts.

NILSEN, Vladimir S.

The cinema as a graphic art: on a theory of representation in the cinema. With an appreciation by S.M. Eisenstein. Translation by Stephen Garry, with editorial advice from Ivor Montagu.

London, Newnes, 1936. 227p. illus.

An exposition on the creative uses of the camera and the dynamics of composition.

QUIGLEY, Martin, 1917-   ed.

New screen techniques.

New York, Quigley, 1953. 208p. illus.

An anthology of 26 articles, explaining such techniques as widescreen and 3-D.

THOMAS, David Bowen

The first colour motion pictures.

London, H.M.S.O., 1969.

44p. illus. *Science Museum monographs.*

A brief history up to 1917.

Set design

1005   CARRICK, Edward, *pseud*.

Art and design in the British film; a pictorial directory
of British art directors and their work, compiled by
Edward Carrick.

London, D. Dobson, 1948. 133p. illus.

*A well illustrated volume covering the work of 47
designers accompanied by brief biographical notes, and
illustrations of characteristic designs.*

1006   CARRICK, Edward, *pseud*.

Designing for films.

London, Studio, 1949. 128p. illus.

*A new edition of the book first published in 1941 as
Designing for moving pictures. It is a practical book on
the work of the film art director and set design, illustrated by examples of the author's work.*

1007   LARSON, Orville Kurth, 1914-   ed.

Screen design for stage and screen; readings on the
aesthetics and methodology of screen design for drama,
opera, musical comedy, ballet, motion pictures, television
and arena theatre.

East Lansing, Mich., Michigan State University Press,
1961. 334p. illus.

*A collection of readings by leading designers, but with
emphasis on stage design.*

1008   MYERSCOUGH-WALKER, Raymond.

Stage and film decor.

London, Pitman, 1940. 192p. illus.

Part II (p. 101-162) deals with set design and decor

for the film.

Writing

1009   BERANGER, Clara

Writing for the screen.

Dubuque, Iowa, W.C. Brown, 1950. 199p.

Presents the problems of screenwriting, illustrated

by film examples, and in the second part of the book

discusses dramatic construction.

1010   BRUNEL, Adrian

Film script: the technique of writing for the screen.

London, Burke, 1948. 192p. illus.

Includes extracts from the shooting and post-

production scripts of The captive heart, showing vari-

ations between the two. Also includes extracts from the

final shooting scripts of Anna Karenina and Broken journey.

CURRAN, Charles W., 1899-

Screen writing and production techniques; the nontechnical

handbook for TV, film and tape.

New York, Hastings House, 1958. 240p. illus.

Arranged in three parts:- The pre-production phase.-

Putting the subject into production.- Screen production costs

Previously published in 1953 as The handbook of TV and film

technique, and in 1952 as The handbook of motion picture

techniques for businessmen.

1011   HERMAN, Lewis Helmar

A practical manual of screen playwriting for theater and television films.

Cleveland, World, 1952. 294p. illus.

Arranged in three parts:- Dramaturgy.- The filmic components.- Writing the screen play. The second part of the book is of interest to students of film language as well as to those engaged in writing for the screen.

1012   LANE, Tamar

The new technique of screen writing; a practical guide to the writing and marketing of photoplays.

New York, Whittlesey House, 1936. 342p.

Of mainly historical interest, covering such topics as censorship and copyright, as well as theory and general technique of screenplay writing. Also includes three specimen manuscripts.

1013   LAWSON, John Howard, 1895-

Theory and technique of playwriting and screenwriting.

New rev. ed. New York, Putnam, 1949.

464p.

About one third of the book is devoted to the screen, covering the historical development of the American cinema, film structure, and motion picture composition. The book relates techniques to actual film examples.

MARGRAVE, Seton

Successful film writing: as illustrated by The ghost
goes west.

London, Methuen, 1936. 216p. illus.

*Following an essay on the principles of film writing,
this volume presents the short story by Eric Keown of Sir
Tristram goes west, a short article by Rene Clair on the
story's cinematic qualities, a first treatment of the
screen adaptation now titled The ghost goes west, and the
final scenario of Clair's film, with detailed times and
measurements.*

MARION, Frances, 1890–

How to write and sell film stories: with a complete
shooting script for Marco Polo by Robert E. Sherwood.

New York, Covici, Friede, 1937. 375p.

*Contents:- The motion picture story.- Characterization.
Plot.- Motivation.- Theme.- Dialogue.- Dramaturgy.- Emotion.
Common errors.- Story ideas.- Censorship.- How stories are
sold.- Author's rights and plagiarism.- Adaptation.-
Continuity.- Marco Polo: a shooting script. (p. 231-364).-
Glossary.*

1014   MARTIN, Ólga Johanna.

Hollywood's movie commandments; a handbook for motion

picture writers and reviewers.

New York, Wilson, 1937.   301p.

The book is mainly concerned with interpretation of the

Motion Picture Production Code of 1930, for screenwriters

and other concerned parties. The Code, addenda and ammend-

ments appear as appendices. Arrrangement:- The movies and

the public.- Moral values in pictures.- Crime in pictures.-

Sex in pictures.- General picture subjects.- Screen writing

proglems.

RAPHAEL, Frederic, 1931-

Two for the road.

London, Cape, 1967.   141p.

A screenplay, prefaced by an illuminating thirty page essay

on writing for the cinema, and on the future of the film

medium generally. Written by the novelist and scriptwriter

of Darling, and Far from the madding crowd.

1015   VALE, Eugene

The technique of screenplay writing; a book about the

dramatic structure of motion pictures.

New York, Crown, 1944.   274p.

A detailed work of general as well as specialized

interest, divided into three sections:- The form.- The

dramatic construction.- The story.

1016   WRITERS CONGRESS, UNIVERSITY OF CALIFORNIA AT LOS ANGELES, 1943.

Writers' Congress; the proceedings of the conference held in October 1943 under the sponsorship of the Hollywood Writers' Mobilization and the University of California. Berkeley, University of California Press, 1944. 663p. front

Film writers discuss the nature of their art.

1017   YOAKEM, Lola Goelet, ed.

TV and screen writing, by Eric Barnouw and others. Berkeley, University of California Press, 1958. 124p.

Contributions from 17 members of the Writers Guild of America, each dealing with one aspect of television and screen writing, such as westerns, comedies, religious and biblical films, etc.

TYPES OF FILM

Adaptations

BALL, Robert Hamilton, 1902–

Shakespeare on silent film; a strange eventful history. New York, Theatre Arts Books, 1968. 403p. illus.

A carefully researched study of the silent film adaptations of Shakespeare's works produced during the silent film era, from 1899. The main work is followed by detailed "Explanations and acknowledgments" a bibliography, and indexes.

1018   BLUESTONE, George

Novels into film.

Baltimore, Johns Hopkins Press, 1957. 237p. illus.

An important book that discusses the aesthetic and
practical problems of film adaptation from the novel.
The bulk of the book illustrates these problems by
considering the adaptation of six novels: The informer,
Wuthering Heights, Pride and prejudice, The grapes of
wrath, The Ox-Bow incident, and Madame Bovary. A
bibliography is included.

COSTELLO, David Paul, 1909-

The serpent's eye: Shaw and the cinema.

Notre Dame, University of Notre Dame Press, c1965. 209p.
illus.

A study of Shaw's theories on the cinema, together
with criticism and discussion of the film versions of
Pygmalion, Major Barbara, and Caesar and Cleopatra.
Includes a listing of motion pictures made from Shaw's
works.

1019   DIMMITT, Richard Bertrand

A title guide to the talkies; a comprehensive listing of 16000 feature-length films from October 1927 until December 1963.

New York, Scarecrow Press, 1965. 2v. (2133p.)

A reference work especially useful for establishing literary sources of films, giving the title of the novel, play, poem, short story, or screen story that was used as the basis for any particular film. Details include author, title, place of publication, publisher, date and pagination. Some analytical entries are included for works not published separately, and cross-references are added for title changes. Film production details are limited largely to date, company and producer. With author index.

1020   ENSER, A. G. S.

Filmed books and plays: a list of books and plays from which films have been made, 1928-1967. Revised edition; revised and with a supplementary list for 1968 and 1969.

London, Deutsch, 1971. 509p.

A revised edition of the work first published, with later supplements, in 1951. Covering primarily British and American sound films, the book is in three main sections. The film title index includes the production company and registration date, together with details of the book or play from which the film was made. Variant titles are noted. There are further indexes under author and under original book or play title where the film title differs.

FICTION INTO FILM: A WALK IN THE SPRING RAIN, by Rachel Maddux,

Stirling Silliphant, and Neil D. Isaacs.

Knoxville, University of Tennessee Press, 1970.

239p. illus.

Contents:- Fiction: A walk in the spring rain, by
R. Maddux.- Screenplay: A walk in the spring rain, by
S. Silliphant.- Fiction into film...by N.D. Isaacs.

KOZINTSEV, Grigorii Mikhailovich

Shakespeare: time and conscience.

New York, Hill and Wang, 1966. 276p. illus.

Written by the director of the Russian film version
of Hamlet. The book, mainly a study of King Lear and Hamlet,
contains considerable information on the writer's approach to
filming Shakespeare. Partial contents:- Hamlet, Prince of
Denmark (p. 105-174).- Ten years with Hamlet, from the director's
diary (p. 211-276).

1021   LIMBACHER, James L.

Remakes, series and sequels on film and television. 2d ed.

Dearborn, Mich., Dearborn Public Library, 1969. 74 leaves.

A revised and expanded edition of the author's Original
film sources and titles with subsequent remakes.

MARCUS, Fred Harold, 1921-   ed.

Film and literature: contrasts in media.

Scranton, Chandler, 1971. 283p. illus.

An anthology in two parts:- The art of the film.-
From words to visual images. The first part presents
the language of film and offers historical perspective.
The second part centers on contrasts between films and
their literary sources. With filmography.

Animal and jungle films

1022   AMARAL, Anthony A., 1930-

       Movie horses: their treatment and training.

       Indianapolis, Bobbs-Merrill, 1967. 152p. illus.

       An expanded version of the author's earlier work,
Motion picture horses (Cruse Pub. Co., 1962) covering
training of horses for film work, stunts, and with brief
notes on the most famous horses.

1023   BEHLMER, Rudy

       Jungle tales of the cinema.

       Hollywood, 1960. 37 leaves. illus.

       Brief notes on jungle films, eg. Tarzan, Simba, etc.

1024   ENGLISH, James W

       The Rin Tin Tin story.

       New York, Dodd, Mead, 1949. 247p. illus.

1025   ESSOE, Gabe

       Tarzan of the movies: a pictorial history of more than fifty
years of Edgar Rice Burrough's legendary hero.

       New York, Citadel Press, 1968. 208p. illus.

       An account of the forty Tarzan films and of the fourtee
actors who have portrayed the Burrough's hero. No index.

1026   FENTON, Robert W.

       The big swingers.

       Englewood Cliffs, N.J., Prentice-Hall, 1967. 258p. illus.

       Scope includes film treatments of the Tarzan books.
With bibliography.

1027   LEE, Raymond   and CORIELL, Vernell.

A pictorial history of the Tarzan movies; 50 years

of the jungle superman and all-time box office champion.

Los Angeles, Golden State News, 1966.

80p. illus.

Magazine-format. Of interest mainly for the stills

and photographs.

1028   WEATHERWAX, Rudd B.   and ROTHWELL, John H.

The story of Lassie: his discovery and training from

puppyhood to stardom.

New York, Duell, Sloan and Pearce, 1950. 126p. illus.

Animated and allied techniques

BRYNE-DANIEL, J

Grafilm: an approach to a new medium.

London, Studio Vista, 1970. 96p. illus.

Deals with graphic (i.e. non-photographic) film

processes and techniques.

1029   HALAS, John   and MANVELL, Roger, 1909-

Design in motion.

New York, Hastings House, 1962. 160p. illus.

Survey of animation around the world, with nearly 400

illustration

HALAS, John   and MANVELL, Roger, 1909-

The technique of film animation. 2d ed.

New York, Hastings House, c1958. 360p. illus.

Discusses forms, techniques, and uses of animation.

With bibliography.

1030   HERDEG, Walter, ed.

Film and TV graphics: an international survey of film
and television graphics. Text by John Halas.
London, Studio Vista, 1967. 199p. illus.

*Text in English, German and French, dealing with
entertainment, advertising films, titles, captions, and
story board. Includes stills selected from all branches
of animated film.*

MADSEN, Roy

Animated film: concepts, methods, uses.
New York, Interland, 1969. 234p. illus.

MARVELL, Roger, 1909-

The animated film. With pictures from the film Animal
farm, by Halas & Batchelor.
London, Sylvan Press, 1954. 63p. illus.

*A non-technical introduction to the processes involved
in the creation of an animated film. Includes a brief
history.*

1031   STEPHENSON, Ralph

Animation in the cinema.
London, Zwemmer, 1967. 176p. illus. *International film
guide series.*

*A survey and assessment of cartoon work and puppetry
in world cinema. With bibliography and filmography. No inde.*

THOMAS, Bob

Walt Disney, the art of animation: the story of the Disney
Studio contribution to a new art, by Bob Thomas, with the Walt
Disney staff, with research by Don Graham.

New York, Simon & Schuster, 1958. 181p. illus.

Films for children

1032   BAUCHARD, Philippe

The child audience; a report on press, film and radio
for children.

Paris, UNESCO, 1952. 198p. *Press, film and radio in the
world today.*

1033   CHILDREN'S FILM FOUNDATION

Saturday morning cinema. New ed.

London, 1969. 52p. illus.

Includes a catalogue of C.F.F. films.

1034   FIELD, Mary

Good company; the story of the Children's Entertainment
Film Movement in Great Britain, 1943-1950.

London, Longmans, Green, 1952. 192p. illus.

*An account of the growth and acceptance in Britain
of the production of entertainment films intended for children,
and the encouragement provided by J. Arthur Rank.*

1035   FORD, Richard

Children in the cinema.

London, Allen & Unwin, 1939. 232p.

Written as a result of experience gained in running children's film programmes. Contents:- The social problem caused by children in the cinema.- Facts and figures.- Psychological and physical aspects.- The films children like.- The organization of children's matinees.- The children's club movement in cinemas.- The attitude of the authorities, teachers and clergy.- Teaching through entertainment.- Summary of work achieved and future outlook.

1036   STORCK, Henri

The entertainment film for juvenile audiences.

Paris, UNESCO, 1950. 240p.

An international survey of films for children, the portrayal of violence on the screen, and the nature of the juvenile audience.

1037   UNESCO. *Department of Mass Communications.*

Film programmes for the young; report on a presentation of children's films organized by the International Centre of Films for Children, Brussels, 19-23 September, 1958. Paris, UNESCO, 1959. 30p.

Reports by five international experts in children's cinema concerning a programme of films submitted by 21 countries.

1038   BLISTEIN, Elmer M

Comedy in action.

Durham, N.C., Duke University Press, 1964. 146p.

Covering both theatre and cinema, this book is an

examination of theories of comedy past and present.

Includes bibliography and filmography.

1039   DURGNAT, Raymond, 1932-

The crazy mirror: Hollywood comedy and the American image.

London, Faber, 1969. 280p. illus.

In five parts:- Jokes and how to spot them.- The great

American silence.- Who's afraid of the big bad wolf.- Kiss

the boys goodbye.- And therefore take the present time. The

book attempts to show American film comedy styles as reflect-

ions of aspects of American society. With bibliography

and filmography.

1040   LAHUE, Kalton C.   and GILL, Samuel, 1946-

Clown princes and court jesters.

South Brunswick, N.J., Barnes, 1970. 406p. illus.

The stories of fifty typical Hollywood silent screen

comedy actors, from "Fatty" Arbuckle to Billy West. Well

illustrated. No filmographics.

1041   LAHUE, Kalton C.

World of laughter; the motion picture comedy short, 1910-1930. Norman, University of Oklahoma Press, 1966. 240p. illus.

A history of the major short comedy films, actors and directors of the period 1910-1930. An appendix lists the sile films made by eleven of the most prominent comedians and teams

McCAFFREY, Donald W.

4 great comedians: Chaplin, Lloyd, Keaton, Langdon. London, Zwemmer, 1968. 175p. illus. *International film guide series.*

A critical study in the form of a re-evaluation of the major films of the four film-makers mentioned in the title. Includes shot-by-shot analyses and scenario extracts. With bibliography.

MALTIN, Leonard.

Movie comedy teams.

New York, New American Library, 1970. 352p. illus.

Of interest for its inclusion of relatively minor screen comedy teams. With filmographies.

1042   MONTGOMERY, John, 1916-

Comedy films, 1894-1954. 2d. rev. ed.

London, Allen & Unwin, 1968. 286p. illus.

Conceived as a factual rather than a critical account of the history and tradition of the comic film, covering the period from 1894 to 1954. The book concentrates on the American and British cinema.

1043   ROBINSON, David, 1915-

The great funnies: a history of film comedy.

London, Studio Vista, 1969.

156p. illus. *Pictureback series.*

A brief illustrated essay, with emphasis on silent

screen comedy.

Crime films

1044   BAXTER, John

The gangster film.

London, Zwemmer, 1970. 160p. illus. *Screen series.*

Notes on 225 directors, actors, and other key

figures connected with the gangster film genre. With film

title index.

1045   LEE, Raymond   and   VAN HECKE, B. C., 1926-

Gangsters and hoodlums; the underworld in the cinema.

With a foreword by Edward G. Robinson.

South Brunswick, N.J., Barnes, 1971. 264p. illus.

Consists of nearly 350 stills illustrating the era

of the Hollywood gangster film. With brief introductory

text.

Experimental and underground films

1046   ART IN CINEMA SOCIETY

Art in cinema; a symposium on the avantgarde film, together with program notes and references for series one
of Art in cinema. Edited by Frank Stauffacher.
San Francisco, Art in Cinema Society and San Francisco
Museum of Art, 1947. 104p. illus.

*An excellent introduction to avantgarde cinema, with
statements by the film-makers and well prepared notes on
numerous films of the genre. With bibliography.*

1047   BATTCOCK, Gregory, 1937- ed.

The new American cinema; a critical anthology.
New York, Dutton, 1967. 256p. illus.

*A collection of 29 essays written by both critics
and filmmakers, including Brakhage, Mekas, Sontag and
Vogel. The book is in three sections: Survey; Theory
and criticism; Films and filmmakers.*

1048   CURTIS, David, 1942-

Experimental cinema.
New York, Universe Books, 1971. 168p. illus.

*A survey of the fifty-year evolution of film experimentat
Contents:- The economic structure.- The European avant-garde.-
America between the wars.- America since the war.- The co-oper
movement, internationalism, new directions. With bibliography*

1049   MANVELL, Roger, 1909-   ed.

            Experiment in the film.

            London, Grey Walls Press, 1949. 285p. illus.

                A collection of essays on the development of experimental

            cinema in America, Britain, France, Russia, and Germany.

            The meaning of the word 'experimental' is interpreted in

            different ways by the contributors.

1050   RENAN, Sheldon

            An introduction to the American underground film.

            New York, Dutton, 1967. 318p. illus.

                A survey of the avant-garde and the growth of underground

            films in America, with a useful appendix listing a number of the

            most interesting films with their American distributors.

            Essentially informative rather than critical.

        SITNEY, P. Adams, *comp.*

            Film culture reader.

            New York, Praeger, 1970. 438p. illus.

                A collection of articles from Film Culture, arranged

            in five sections:- The formative years, 1955-58.- The new

            American cinema.- The commercial cinema and the auteur theory.-

            The American avant-garde.- Overviews and theoretical

            considerations. The collection is of particular value as a

            survey of American avant-garde film, with many essays by the

            filmmakers themselves.

1051   TYLER, Parker

Underground film: a critical history.

New York, Grove Press, 1969. 249p. illus.

A history and critical survey of the experimental

cinema with emphasis on the American underground film.

Includes assessements of the major film-makers and examines

the possible future developments.

Factual films and documentaries

1052   THE ARTS ENQUIRY

The factual film; a survey sponsored by the Dartington

Hall trustees.

London, Oxford University Press, 1947. 259p.

"Published on behalf of the Arts Enquiry by PEP

(Political and Economic Planning)". A report presented

by the Dartington Hall trustees, and written anonymously

between 1943 and 1945 by a group of experts in the field.

The theme is the use of the film medium, mainly in

Britain, for purposes other than entertainment.

1053   BACHLIN, Peter, 1916-   and MULLER-STRAUSS, Maurice

Newsreels across the world.

Paris, UNESCO, 1952. 100p.

An English-language adaptation of a study of all

facets of newsreels - production, development, technique,

distribution, etc. Includes reference to television news-

reels. With bibliography.

BADDELEY, Walter Hugh

The technique of documentary film production. 2nd rev. ed.

London, Focal Press, 1969. 268p. illus.

A manual dealing with all aspects of the production of

documentary films, discussed in a technical manner. Includes

all stages, from scripting to distribution.

1054   BUCHANAN, Donald William, 1908-

Documentary and educational films in Canada, 1935-1950;

a survey of problems and achievements. Revised April 1952.

Ottawa, Canadian Film Institute, 1952. 24p.

A pamphlet that includes notes on the National Film

Board of Canada, Canadian Film Institute, Film Councils,

etc.

1055   EDINBURGH. INTERNATIONAL EDINBURGH FILM FESTIVAL.

Documentary 47. A time for enquiry, by John Grierson.

Other contributors: Donald Alexander and others.

Edinburgh, Albyn Press, 1947.

36p. illus.

1056   GRIERSON, John, 1898-

Grierson on documentary. Edited and compiled by Forsyth

Hardy.

Berkeley, University of California Press, 1966. Rev. ed.

411p. illus.

First published in 1946, this enlarged edition contains

the observations of the most influential name in the area

of documentary film, both as a director and as a critic.

Of particular interest for reviews and criticism of films

of the 1930's.

278

1057   INFORMATIONAL FILM YEAR BOOK.

Edinburgh, Albyn Press, 1947-   v. illus.

Later editions published under title: Informational

film and television year book.

LEVIN, G. Roy.

Documentary explorations; 15 interviews with filmmakers.

Garden City, N.Y., Doubleday, 1971. 420p. illus.

Film-makers interviewed include such names as Richard

Leacock, the Maysles brothers, D.A. Pennebaker, Frederick

Wiseman, etc. With filmographies and bibliography.

1059   LEYDA, Jay, 1910-

Films beget films.

London, Allen & Unwin, 1964. 176p.

An authoritative survey of the "compilation" film,

a term used to describe films made up from historical

material from film archives. Appendices include a list

of significant compilation films from 1914 to 1963. With

bibliographical references.

NEEGAARD, Ebbe, 1901-1957.

Documentary in Denmark; one hundred films of fact in war,

occupation, liberation, peace, 1940-1948; a catalogue with

synopses.

Copenhagen, Statens Filmcentral, 1948. 89p.

1060   ROSENTHAL, Alan

The new documentary in action: a casebook in film making.

Berkeley, University of California Press, 1971.

287p.

A collection of interviews with film and television documentary film-makers, arranged under the following headings:- Direct cinema.- Television journalism.- Reconstructions and reenactments.- Specials.- Sponsored films.- Candid camera.- Optical transformations.

1061   ROTHA, Paul, 1907-

Documentary film; the use of the film medium to interpret creatively and in social terms the life of the people as it exists in reality. 3d ed., rev. & enl.

London, Faber, 1952. 412p. illus.

The third edition of a standard work, written in collaboration with Sinclair Read and Richard Griffith. Serves both as a history of documentary film and as a discussion of production techniques and artistic principles.

SNYDER, Robert L

Pare Lorentz and the documentary film.

Norman, University of Oklahoma Press, 1968. 232p. illus.

A detailed examination of the documentary film work of Pare Lorentz and the establishment of the United States Film Service. With bibliography.

280

1062   WALDRON, Gloria

The information film; a report of the Public Library

Inquiry, by Gloria Waldron with the assistance of Cecile

Starr.

New York, Columbia University Press, 1949. 281p. illus.

A report sponsored by the Public Library Inquiry and

the Twentieth Century Fund, dealing with the production,

distribution and exhibition in America of information films,

with emphasis on the role played by public libraries.

1063   WRIGHT, Basil, 1907-

The use of the film.

London, Bodley Head, 1948. 72p.

Discusses the social value of documentary and also

entertainment films. Written by a veteran English documentary

film-maker.

Fantasy, horror, and science fiction films

1064   BAXTER, John

Science fiction in the cinema

New York, Barnes, 1970. 240p. illus. *International*

film guide series.

A survey of science fiction films from Melies to

Kubrick's 2001, with a bibliography and selected

filmography.

1065   BUTLER, Ivan

Horror in the cinema. 2d rev. ed.

London Zwemmer, 1970. 208p. illus. *International film*

guide series.

> *The first edition of this book was published under*
>
> *the title: The horror film. It is "a consideration of*
>
> *the use of horror...in the cinema as a whole" (Introd.)*
>
> *Contents:- Horror through the ages.- The macabre in the*
>
> *silent cinema.- Dracula and Frankenstein.- Three early*
>
> *sound horror classics.- Val Lewton and the forties cycle*
>
> *.- British horror.- Two British classics.- Clouzot: Le*
>
> *Corbeau and Les diaboliques.- Hitchcock and Psycho.- Roger*
>
> *Corman and Edgar Allan Poe.- Polanski and Repulsion. Includes*
>
> *an annotated chronology of notable or historically interesting*
>
> *horror films, and a bibliography.*

BYRNE, Richard S

Films of tyranny: shot analyses of The cabinet of Dr.

Caligari, The golem, Nosferatu.

Madison, Wis., College Printing & Typing Co., 1966.

152p. illus.

1066   CLARENS, Carlos

Horror movies; an illustrated survey.

London, Secker & Warburg, 1968. 264p. illus.

> *A new revised and enlarged edition of the work first*
>
> *published in 1967 as An illustrated history of the horror*
>
> *film. A study of the horror film which blends history*
>
> *and criticism. With many illustrations and filmography.*

1067   DOUGLAS, Drake, *pseud*.

Horror!

New York, Macmillan, c1966. 309p.

An entertaining book, with chapters devoted to each of the major categories of the horror film genre, eg. the vampire, the werewolf, the mummy, etc. Includes bibliography and a film list, but no illustrations.

1068   GIFFORD, Denis

Movie monsters.

London, Studio Vista, 1969. 158p. illus. *Pictureback series.*

Contents:- Part I, Creation: The monster; The golem.- Part II, Resuscitation: The mummy; The zombie.- Part III, Metamorphosis: The vampire; The werewolf; The cat; The ape; The beast; The brute; The mutant; The mask. The filmography lists titles of films under each of the above categories. With many illustrations.

1069   GIFFORD, Denis

Science fiction film.

London, Studio Vista, 1971. 160p. illus. *Pictureback series.*

A pictorial survey of the genre, arranged in three parts:- Invention.- Exploration.- Prediction. With filmography.

1070   JONES, Jack Ray, 1934-

               Fantasy films and their fiends.

               Oklahoma City. 1964. 131p. illus.

                   With checklist, who's who, etc., and bibliography.

1071   LEE, Walter W

               Science-fiction and fantasy film checklist, summer 1958.

               Los Angeles, 1958. 59p.

Musical films including opera and ballet

1072   BURTON, Jack

               The blue book of Hollywood musicals; songs from the

               sound tracks and the stars who sang them since the birth

               of the talkies a quarter-century ago.

               Watkins Glen, N.Y., Century House, c1953. 296p. illus.

                   A survey of Hollywood musicals and films with songs

               that complements The blue book of Tin Pan Alley (1951) and

               The blue book of Broadway musicals (1952) Brief credits

               and song titles for each film are given, and there is a

               comprehensive index.

1073   FRANKS, Arthur Henry

               Ballet for film and television.

               London, Pitman, 1950. 85p. illus.

                   Offers criticism and analysis of selected ballet films

               and television productions, and discusses technical problems

               involved in filming ballet. With bibliography and filmography.

284

1074   KOBAL, John.

Gotta sing, gotta dance; a pictorial histroy of film musicals.
London, Hamlyn, 1970. 319p. illus.

*A well illustrated survey under the following chapter
headings:- Early sound.- Lost in translation: the foreign film
musical.- The great escape: the Hollywood musical in the thirtie
The golden years: the Hollywood musical in the forties.- Thank
God for Sweet Charity.- Bring on the girls. With index.*

1075   McCARTY, Clifford, 1929-   ed.

Film composers in America; a checklist of their work.
Glendale, Calif., J. Valentine, 1953. 193p.

1076   MCVAY, James Douglas.

The musical film, by Douglas McVay.
London, Zwemmer, 1967. 175p. illus. *International film
guide series.*

*A chronological survey of film musicals seen by the
author and produced from 1927 to date, with brief notes on
each film. The scope of the book includes films with
musical sequences. With bibliography.*

1077   MINTON, Eric, *comp.*

American musicals, 1929-1933.
Ottawa, 1969. 75p. illus.

*A collection of reviews from the New York Times of
film musicals from 1929 to 1933.*

MOISEIWITSCH, Maurice, ed. <u>and</u> WARMAN, Eric, 1904-   ed.

The Royal Ballet on stage and screen: the book of the

Royal Ballet film.

London, Heinemann, c1960. 56p. illus.

A companion to the Paul Czinner film, The Royal

Ballet, with a chapter by the director on the film's

production, and other chapters about the ballet company

and the ballets staged for the film.

1078   SPRINGER, John Shipman, 1916-

All talking. All singing. All dancing. A pictorial history·

of the movie musical.

New York, Citadel Press, 1966. 256p. illus.

Consists largely of stills, accompanied by brief text.

1079   VALLANCE, Tom

The American musical.

London, Zwemmer, 1970. 192p. illus. *Screen series.*

Alphabetical arrangements of "artists who gave Hollywood

supremacy in the form of the musical. It lists their

musical credits with a small amount of biographical material

and comment." (Introd.) With film title index.

Propaganda films

1080   .BOX, Sidney

Film publicity: a handbook on the production and

distribution of propaganda films.

London, L. Dickson, 1937. 142p. illus.

Concentrates on the practical use of the film media

for publicity purposes, or what is better known today as

the sponsored film.

HULL, David Stewart

Film in the Third Reich: a study of the German cinema

1933-1945.

Berkeley, University of California Press, 1969. 291p. illus

A chronological study of the films of the Nazi era,

with emphasis on the factual background to production

rather than pychological analysis. With bibliography.

1081   JOHNSTON, Winifred

Memo on the movies: war propaganda, 1914-1939.

Norman, Cooperative Books, 1939. 68p.

1082   JOHNSTON, Winifred

Visual "education"? The serious student's guide to social

misinformation. The movies and public opinion no. 2.

Norman, Cooperative Books, 1941. 55p.

A sequel to the author's Memo on the movies. With

bibliographical note.

KRACAUER, Siegfried, 1889-

From Caligari to Hitler; a psychological history of the German film. Princeton, N.J., Princeton University Press, c1947. 361p. illus.

A standard work on the pre-War German cinema and its psychological implications, relating it to the contemporary social, political and economic conditions in Germany. With a detailed bibliography and an appendix examining the techniques of Nazi propaganda films.

KRACAUER, Siegfried, 1889-

Propaganda and the Nazi war film.

New York, Museum of Modern Art Film Library, 1942. 90p.

Religious films

1083   BUTLER, Ivan

Religion in the cinema.

New York, Barnes, 1969. 208p. illus. *International film guide series.*

An illustrated survey not only of biblical and re ligious themes, but also of witchcraft, Satanism, and allied subjects as presented in the commercial cinema. Includes bibliography.

Serials

1084   BARBOUR, Alan G

Days of thrills and adventure.

London, Collier Books, 1970. 168p. illus.

A pictorial history of the American film serial. Includes a complete list of sound serials arranged chronologically by studio.

1085   BARBOUR, Alan G

Great serial ads.

Kew Gardens, N. Y., Screen Facts Press, c1965. unpaged
illus.

*A collection of black & white reproductions of
advertisements for motion picture serials.*

1086   BARBOUR, Alan G

The serial.

Kew Gardens, N. York, 1967-   v. illus.

*A continuing series (2 volumes issued to date)
offering credits and synopses from selected film serials.*

1087   BARBOUR, Alan G

Serial showcase.

Kew Gardens, N.Y., Screen Facts Press, c1968. unpaged.
illus.

Briefly annotated stills and posters of film serials.

1088   BARBOUR, Alan G

The serials of Columbia.

Kew Gardens, N.Y., Screen Facts Press, 1967. unpaged.
illus.

*Consists of credits and chapter titles for each
serial from 1937 to 1956, arranged chronologically.*

1089   BARBOUR, Alan G

The serials of Republic.

Kew Gardens, N.Y., Screen Facts Press, 1965. unpaged.
illus.

*Consists of credits and chapter titles for each
serial from 1936 to 1955, arranged chronologically.*

1090   LAHUE, Kalton C.

Bound and gagged; the story of the silent serials.

South Brunswick, N.J., Barnes, 1968. 352p. illus.

The story of the development and demise of the American

silent film serial. Includes the script of the first chapter

of a 1920 serial, Pirate gold. The book provides indexes

of names and serial titles, but lacks production details of

specific films as found in the author's earlier work, Continued

next week.

1091   LAHUE, Kalton C.

Continued next week: a history of the moving picture serial.

Norman, University of Oklahoma Press, 1964.

293p. illus.

A record of the silent film serial, highlighted by

a 124 page listing of serials produced between 1913 and

1930, each with credits and chapter titles where known.

1092   STEDMAN, Raymond William

The serials: suspense and drama by installment.

Norman, University of Oklahoma Press, 1971. 514p. illus.

A study of the serial format, extending into radio,

television and comic-books. The opening 142 pages deal with the

motion picture serial.

<u>Sex, "blue" and pornographic films</u>

AXEL, Gabriel

Danish blue; a film by Gabriel Axel.

New York, Grove Press, 1970. 126p. illus.

Illustrated scenario of the Danish semi-documentary

about pornographic films.

1093   BRUSENDORFF, Ove   and HENNINGSEN, Poul, 1894--·

        Erotica for the millions: love in the movies.

        Los Angeles, Book Mart, 1960. 147p. illus.

1094   DURGNAT, Raymond, 1932-

        Eros in the cinema.

        London, Caldar & Boyars, 1966. 207p. illus.

           An expansion of a series of articles in the journal

        Films and filming, on the subject of eroticism in the

        cinema. The approach is historical and the tone scholarly.

        Includes bibliography, but no index is provided.

1095   HANSON, Gillian

        Original skin; nudity and sex in cinema and theatre.

        London, T. Stacey, 1970. 192p. illus.

           Sex and nudity in the cinema is dealt with from p. 41

        to p. 122, with emphasis on recent films.

1096   KNIGHT, Arthur   and ALPERT, Hollis, 1916-

        Playboy's sex in cinema, 1970.

        Chicago, Playboy Press, 1971. 144p. illus.

1097   MILNER, Michael

        Sex on celluloid.

        New York, Macfadden-Bartell, 1964. 224p. illus.

           Contents:- The movie-maker and his intentions: honor-

        able or otherwise.- Survey of sex: the censorable subjects.-

        The sex symbol: the star.- Regulating sex on the screen.

1098   WALKER, Alexander

The celluloid sacrifice; aspects of sex in the movies.
London, Joseph, 1966. 241p. illus.

*An examination of the sexual appeal of the female star
personality, with chapters devoted to Pickford, Mae West,
Dietrich, Garbo, etc., also considers film censorship in
Britain and the United States. A final section deals with
Italian and American sex comedies. Published in United States,
and in England in a later paperback edition under title:- Sex
in the movies: the celluloid sacrifice.*

Short films

1099   KNIGHT, Derrick   and PORTER, Vincent

A long look at short films; an A.C.T.T. report on the short
entertainment and factual film, by Derrick Knight and Vincent
Porter.
London, Association of Cinematograph, Television and Allied
Technicians in association with Pergamon Press, 1967.
185p.

*A factual detailed report written for the A.C.T.T..
illuminating the difficulties of production and distribution
of short films in Britain. With bibliography.*

LAHUE, Kalton C.

World of laughter; the motion picture comedy short, 1910-
1930. Norman, University of Oklahoma Press, 1966.
240p. illus.

*A history of the major short comedy films, actors and
directors of the period 1910-1930. An appendix lists the silent
films made by eleven of the most prominent comedians and teams.*

Student-made films

1100   FENSCH, Thomas

Films on the campus.

South Brunswick, N.J., Barnes, 1970. 534p. illus.

The author states that this is "the first complete comprehensive analysis of film programs, student films, and film work in colleges and universities throughout the country." The book deals exclusively with activities in the U. S. With brief lexicon of film terms, and a detailed index.

1101   SULLIVAN, *Sister* Bede

Movies: universal language; film study in high school.

Notre Dame, Ind., Fides, 1967. 160p.

Presents the author's experiences in film teaching, with suggestions on student film-making.

Westerns

1102   BARBOUR, Alan G., comp.

The "B" western.

Kew Gdns., N.Y., Screen Facts Press, 1966. unpaged. illus. *Movie ads of the past series.*

1103   CORNEAU, Ernest N

The hall of fame of western film stars.

North Quincy Mass., Christopher Publishing House, 1969. 307p. illus.

A nostalgic survey of the Hollywood western, consisting of biographies and filmographies of most of the western stars, with additional entries under such topics as The western serial, The wonder horse, The sidekicks, etc.

1104   EVERSON, William K

A pictorial history of the western film.

New York, Citadel Press, 1969. 246p. illus.

Traces the development of the western genre from
The great train robbery to the present day. Includes
over 500 stills.

1105   EYLES, Allen

The western: an illustrated guide.

London, Zwemmer, 1967. 183p. illus. *International*
film guide series.

A reference book consisting of more than 350 entries
for stars, supporting actors, directors, screenwriters,
cameramen, etc. of the Hollywood western, arranged
alphabetically and including brief filmographies. Entries
also appear for famous characters and personalities of the
American west, with details of screen portrayals. There
is a comprehensive index of film titles, and a bibliography.

1106   FENIN, George N   and   EVERSON, William K

The western from silents to cinerama.

New York, Orion Press, 1962. 362p. illus.

A detailed illustrated history and critical survey
of the genre, following a basically chronological approach.
Lacks bibliography and filmography.

1107   KITSES, Jim, *pseud.*

Horizons west: Anthony Mann, Budd Boetticher, Sam Peckinpah;
studies of authorship within the western.

London, Thames & Hudson in association with the British
Film Institute, 1969. 176p. illus. *Cinema one series.*

A critical analysis of the westerns directed by Mann,
Boetticher and Peckinpah. With filmographies.

1108   LAHUE, Kalton C.

        Winners of the west; the sagebrush heroes of the

        silent screen.

        South Brunswick, N.J., Barnes, 1970. 353p. illus.

        Biographical portraits of 38 western stars of the

        silent cinema. No filmographies.

1109   WARMAN, Eric, 1904-   <u>and</u> VALLANCE, Tom, *eds.*

        Westerns: a preview special.

        London, Golden Pleasure Books, 1964. 151p. illus.

1110   THE WESTERN FILM AND T.V. ANNUAL.

        London, Macdonald, 1951.

        v. illus. *annual.*

        Editor: 1951-   F. M. Speed. Title varies: 1951-1956.

        The Western film annual.

Other specific types of film

1111   BARBOUR, Alan G., comp.

        The wonderful world of B-films.

        Kew Gdns., N.Y., Screen Facts Press, 1968. unpaged. illus.

1112   BYRNE, Richard S

        Films of tyranny: shot analyses of The cabinet of Dr.

        Caligari, The golem, Nosferatu.

        Madison, Wis., College Printing & Typing Co., 1966.

        152p. illus.

EVERSON, William K.

The bad guys: a pictorial history of the movie villain.
New York, Citadel Press, c1964. 241p. illus.

*A well illustrated survey of film villains, arranged
by category, e.g. monsters, social villains, swashbucklers,
etc.*

1113 HUGHES, Robert, ed.

Film, book 2: Films of peace and war.
New York, Grove Press, c1962. 255p. illus.

*A discussion by leading filmmakers on war and anti-
war films, together with the scripts for two films: Let
there be light, and Night and fog.*

YOUNGBLOOD, Gene, 1942-

Expanded cinema.
New York, Dutton, 1970. 432p. illus.

*Examines new developments such as laser and computer-
generated films, and multi-screen environments. Includes
interviews with the people involved, and has an introduction
by R. Buckminister Fuller.*

FILM AND SOCIETY (INCLUDING CENSORSHIP)

1114 BARCLAY, John Bruce

Viewing tastes of adolescents in cinema and television.
Glasgow, Scottish Educational Film Association and
Scottish Film Council, 1961. 73p.

*The results of a questionnaire distributed to
adolescents and based on 5000 replies from Scottish
teenagers between the ages of 14 and 18.*

BAUCHARD, Philippe

The child audience; a report on press, film and radio
for children.

Paris, UNESCO, 1952. 198p. *Press, film and radio in the
world today.*

1115   BENOIT-LEVY, Jean Albert, 1888-

The art of the motion picture.

New York, Coward-McCann, 1946. 263p. illus.

*Arranged in two parts:- The motion picture in
education.- The motion picture in the art of entertainment. An authoritative book by an educator concerned
with both the social and educational functions of film.*

1116   BOX, Kathleen Lois

The cinema and the public; an inquiry into cinema going
habits and expenditure made in 1946.

London, Social Survey, 1948. 17p.

*Of interest for its survey of cinema attendance in
England before the major impact of television.*

1117   BRITISH FILM INSTITUTE, LONDON.

Children and the cinema; a report of a conference organized by the British Film Institute & National Council of
Women.

London, 1946. 31p.

*A report of the speeches made at a conference on
children and the cinema, held in London in 1946.*

1118   BRITISH FILM INSTITUTE, LONDON.

The film in national life; being the proceedings of a
conference held by the British Film Institute in
Exeter, April, 1943.

London, 1943. 39p.

*Content:- Adolescents and the cinema.- Developments
in non-theatrical cinemas.- The psychology of cinema-
going.- International influence of the film.- Reports of
discussion groups.*

1119   BRITISH FILM INSTITUTE, LONDON.

Report of the conference on films for children, November
20th and 21st, 1936.

London, 1937. 48p.

*Speeches given at a conference held by the British
Film Institute. Content:- The dimensions of the problem.-
The psychology of children in relation to film-going.-
Attempts made by the film trade to meet the problem and
the difficulties encountered.- What might be done.*

1120   BUCHANAN, Andrew, 1897-

Film and the future.

London, Allen & Unwin, 1945. 104p. illus.

*A series of essays studying the influence and
obligations of film, particularly for the future.*

1121   CARMEN, Ira H

Movies, censorship and the law.

Ann Arbor, University of Michigan Press, 1966. 339p.

History and analysis of film censorship in the
United States from 1915 to date, including accounts of
important court cases. Includes interviews with various
film censors, each interview being based on a sixty point
questionnaire.

1122   COMMISSION ON FREEDOM OF THE PRESS

Freedom of the movies; a report on self-regulation, from
the Commission On Freedom of the Press, by Ruth Inglis.
Chicago, University of Chicago Press, 1947. 240p.

A study prepared by Ruth Inglis of the Commission
staff Partial contents:- The social role of the screen.-
History and economics.- Early attempts to control.- The
evolution of self-regulation.- Self-regulation in operation.
Conclusions and recommendations.

1123   CROWTHER, Bosley

Movies and censorship.

New York, Public Affairs Committee, 1962. 28p. illus.

A summary by the well-known New York critic.

1124   DEMING, Barbara, 1917-

Running away from myself; a dream portrait of America
drawn from the films of the forties.
New York, Grossman, 1969. 210p. illus.

A look at the way in which Hollywood films of the
forties reflected the image of society, not as a mirror,
but as in a dream: wish fulfilling and vicarious.

DURGNAT, Raymond, 1932-

The crazy mirror: Hollywood comedy and the American image.

London, Faber, 1969. 280p. illus.

In five parts:- Jokes and how to spot them.- The great American silence.- Who's afraid of the big bad wolf.- Kiss the boys goodbye.- And therefore take the present time. The book attempts to show American film comedy styles as reflections of aspects of American society. With bibliography and filmography.

1125   FIELD, Mary

Children and films: a study of boys and girls in the cinema; a report to the Carnegie United Kingdom Trustees on an enquiry into children's response to films.

Dunfermline, Fife, Carnegie United Kingdom Trust, 1954.

56p. illus.

A report consisting of photographs of ten audiences of children viewing two selected film programmes in England and Scotland, with detailed ancillary written material on the responses produced.

FORD, Richard

Children in the cinema.

London, Allen & Unwin, 1939. 232p.

Written as a result of experience gained in running children's film programmes. Contents:- The social problem caused by children in the cinema.- Facts and figures.- Psychological and physical aspects.- The films children like.- The organization of children's matinees.- The children's club movement in cinemas.- The attitude of the authorities, teachers and clergy.- Teaching through entertainment.- Summary of work achieved and future outlook.

GETLEIN, Frank   and GARDINER, Harold Charles, 1904-

Movies, morals and art.

New York, Sheed and Ward, 1961. 179p.

Contents:- The art of the movie, by F. Getlein.-
Moral evaluation of the films, by H.C. Gardiner. The latter
part of the book by Father Gardiner offers a Catholic
approach to film evaluation.

1126   GLUCKSMANN, Andre, 1937-

Violence on the screen; a report on research into the
effects on young people of scenes of violence in films and
television.

London, British Film Institute Education Department, 1971.
78p.

A well-researched analysis produced in 1966, with a
summary of research since that date by Dennis Howitt.

HANDEL, Leo A

Hollywood looks at its audience; a report of film
audience research.

Urbana, Ill., University of Illinois Press, 1950. 240p.
illus.

An introduction to the methods used by Hollywood to
determine audience wishes. With bibliography.

1127   HARLEY, John Eugene, 1892-

World-wide influence of the cinema: a study of official

censorship and the international cultural aspects of

motion pictures.

Los Angeles, University of Southern California Press,

1940. 320p.

1128   HUACO, George A

The sociology of film art.

New York, Basic Books, c1965. 229p.

A sociological study dealing with the following

schools of film-making:- German expressionism.- Soviet

expressive realism.- Italian neo-realism, and relating

them to the social and cultural background of the period.

1129   HUNNINGS, Neville March

Film censors and the law.

London, Allen & Unwin, 1967. 474p. illus.

A description of the development of film censorship

in England, U.S.A., India, Canada, Australia, Denmark,

France and Soviet Russia, written by a legal expert. With

bibliography.

1131   JARVIE, I. C.

Towards a sociology of the cinema; a comparative essay on the structure and functioning of a major entertainment industry.

London, Routledge & Kegan Paul, 1970.   394p.

An introduction to the sociology and economics of the cinema, arranged in four parts:- The sociology of an industry: who makes films, how and why?- The sociology of an audience : who sees films and why?- The sociology of an experience: who sees films and why?- The sociology of evaluation: how do we learn about, and appraise films? With major bibliography.

JONES, George William

Sunday night at the movies.

Richmond, Va., John Knox Press, 1967.

127p. illus.

Discusses the involvement of the church in film criticism. Provides hints on running film discussion groups. With filmography and bibliography.

1132   KOENIGIL, Mark.

Movies in society: sex, crime and censorship.

New York, R. Speller, 1962. 214p. illus.

Discusses the influence of the cinema on crime, and surveys films from America, Europe, Russia, Brazil and Japan.

KRACAUER, Siegfried, 1889-

From Caligari to Hitler; a psychological history of the German film. Princeton, N.J., Princeton University Press, c1947. 361p. illus.

A standard work on the pre-War German cinema and its psychological implications, relating it to the contemporary social, political and economic conditions in Germany. With a detailed bibliography and an appendix examining the techniques of Nazi propaganda films.

1133   LAWSON, John Howard, 1895-

Film in the battle of ideas.

New York, Masses & Mainstream, 1953. 126p.

A left-wing analysis, divided into three parts:- The battle of ideas.- The social pattern of Hollywood films.- Toward a people's film art. Includes studies of such films as Viva Zapata and The red badge of courage.

1134   LYNCH, William F., 1908-

The image industries.

New York, Sheed and Ward, 1959. 159p.

An analysis of the morality of the contemporary film and television industries written by a Catholic theologian.

1135   MACCANN, Richard Dyer, ed.

Film and society.

New York, Scribner, 1964. 182p.

A collection of source material on film and its relationship to society, arranged in seven parts:- Films past, present, and future.- What does the audience want?- Does the screen reflect society?- Can the screen influence society?- Should the screen be controlled?- Should film distribution overseas be restricted?- Should films for television be controlled?

1136   MANVELL, Roger, 1909-

The film and the public.

Harmondsworth, Eng., Penguin Books, 1955. 351p. illus.

An outline survey of the cinema as an art, including
studies of 23 significant films, followed by discussions
of problems affecting film production, social effects of
the popularity of the cinema, and the relationship of
television to the film. With bibliography.

1137   MAYER, Jacob Peter, 1903-

British cinemas and their audiences: sociological studies.
London, Dobson, 1948. 279p.

Includes original documents written by the film-going
public, selected to illustrate the effect that films can
have on the lives of those who see them. The book is a
development from the author's earlier work, Sociology of
film (q.v.). The documents are responses to competitions
in which the public were asked to write about their interest
in films and influences upon them.

1138   MAYER, Jacob Peter, 1903-

Sociology of film: studies and documents.
London, Faber, 1946. 328p.

An investigation into the effects of films on average
cinemagoers, with particular attention being given to
children and the English cinema clubs for young people.
The book includes 68 answers to a questionnaire-competition
regarding the influence of films on personal behaviour and
decisions, and whether films appeared in dreams.

MILNER, Michael

Sex on celluloid.

New York, Macfadden-Bartell, 1964. 224p. illus.

Contents:- The movie-maker and his intentions: honorable or otherwise.- Survey of sex: the censorable subjects.- The sex symbol: the star.- Regulating sex on the screen.

1139 MOSS, Louis   and BOX, Kathleen Lois

The cinema audience; an inquiry made by Wartime Social Survey for the Ministry of Information.

London, Wartime Social Survey, 1949. 24p.

1140 PAINE, Stephen William, 1908-

The Christian and the movies.

Grand Rapids, Eerdmans, 1957. 79p.

1141 PERLMAN, William J., ed.

The movies on trial; the views and opinions of outstanding personalities anent screen entertainment past and present.

New York, Macmillan, 1936. 254p.

Offers the arguments presented during the thirties for and against control and censorship of American cinema.

POWDERMAKER, Hortense, 1903-

Hollywood, the dream factory; and anthropologist looks at the movie-makers.

Boston, Little, Brown, 1950. 342p.

A study of Hollywood, using the same processes that would be used to study primitive societies to uncover "the patterns and ideas which control or influence the activities of its members" and therefore affect the films being produced. Gives and insight into the Hollywood power structure.

1142   QUIGLEY, Martin , 1890-

Decency in motion pictures.

New York, Macmillan, 1937. 100p.

Written by the man who drafted the Production Code
and brought it into being in 1930, this book presents
his viewpoint which "undertakes to consider the moral
and social influence of the cinema upon a mass adience,
to analyze the reasons for such influence, and to discuss
the meth·ds by which this influence may be made and must
be kept healthy in its consequences".

1143   QUINN, James, 1919-

The film and television as an aspect of European culture.
Foreword by Jennie Lee.

Leyden, A.W. Sijthoff, 1968. 168p. illus.

The stated purpose of this book is "to explore how
far the cinema and television have come to be accepted as
culturally and educationally significant in the member
countries of the Council of Europe." (pref.) Covers the
period from 1955 to 1965.

1144   RANDALL, Richard S.

Censorship of the movies; the social and political control
of a mass medium.

Madison, University of Wisconsin Press, 1968. 280p. illus.

Arranged in five parts:- Introduction.- The movies and
the law.- Prior censorship in operation.- The wider milieu
of censorship.- Conclusion. The book is a serious study,
including a history of censorship in the United States, legal
requirements, classification and rating systems, and other
forms of censorship. With bibliographical references and tables
of legal cases mentioned in the text.

1145   RICE, John R., 1895-

What is wrong with the movies?

Grand Rapids, Mich., Zondervan, 1938. 117p.

An evangelist expresses the opinion that films are "made by sinful wicked people" and warns against the cinema as a suitable place for entertainment.

1146   ROBSON, Emanuel W., 1897-   and ROBSON, Mary Major, 1901-

The film answers back; an historical appreciation of the cinema.

London, Lane, Bodley Head, 1939. 336p. illus.

Attempts to illustrate how the "basic national culture imprints itself upon the film output in a given country". Arranged in two parts:- The cinema: Europe and America.- The American cinema.

1147   ROBSON, Emanuel W., 1897-   and ROBSON, Mary Major, 1901-

The world is my cinema.

London, Sidneyan Society, 1947. 205p. illus.

The authors express their views on the rise of anti-Americanism in films and film criticism. Also discusses sadism and violence and offers unusual opinions on the merits of many film classics.

1148   SCHILLACI, Anthony

Movies and morals.

Notre Dame, Ind., Fides, 1968. 181p.

Covers such topics as movies and moral sensitivity, religion and the cinema, Bergman's vision of good and evil, etc. With bibliography.

1149   SCHMIDT, Georg, 1896-   <u>and others</u>.

The film: its economic, social and artistic problems.

Basle, Holbein Pub. Co., 1948.

Written by Georg Schmidt, Werner Schmalenbach, and

Peter Bachlin and prepared by the Swiss Film Archive, as a

result of an exhibition 'The film, yesterday and today', the

book consists of revised versions of the exhibition illustration

and programme text as related to the economic, social and

artistic problems of the fiction film and its various

interrelations.

1150   SCHUMACH, Murray

The face on the cutting room floor; the story of movie and

television censorship.

New York, Morrow, 1964. 305p. illus.

Concentrates on censorship in the United States, with

the addition of an appendix dealing with foreign censorship.

Includes the Production Code.

1151   SELDES, Gilbert Vivian, 1893-

The public arts.

New York, Simon & Schuster, 1956. 303p.

A successor to the author's The 7 lively arts, examining

films, radio and television. Emphasis is placed on their

effects upon the American public. No index.

STORCK, Henri

The entertainment film for juvenile audiences.

Paris, UNESCO, 1950. 240p.

An international survey of films for children, the

portrayal of violence on the screen, and the nature of the

juvenile audience.

SUMNER, Robert Leslie, 1922-

Hollywood cesspool; a startling survey of movieland lives

and morals, pictures and results.

Wheaton, Ill., Sword of the Lord, 1955. 284p.

An evangelist's attack on Hollywood stars' lives and morals.

1152   THOMSON, David, 1941-

Movie man.

New York, Stein and Day, c1967. 233p. illus.

"Movie man is the unit in a society that has so

assimilated the methods and effects of moving film that

they are determining his understanding of the present and

his discovery of the future". (Author) The book attempts to

show how the use of the motion picture medium is determined

by society, and in doing so discusses the work of such

film-makers as Hitchcock, Renoir and Godard.

1153   THORP, Margaret (Farrand)

America at the movies.

New Haven, Yale University Press, 1939. 313p. illus.

An account of the cultural influence of film in the

United States during the thirties.

1154   TYLER, Parker

The Hollywood hallucination.

New York, Creative Age Press, 1944. 246p.

Examines the cinema as "the psychoanalytical clinic

for the average worker's daydreams" and looks at Hollywood

as a manufacturer of daydreams and hallucinations.

310

1155   TYLER, Parker

Magic and myth of the movies.

New York, Holt, 1947. 283p. illus.

A development of the author's proposition that "the
true field of the movies is not art but myth" and that
this mythology and its effects must be understood.

UNESCO. *Department of Mass Communications.*

Film programmes for the young; report on a presentation
of children's films organized by the International Centre
of Films for Children, Brussels, 19-23 September, 1958.
Paris, UNESCO, 1959. 30p.

Reports by five international experts in children's
cinema concerning a programme of films submitted by 21
countries.

1156   UNESCO. *Department of Mass Communications.*

The influence of the cinema on children and adolescents;
an annotated international bibliography.

Paris, UNESCO, 1961. 106p.

1157   U. S. CONGRESS. SENATE. COMMITTEE ON THE JUDICIARY.

Motion pictures and juvenile delinquency...
Washington, U.S. Govt. Printing Office, 1956.
122p.

VIZZARD, Jack

See no evil; life inside a Hollywood censor.

New York, Simon & Schuster, 1970. 381p.

Offers an insight into film censorship in the United
States.

WALKER, Alexander

The celluloid sacrifice; aspects of sex in the movies.
London, Joseph, 1966. 241p. illus.

*An examination of the sexual appeal of the female star
personality, with chapters devoted to Pickford, Mae West,
Dietrich, Garbo, etc.; also considers film censorship in
Britain and the United States. A final section deals with
Italian and American sex comedies. Published in United States,
and in England in a later paperback edition under title:- Sex
in the movies: the celluloid sacrifice.*

1158   WHITE, David Manning   and AVERSON, Richard, eds.

Sight, sound, and society: motion pictures and television
in America.

Boston, Beacon Press, 1968. 466p.

*32 contributors "describe the extent of American
society's involvement with the sight-and-sound media, and
to indicate the special problems engendered by that involvement." Nearly all the articles are reprinted from periodicals.
With bibliography.*

1159   WOLFENSTEIN, Martha, 1911-   and LEITES, Nathan

Movies: a psychological study.
Glencoe, Ill., Free Press, 1950. 316p. illus.

*An examination by two psychologists of the ways in
which films reflect the psychology of their audiences -
"to see what are the recurrent day-dreams which enter
into the consciousness of millions of movie goers".
(introd.) Arranged in four sections:- Lovers and loved
ones.- Parents and children.- Killers and victims.- Performers
and onlookers.*

WRIGHT, Basil, 1907-

The use of the film.

London, Bodley Head, 1948. 72p.

Discusses the social value of documentary and also entertainment films. Written by a veteran English documentary film-maker.

THE FILM INDUSTRY

General works

1160   GUBACK, Thomas H.

The international film industry: Western Europe and America since 1945.

Bloomington, Indiana University Press, c1969. 244p.

An analysis of the relationships between the American and Western European film industries since the war. With bibliography.

JARVIE, I. C.

Towards a sociology of the cinema; a comparative essay on the structure and functioning of a major entertainment industry.

London, Routledge & Kegan Paul, 1970. 394p.

An introduction to the sociology and economics of the cinema, arranged in four parts:- The sociology of an industry: who makes films, how and why?- The sociology of an audience : who sees films and why?- The sociology of an experience: who sees films and why?- The sociology of evaluation: how do we learn about, and appraise films? With major bibliography.

Awards and festivals

1161   ACADEMY OF MOTION PICTURE ARTS AND SCIENCES

        Academy award: a complete list of Academy award winners

        for the twenty-two years they have been conferred.

        Hollywood, 1950. 29p.

        A chronological listing of all Academy awards from

        the first winners for the period 1927-28 to 1949. Later

        editions also published with appropriate sub-title changes.

1162   BERTINA, Bob   and others.

        Film festival.

        London, Deutsch, 1962. 47p. illus.

        95 pages of photographs by Kees Scherer of the Cannes

        International Film Festival. Text by Bob Bertina and others,

        translated from the Dutch.

1163   CLARK, Henry, 1922-

        Academy award diary, 1928-1955; a motion picture

        history.

        New York, Pageant Press, 1959. 188p.

1164   FREDRIK, Nathalie

        Hollywood and the Academy awards.

        Los Angeles, Award Publications, c1968. 191p. illus.

        Arranged chronologically, concentrating on awards for

        best pictures, actors, and actresses, and briefly listing

        awards in other categories.

LIKENESS, George C

The Oscar people: from Wings to My fair lady.

Mendota, Ill., Wayside Press, 1965. 415p. illus.

The Oscar winners and the films they appeared in,

with category appendices and index.

1165   MICHAEL, Paul, comp.

The Academy awards: a pictorial history. Rev. ed.

New York, Crown, 1968. 374p. illus.

A record, arranged chronologically, of all award

winners, but with emphasis on the stars. Includes stills

from representative films.

1166   OSBORNE, Robert A.

Academy awards illustrated; a complete history of

Hollywood's Academy awards in words and pictures.

Hollywood, Marvin Miller Enterprises, 1965. 290p. illus.

Cover title:- Hollywood and Oscar: 37 years of film

history; Academy awards illustrated. All awards are listed

with entries arranged chronologically. Additional notes are

provided on the awards for Best Picture, Best Actor, and

Best Actress.

1167   **VENICE.** MOSTRA INTERNAZIONALE D'ARTE CINEMATOGRAFICA.

Twenty years of cinema in Venice. Edited by the management. Rome, 1952. 698p. illus.

A documentation of the twenty years of the International Exhibition of Cinematographic Art, from 1932 to 1952. Partial contents:- Twenty years of cinema in Venice.- Films of forty countries in twenty years.- 336 still photographs.- Twenty years of film making history.- International Festival of Film for Children. A lengthy filmography lists all films screened at the festival from 1932 to 1951, and a further section lists awards. The work is indexed in detail.

1168   ZWERDLING, Shirley

Film & TV festival directory. Researched and edited by Shirley Zwerdling.

New York, Back Stage Publications, 1970.

174p.

A directory of American and international festivals, including amateur and college festivals, conventions, exhibitions, and organizations.

The film industry of individual countries and regions

Asia

1169   DORAISWAMY, V., ed.

Asian film directory & who's who. 2d ed.

Bombay, 1956. 392p. illus.

Production information, statistics, distribution, etc. in the Asian countries.

Australia

1170   FILM WEEKLY (SYDNEY)

         Motion picture directory; who's who in the motion

         picture industry of Australia and New Zealand.

         Sydney.   v.

<u>Canada</u>

        MCKAY, Marjorie

         History of the National Film Board of Canada.

         Montreal, National Film Board of Canada, 1964.

         147p.

           Issued on the occasion of the 25th anniversary of the

         founding of the National Film Board of Canada.

        MORRIS, Peter, ed.

         The National Film Board of Canada: the war years; a

         collection of contemporary articles and a selected index

         of productions.

         Ottawa, Canadian Film Institute, 1965. 32p. *Canadian*

         filmography series.

1171   YEAR BOOK, CANADIAN ENTERTAINMENT INDUSTRY. Editor and publisher

         Ed Hocura.

         Toronto, Film Publications of Canada. v. illus. *annual.*

           At head of title: Canadian film and TV bi-weekly.

         First edition published in 1951 as Year book, Canadian motic

         picture industry.

317

Denmark

1172   THE CINEMA IN DENMARK.

        Copenhagen, Danish Government Film Foundation, 1970? 35p.

        A brief study of the work of the Danish Film Foundation, with notes on Danish film distribution and exhibition.

    FILM CENTRE (INTERNATIONAL)

        The film industry in six European countries; a detailed study of the film industry in Denmark as compared with that in Norway, Sweden, Italy, France, and the United Kingdom.

        Paris, UNESCO, 1950. 156p.

Egypt

    KHAN, Mohamed.

        An introduction to the Egyptian cinema.

        London, Informatics, 1969. 93p. illus.

        A brief survey of Egyptian films and film industry. With filmographies. No index.

Europe

1173   FILM CENTRE (INTERNATIONAL)

        The film industry in six European countries; a detailed study of the film industry in Denmark as compared with that in Norway, Sweden, Italy, France, and the United Kingdom.

        Paris, UNESCO, 1950. 156p.

HIBBIN, Nina

Eastern Europe; an illustrated guide.

London, Zwemmer, 1969. 239p. illus. *Screen series*.

An illustrated guide to directors, actors and others involved in film-making in Albania, Bulgaria, Czechoslovakia, East Germany, Hungary, Poland, Romania, U.S.S.R., and Yugoslavia since the Second World War. A dictionary arrangement is used for each country, prefaced by notes about its film industry and production. A general film title index to all films mentioned in the book is included.

Great Britain

BALCON, *Sir* Michael, 1896-

Michael Balcon presents... a lifetime of films.

London, Hutchinson, 1969. 239p. illus.

The autobiography of a pioneer film-maker since the twenties and one of the most influential producers in the history of British film. Particularly useful for information on the films of Ealing Studios.

1174   BETTS, Ernest, 1896-

Inside pictures; with some reflections from the outside.

London, Cresset Press, 1960. 161p. illus.

A personal account of the British film industry from the thirties to the late fifties, dealing with such facets as production, dependence on the United States, the star system, etc.

BIRD, John H

Cinema parade; fifty years of film shows.

Birmingham, Eng., Cornish Brothers, 1947. 106p. illus.

Largely deals with the life and work of the English showman and filmmaker Waller Jeffs, together with other subjects concerned with the early years of the cinema, particularly in England.

BRITISH FILM AND TELEVISION YEARBOOK. 1946–

London, British and American Press, etc. v. illus.

Title varies: 1946–   The British film yearbook.

Editor: 1946–   P. Noble.

Early editions included articles on various aspects of the British cinema, with a biographical index of actors, writers, directors, technicians, etc. This latter feature forms the major part of later editions, together with information on the British film and television industry.

1176   THE BRITISH FILM INDUSTRY: A REPORT ON ITS HISTORY AND PRESENT ORGANIZATION, WITH SPECIAL REFERENCE TO THE ECONOMIC PROBLEMS OF BRITISH FEATURE FILM PRODUCTION. A report by P.E.P.

London, P.E.P., 1952. 307p.

A report prepared by Political and Economic Planning, arranged in three parts:- The development of the industry.- The topical background.- The operations of the industry. A supplement, titled The British film industry, (London, British Film Institute, 1958; 40p.) provided an account of the economics of the industry since the publication of the P.E.P. report.

BOX, Kathleen Lois

The cinema and the public; an inquiry into cinema going

habits and expenditure made in 1946.

London, Social Survey, 1948. 17p.

Of interest for its survey of cinema attendance in

England before the major impact of television.

BRUNEL, Adrian

Nice work; the story of thirty years in British film

production.

London, Forbes Robertson, 1949. 217p. illus.

An autobiography of the British film editor and

director; also interesting as an insight into aspects of

the British film industry.

1176   CHADWICK, Stanley

The mighty screen: the rise of the cinema in Huddersfield.

Huddersfield, Eng., Venturers Press, 1953. 128p. illus.

1177   GREAT BRITAIN. MONOPOLIES COMMISSION.

Films: a report on the supply of films for exhibition

in cinemas.

London, H.M.S.O., 1966. 113p.

1178   KELLY, Terence Peter,   and others.

A competitive cinema, by Terence Kelly, with Graham Norton

and George Perry.

London, Institute of Economic Affairs, 1966. 204p. illus.

An analysis of the problems of all aspects of the

British film industry, with proposals for reform and re-

organization. With bibliography.

1179   KINEMATOGRAPH AND TELEVISION YEAR BOOK.

London, Longacre Press, 1914–   v. illus. *annual.*

First published in 1914 by the Kinematograph & Lantern Weekly under the title Kinematograph year book, diary and directory. This British equivalent of the International motion picture almanac provides directory-style information on the British film industry, and since 1961, television industry. It provides detailed listings of cinemas in the United Kingdom, and lists films released during the preceding year.

1180   KLINGENDER, F.D.   <u>and</u> LEGG, Stuart

Money behind the screen: a report prepared on behalf of the Film Council. With a preface by John Grierson.

London, Lawrence and Wishart, 1937. 79p. illus.

A volume of research into the economic structure of the British film industry before the war, and the influence of Hollywood.

KNIGHT, Derrick   <u>and</u> PORTER, Vincent

A long look at short films; an A.C.T.T. report on the short entertainment and factual film, by Derrick Knight and Vincent Porter.

London, Association of Cinematograph, Television and Allied Technicians in association with Pergamon Press, 1967. 185p.

A factual detailed report written for the A.C.T.T.. illuminating the difficulties of production and distribution of short films in Britain. With bibliography.

1181   LE HARIVEL, Jean Philippe.

Focus on films.

London, Watts, 1952. 90p.

A brief introductory book, almost entirely concerned with cinema in Britain.

LOW, Rachael.

The history of the British film.

London, Allen & Unwin, 1948- v. illus.

An important work covering the following periods:- 1896-1906 (vol.1).- 1906-1914 (vol. 2).- 1914-1918 (vol. 3).- 1918-1929 (vol. 4). Each volume deals with both the industry and the films produced during the period covered. The first volume was written with the collaboration of Roger Manvell. Volume 4 was published in 1971, twenty years after volume 3 was produced.

1182   MINNEY, Rubeigh James, 1895-

Talking of films.

London, Home & Van Thal, 1947. 80p.

MORGAN, Guy.

Red roses every night; an account of London cinemas under fire.

London, Quality Press, 1948. 127p. illus.

A factual account of the activities of selected London cinemas during World War II and their difficulties in remaining open. An appendix lists British films shown between the outbreak of war and V.E. Day, arranged by date of release.

OAKLEY, Charles Allen.

Where we came in: seventy years of the British film
industry.

London, Allen & Unwin, 1964. 245p. illus.

*A concise history of the British film industry, written
after it became apparent that the Low-Manvell work would not
be completed in the form originally intended.*

1183   SPRAOS, John

The decline of the cinema; an economist's report.

London, Allen & Unwin, 1962. 168p.

*A report, with recommendations, on the causes of the
declining cinema audience in Great Britain. In three parts:-
The shrinking numbers:- The process of adjustment to humbler
dimensions.- The policy issues.*

WOOD, Alan

Mr. Rank; a study of J. Arthur Rank and British films.

London, Hodder & Stoughton, 1952.

228p. front.

*The story of J. Arthur Rank and the growth of the
Rank Organisation. In five sections:- Background and
beginnings.- Building an empire.- The best films of our
lives.- Storm and disaster.- Envoi.*

India

BARNOUW, Erik, 1908-   and KRISHNASWAMY, S

Indian film.

New York, Columbia University Press, 1963. 301p. illus.

*A history of India's vast film industry. Includes
bibliography.*

CHATTERJEA, Bankim Chandra, ed.

Dipali year-book of motion pictures, 1943.

Calcutta, Dipali Granthashala, 1944. 150p. illus.

General information on the Indian film industry and the films released in India in 1943.

1184   JAIN, Rikhab Dass

The economic aspects of the film industry in India.

Delhi, Atma Ram, 1960.

28, 327p.   illus.

A revision of the author's thesis, Agra University. With bibliography.

Ireland

1185   O LAOGHAIRE, Liam, 1910-

Invitation to the film.

Tralee, Kerryman, 1945. 203p. illus.

A survey of the cinema with special reference to Irish problems in establishing a film industry.

Japan

CINEMA YEARBOOK OF JAPAN. 1936/1937-   By the International Cinema Association of Japan.

Tokyo, Sandeido, 1937- v. illus. *annual.*

Annual survey of the Japanese film industry by the International Cinema Association of Japan. 1936/37 edition edited by Tadasi Iizima and others. 1938 edition published by the Society for International Relations. Text in English.

JAPAN MOTION PICTURE ALMANAC, 1957. Compiled by Jiri

Tsushinsha. Tokyo, Promotion Council of Motion Picture

Industry of Japan, 1957. 1v. illus.

An illustrated survey and directory of the Japanese

film industry, with notes on Japanese films produced and

released in the previous year, as well as foreign films shown

in Japan.

JAPANESE FILMS.

Tokyo, Association for the Diffusion of Japanese Films

Abroad. v. illus. *annual.*

First published in 1958, this annual consists of

synopses and stills from selected Japanese films produced

in the year of publication, together with listings of films

by production company, and brief industry statistical in-

formation.

1186   JAPANESE MOTION PICTURE INDUSTRY.

Tokyo, Motion Picture Association of Japan.

v. illus.

Title varies. Some editions titled Motion picture

industry of Japan.

New Zealand

FILM WEEKLY (SYDNEY)

Motion picture directory; who's who in the motion

picture industry of Australia and New Zealand.

Sydney, v.

Pakistan

KABIR, Alamgir, 1938-

The cinema in Pakistan.

Dacca, Sandhani Publications, 1969. 194p. illus.

PAKISTAN. FILM FACT FINDING COMMITTEE.

Report of the Film Fact Finding Committee, Govt. of Pakistan,

Ministry of Industries, April 1960-April 1961.

Karachi, Manager of Publications, 1962. 410p.

The report of the Government of Pakistan's enquiry

into the film industry of that country. Extremely detailed.

U. S. A.

1187   BERTRAND, Daniel, 1901-   and others.

...The motion picture industry: a pattern of control...

Washington, U.S. Government Printing Office, 1941. 92p.

A study prepared for Congress by Daniel Bertrand, W.

Duane Evans, and E.L. Blanchard, dealing with the concentratior

of economic power in, and financial control over, American

film production and distribution.

COMMISSION ON FREEDOM OF THE PRESS

Freedom of the movies; a report on self-regulation, from

the Commission On Freedom of the Press, by Ruth Inglis.

Chicago, University of Chicago Press, 1947. 240p.

A study prepared by Ruth Inglis of the Commission

staff Partial contents:- The social role of the screen.-

History and economics.- Early attempts to control.- The

evolution of self-regulation.- Self-regulation in operation.-

Conclusions and recommendations.

1188   DUNNE, John Gregory, 1932-

The studio.

New York, Farrar, Straus & Giroux, 1969. 255p.

The story of the events of one year behind the

scenes at Twentieth Century-Fox Film Corporation.

FILM DAILY YEAR BOOK OF MOTION PICTURES.

New York, Film and Television Daily, 1918-   v. illus.

annual.

A large annual which is an extremely useful reference work.

The exact title and publisher have changed since the first

edition in 1918. A cumulative index of feature films released

in the United States since 1915 (33,000 titles in the 1969 ed.)

gives sources of distribution and dates of reviews in the Film

daily. Films produced during the year of review are listed with

credits, and additional sections list recent work done by

editors, cameramen, directors, etc.   U.S. trade information is

included as well as a bibliography.

GREEN, Abel, 1900-   and LAURIE, Joseph

Show biz from vaude to video, by Abel Green and Joe Laurie,

Jr.

New York, Holt, 1951. 613p.

A light-hearted survey of the highlights of show

business from 1905 to 1950. A useful index makes this

book of interest for its information about the American film

industry. Contents:- Vaude socko (1905-1913).- War comes

to show biz (1914-1918).- Big boom (1919-1929).- Big bust

(1930-1932).- New deal (1933-1940).- Big show (1941-1945).-

Video era (1946-195-)

1189   HANDEL, Leo A

            Hollywood looks at its audience; a report of film

            audience research.

            Urbana, Ill., University of Illinois Press, 1950. 240p.

            illus.

                An introduction to the methods used by Hollywood to

            determine audience wishes. With bibliography.

1190   HARMON, Francis Stuart, 1895-

            The command is forward; selections from addresses on the

            motion picture industry in war and peace.

            New York, R.R. Smith, 1944. 56p.

            HOLLYWOOD STUDIO BLU-BOOK; MOTION PICTURES, TELEVISION,

            RADIO DIRECTORY.

            Hollywood.   v.

1191   HUETTIG, Mae Dena, 1911-

            Economic control of the motion picture industry: a study

            in industrial organization.

            Philadelphia, University of Pennsylvania Press, 1944. 163p.

                An investigation into the economics of film production

            and distribution in the United States. Still of interest

            for its historical approach. Contents:- Development of

            the motion picture industry.- The motion picture industry

            today.- How profitable is the motion picture business.-

            The marketing of films. With bibliography.

INGLIS, Ruth A.

Freedom of the movies; a report on self-regulation from The
Commission on Freedom of the Press.

Illinois, University of Chicago Press, 1947. 240p.

A special study by The Commission on Freedom of the Press
dealing with the Production Code, censorship, responsibility,
and self-regulation in the American film industry.

INTERNATIONAL MOTION PICTURE ALMANAC.

New York, Quigley, 1929- v. illus. *annual.*

The first edition of this annual publication under the
title The motion picture almanac was compiled and edited by the
staff of Exhibitors Herald-World and published in 1929. The
largest section was devoted to biographical data about actors,
producers, directors, writers, executives, and others in production
and distribution. Further sections dealt with various aspects
of the American film industry. Films released in 1929 and the
preceding few years were listed. The 42nd edition published
in 1971 and edited by Richard Gertner contains greatly expanded
listings. The film lists cover feature releases from 1955-1970,
and emphasis in other sections is placed on directory-style
information on the film industry.

MAYER, Michael F.

Foreign films on American screens.

New York, Arco, c1965. 119p. illus.

Surveys the trends in post-war non-American cinema,
and discusses the problems involved in U.S. distribution
and censorship. With appendices listing award-winning
films, major distributors, exhibitors, etc.

1192   MOLEY, Raymond, 1886-

The Hays Office.

Indianapolis, Bobbs-Merrill, 1945. 266p. illus.

The history and activities of the Motion Picture

Producers and Distributors of America, Inc., commonly

known as the Hays Office, which later led to the Production

Code Administration. The book is in five parts:- The

origins and nature of the Hays Office.- The evolution of

self-regulation.- Good taste and good fruit.- The Hays

Office abroad.- Hays the catalyst. With appendices.

1193   MOTION PICTURE ASSOCIATION OF AMERICA.

Film facts, 1942...20 years of self government.

New York, Motion Picture Producers and Distributors of

America, 1942. 64p.

MOTION PICTURE PRODUCTION ENCYCLOPEDIA. 1948-

Hollywood, Hollywood Reporter. v. illus.

A directory listing credits for the five years prior

to year of publication for American actors, producers, direct

writers, etc., followed by credits for films produced in

the same period by title and by company. Includes American

film industry information.

1194   POWDERMAKER, Hortense, 1903-

       Hollywood, the dream factory; an anthropologist looks
at the movie-makers.

       Boston, Little, Brown, 1950. 342p.

       *A study of Hollywood, using the same processes
that would be used to study primitive societies to uncover
"the patterns and ideas which control or influence the
activities of its members" and therefore affect the films
being produced. Gives an insight into the Hollywood
power structure.*

1195   ROSS, Murray, 1912-

       Stars and strikes: unionization of Hollywood.

       New York, AMS Press, 1967, c1941. 233p.

       *The story of organized labour in the American film industry.
A reprint edition of the thesis originally published in 1941
by Columbia University Press.*

ZIEROLD, Norman J.

       The moguls.

       New York, Coward-McCann, 1969. 354p. illus.

       *Published in England under the title: The Hollywood
tycoons, this book presents reminiscences and anecdotes
under the following chapter headings:- The Selznick
saga.- "Uncle Carl" Laemmle.- "Samuel Goldwyn presents".-
The gentlemen from Paramount.- White Fang.- The films'
forgotten man: William Fox.- The brothers Warner.- The "goy"
studio: Twentieth Century-Fox.- Mayer's-ganz-mispochen.*

332

U. S. S. R.

1196   BABITSKY, Paul,   and RIMBERG, John

The Soviet film industry.

New York, Praeger, 1955. 377p.

Comprehensive and informative. Includes appendices
of decrees and directives, also brief notes on important
directors, with title, person and subject indexes to the
films mentioned in the text.

GENERAL WORKS

1197   ALLEN, Kenneth S.

The silver screen.

London, Gifford, 1948. 66p. illus.

A general book on the cinema and film production for
younger readers.

BAZIN, Andre, 1918-1958

What is cinema?

Berkeley, University of California Press, c1967. 183p.

Ten essays exploring the history, aesthetics, philosophy, and techniques of the film, selected and translated
from the original four volume work published in French.
Bazin was co-editor of the influential journal Cahiers
du cinema.

1198   BECKOFF, Samuel

Motion pictures.

New York, Oxford Book Co., 1953.

114p. illus. Oxford communication-arts series.

1199   BOBKER, Lee R

        Elements of film.

        New York, Harcourt, Brace & World, c1969. 303p. illus.

        An introduction to the techniques and aesthetics of filmmaking. Contents:- Story and script.- Image.- Sound.- Editing.- The director.- Acting for film.- The contemporary filmmaker.- Film criticism.- Includes filmographies and bibliographical references.

1200   BOWER, Dallas

        Plan for cinema.

        London, Dent, 1936. 147p.

        Includes excerpts from the unproduced screenplay by the author of Thomas Hardy's The Dynasts.

1201   BOWSER, Eileen, ed.

        Film notes.

        New York, Museum of Modern Art, 1969. 128p.

        Notes on films that were intended primarily for use with the Museum of Modern Art's circulating film programmes. The arrangement of the programme notes is chronological, from 1894 to 1950. Information includes credits and critical commentary. Film-maker and film title indexes and a bibliography are provided.

1202   BRITISH FILM INSTITUTE, LONDON.

        Fifty famous films, 1915-1945.

        London, 1960. 106p. illus.

        A collection of National Film Theatre programme notes covering fifty major films in the history of the cinema.

1203   BUCHANAN, Andrew, 1897-

Going to the cinema. 3d rev. ed.

London, Phoenix House, 1957. 160p. illus.

A general introduction to the cinema, intended for young people. This edition revised by Stanley Reed.

1204   CALLENBACH, Ernest

Our modern art, the movies,

Chicago, Centre for The Study of Liberal Education for Adults, 1955. 116p. illus.

Illustrates the different categories of films by discussing one example of each. Includes questions for discussion.

1205   THE CINEMA

Harmondsworth, Eng., Penguin Books, 1950-52. 3v. illus.

Each volume of this short-lived series consisted of a collection of essays on various aspects of the cinema. The first two volumes included book reviews and lists of foreign feature films produced in the preceeding one or two years. The third volume included six extracts from British screen plays in addition to a collection of general articles. Editors:- R. Manvell and R.K.N. Baxter.

CROWTHER, Bosley

The great films; fifty golden years of motion pictures. New York, Putnam, 1967. 258p. illus.

Analytical studies of fifty significant films, ranging from Birth of a Nation (1916) to Ulysses (1967). Includes credits, together with a supplementary list of one hundred distinguished films.

1206   CRUMP, Irving

Our movie makers.

New York, Dodd, Mead, 1940. 231p. illus.

A general 'behind the scenes' look at motion pictures.

1207   DAVY, Charles, ed.

Footnotes to the film.

London, Lovat Dickson, 1937. 346p. illus.

An anthology by such writers as Hitchcock, Grierson
and Korda, arranged in four sections:- Studio work: how
a film is made.- Screen material: help from other arts.-
Film industry problems.- Films and the public.

DIMMITT, Richard Bertrand

An actor guide to the talkies; a comprehensive listing
of 8000 feature-length films from January 1949 until
December 1964.

Metuchen, N.J., Scarecrow Press, 1967-8. 2v. (1555p.)

The first volume is an alphabetical listing of films,
with entries including date and production company followed
by a list of the actors, but often with little or no
indication of the roles played. The second volume is
an actor index. The emphasis of the work is on American
productions.

DIMMITT, Richard Bertrand

A title guide to the talkies; a comprehensive listing of 16000 feature-length films from October 1927 until December 1963.

New York, Scarecrow Press, 1965. 2v. (2133p.)

A reference work especially useful for establishing literary sources of films, giving the title of the novel, play, poem, short story, or screen story that was used as the basis for any particular film. Details include author, title, place of publication, publisher, date and pagination. Some analytical entries are included for works not published separately, and cross-references are added for title changes Film production details are limited largely to date, company and producer. With author index.

1208   ELSEVIER'S DICTIONARY OF CINEMA, SOUND AND MUSIC IN SIX LANGUAGES: ENGLISH/AMERICAN, FRENCH, SPANISH, ITALIAN, DUTCH AND GERMAN. Compiled and arranged on an English basis by W.E. Clason.

New York, Elsevier, 1956. 948p.

1209   FILM MONTHLY REVIEW ANNUAL. 1948-

London, Precinct Publications.   v. illus. annual.

FILM DAILY YEAR BOOK OF MOTION PICTURES.

New York, Film and Television Daily, 1918-   v. illus.

annual.

A large annual which is an extremely useful reference work.
The exact title and publisher have changed since the first
edition in 1918. A cumulative index of feature films released
in the United States since 1915 (33,000 titles in the 1969 ed.)
gives sources of distribution and dates of reviews in the Film
daily. Films produced during the year of review are listed with
credits, and additional sections list recent work done by
editors, cameramen, directors, etc. U.S. trade information is
included as well as a bibliography.

FILM REVIEW.

London, Macdonald, 1944-   v. illus. annual.

This annual publication has been edited by F. Maurice
Speed since its first edition in 1944. Each edition
contains a pictorial survey of the year's releases in
Britain, giving annotations, brief credits, and distribution
information. More recent volumes have included additional
notes on awards and festivals as well as articles on
various aspects of the cinema.

FILMLEXICON DEGLI AUTORI E DELLE OPERE

Rome, Bianco e nero, 1958-   v. illus.

A multi-volume reference work constructed upon

Francesco Pasinetti's Filmlexicon - piccola enciclopedia

cinematografica. Although the text is in Italian, film

titles are given in the language of the country of production.

The introduction is in Italian, French, English, German

and Spanish. The first seven volumes so far published

present entries under names of directors, story and script

writers, producers, actors, cameramen, composers, art

directors and costume designers in world cinema, past and

persent. Entries include biographical information, filmo-

graphies, and, where relevant, bibliographies.

1210   FILMS: A QUARTERLY OF DISCUSSION AND ANALYSIS. Edited by Lincoln

Kirstein, Jay Leyda, Mary Losey, Robert Stebbins, Lee Strasberg.

New York, Arno Press, 1968. 1v.

A reprint of the only four issues issued of Films, published

between 1939 and 1940. Contributors include James Agee,

Richard Griffith, Joris Ivens, Rudolf Arnheim and others.

1211   FULTON, Albert Rondthaler, 1912-

Motion pictures; the development of an art from silent

films to the age of television.

Norman, University of Oklahoma Press, c1960. 320p. illus.

Explains the film process in chapters such as Editing,

Expressionism, Naturalism, etc. Reference is made to the

adaptation to film from other literary forms.

GRAHAM, Peter John, 1939-

A dictionary of the cinema. Rev. ed.

London, Zwemmer, 1968. 175p. illus. *International film guide series.*

A useful dictionary with emphasis on directors rather than on actors, and with the addition of a few subject entries, such as Avant-garde. Filmographies are usually reliable, and the film title index includes approximately 20,000 references to the text.

HALLIWELL, Leslie

The filmgoer's companion. 3d ed.

London, Macgibbon & Kee, 1970. 1072p.

An encyclopaedia of film information intended for the general filmgoer, with emphasis on British and American cinema. In addition to biographical entries, information is provided under approximately 200 subject and genre entries, fictional screen characters, and technical terms.

1212   HERRING, Robert   and others

Cinema survey.

London, Brendin, 1937. 31p.

Theee essay:- Film in entertainment, by Robert Herring.- Film in education, by Bryher.- Film in the social scene, by Dallas Bower.

HOUSTON, Penelope

The contemporary cinema.

Harmondsworth, Eng., Penguin Books, 1963. 222p. illus.

A well written survey of film making since World War II by the English film critic showing the various trends and important developments.

1213   INTERNATIONAL FILM ANNUAL.

New York, Doubleday, 1957-   v. illus. *annual.*

Editor: 1957-8, C. Dixon; 1959-   W. Whitebait.

An annual survey of international cinema, with an appendix listing major films produced during the preceding year.

1214   INTERNATIONAL FILM GUIDE.

London, Tantivy Press, 1964- v. illus. *annual.*

Edited by Peter Cowie, this useful annual publication includes annual surveys of world film production, international surveys of specialist cinemas and cinema bookstores, and information on film schools, festivals, etc. Five outstanding directors are chosen for study in each edition, and various special articles and features are included as well as a selective bibliography.

INTERNATIONAL MOTION PICTURE ALMANAC.

New York, Quigley, 1929- v. illus. *annual.*

The first edition of this annual publication under the title The motion picture almanac was compiled and edited by the staff of Exhibitors Herald-World and published in 1929. The largest section was devoted to biographical data about actors, producers, directors, writers, executives, and others in production and distribution. Further sections dealt with various aspects of the American film industry. Films released in 1929 and the preceding few years were listed. The 42nd edition published in 1971 and edited by Richard Gertner contains greatly expanded listings. The film lists cover feature releases from 1955-1970, and emphasis in other sections is placed on directory-style information on the film industry.

15   JENNINGS, Gary

       The movie book.

       New York, Dial Press, 1963. 212p.

       A general introduction to film for young people, with emphasis on the American cinema.

16   JORDAN, Thurston C., ed.

       Glossary of motion picture terminology.

       Menlo Park, Calif., Pacific Coast Publishers, 1968. 63p. illus.

       An illustrated glossary intended for use by anyone with a general interest in the motion picture industry.

342

1217   KEMP'S INTERNATIONAL FILM & TELEVISION DIRECTORY.

London, Kemp's.

v. illus. *annual.*

An industry directory of services, facilities, agents, actors, etc. With Austrian, Danish, Finnish, French, German, Dutch, Irish, Italian, Norwegian, Spanish, American, and Yugoslavian sections. Title varies in earlier editions.

1218   KENNEDY, Margaret, 1896-1967.

The mechanized muse.

London, Allen & Unwin, 1942. 52p.

An essay about the development of the cinema and its problems and literary limitations, written in a light-hearted manner. No index.

KINEMATOGRAPH AND TELEVISION YEAR BOOK.

London, Longacre Press, 1914- v. illus. *annual.*

First published in 1914 by the Kinematograph & Lantern Weekly under the title Kinematograph year book, diary and directory. This British equivalent of the International motion picture almanac provides directory-style information on the British film industry, and since 1961, television industry. It provides detailed listings of cinemas in the United Kingdom, an lists films released during the preceding year.

1219   KIRSCHNER, Allen, 1930-   and KIRSCHNER, Linda

Film: readings in the mass media.

New York, Odyssey Press, 1971. 315p.

An anthology of essays arranged by the editors under three topics:- Form and technique.- Audience and effect.- Critics and criticism. With bibliography.

1220   KITSES, Jim, *pseud.*

Talking about the cinema: film studies for young people,

by Jim Kitses with Ann Mercer.

London, British Film Institute Education Department, 1966.

98p. illus.

Young people from Colleges of Further Education discuss

groups of films on specific themes. Supplement issued also

in 1966 under title Film and general studies. (22p.)

1221   KUHNS, William   <u>and</u> Stanley, Robert, 1942-

Exploring the film.

Dayton, Ohio, Pflaum, 1968. 190p. illus.

A secondary school-level text covering most aspects

of film production and visual language. With bibliography.

Teaching notes (94p.) also available.

1222   LARSEN, Egon

Spotlight on films; a primer for film-lovers.

London, Parrish, 1950. 301p. illus.

A general introduction to the cinema.

1223   LEWIS, Leon, 1940-   <u>and</u> SHERMAN, William David.

The landscape of contemporary cinema.

Buffalo, Buffalo Spectrum Press, 1967. 97p.

Short notes and essays on films, film-makers and per-

formers, arranged in three sections:- Directors; Hollywood

in the sixties; Films around the world.

1224   LONDON. NATIONAL FILM ARCHIVE.

Catalogue.

London, British Film Institute, 1960-   v. illus.

Contents:- v.I. Silent news films, 1895-1933. 2d

ed., 1965.- v.II. Silent non-fiction films, 1895-1934.-

v.III. Silent fiction films, 1895-1930. In volume I, entries

are arranged chronologically; in volumes II and III, entries

are arranged by country of origin.

1225   LOVELL, Alan

Art of the cinema in ten European countries, by Alan

Lovell (Editor), Jacques Chevallier and others.

Strasbourg, Council of Europe, 1967. 265p.

1226   LOWE, Thomas Alfred, 1888-

We all go to the pictures. Illustrated and charicat-

ured by Coia. With an introduction by Anthony Arm-

strong (A.A. of Punch).

London, Hodge, 1937. 214p. illus.

1227   McANAVY, Emile G.   and WILLIAMS, Robert

The filmviewers handbook.

Glen Rock, N.J., Paulist Press, 1965. 208p.

1228   MACGOWAN, Kenneth, 1888-1963.

Behind the screen; the history and techniques of the motion

picture. New York, Delacorte Press, c1965. 528p. illus.

A comprehensive work on the history and techniques of film-

making and the cinema, with additional chapters on such topics

as censorship and distribution.

1229   MALTIN, Leonard, ed.

TV movies.

New York, New American Library, 1969. 535p. illus.

> The most comprehensive guide to more than 8000 films currently being shown on television in North America. Entries include capsule plot summary and rating as well as identification of director, stars, release date and original running time for each title listed.

1230   MANVELL, Roger, 1909-

Film. Rev. ed.

Harmondsworth, Eng., Penguin Books, 1950. 287p. illus.

> An outline of the essentials of film art, arranged in three parts:- The film as a new art form.- The influence of the film on present-day society.- The film today. With bibliography.

MANVELL, Roger, 1909-

The film and the public.

Harmondsworth, Eng., Penguin Books, 1955. 351p. illus.

> An outline survey of the cinema as an art, including studies of 23 significant films, followed by discussions of problems affecting film production, social effects of the popularity of the cinema, and the relationship of television to the film. With bibliography.

1231   MANVELL, Roger, 1909-

A seat at the cinema.

London, Evans, 1951. 192p. illus.

> An introduction to film appreciation and production, arranged in two parts:- The cinema and you.- The cinema and the artist.

1232   MANVELL, Roger, 1909-

What is a film?

London, Macdonald, 1965. 184p. illus.

A step-by-step explanation of all aspects of film
production, from D.W. Griffith to Cleopatra. Intended
for younger readers, but also of general interest.

MICHAEL, Paul.

The American movies reference book: the sound era.
Paul Michael, editor in chief; James Robert Parish,
Associate editor.

Englewood Cliffs, N.J., Prentice-Hall, 1969. 629p. illus.

Entries arranged under the following headings:- The
history.- The players.- The films.- The directors.- The
producers.- The awards. The information included is highly
selective and greatly varying in length and detail. With
bibliography.

1233   MINNEY, Rubeigh James, 1895-

The film-maker and his world; a young person's guide.
London, Gollancz, 1964. 160p.

1234   MONTAGU, Ivor Goldsmid Samuel, 1904-

Film world: a guide to cinema.

Harmondsworth, Eng., Penguin Books, 1964. 327p. illus.

An introduction to the art, technique, and nature of
film. Arranged in four parts:- Film as science.- Film as
art.- Film as commodity.- Film as vehicle.

1235   MOVIES FOR TV: 6180 RATINGS; THE RESULTS OF CONSUMER REPORTS'
CONTINUING MOVIE POLL, 1947-1969. 3d ed., updated and
expanded.

New York, Consumers Union, 1969. 52p.

Cover title.

1236   NATIONAL BOARD OF REVIEW OF MOTION PICTURES, NEW YORK.

30 years of the "ten best"; the movies, players, directors, etc. designated as the best, 1930 through 1959.
Compiled, with an introduction, by Henry Hart.

New York, 1959. unpaged.

THE NEW YORK TIMES FILM REVIEWS, 1913-

New York, The New York Times, 1970-   v. illus.

The main part of this major reference work is in six
volumes and comprises more than 16000 film reviews originally
published in The New York Times between 1913 and 1968.
Arrangement is chronological, with an index, addenda, lists
of awards, and nearly 2000 portraits of film stars included
in the sixth volume. A seventh volume covers the period
1969 to 1970, and further volumes are promised.

1237   NOBLE, Peter, 1917-

Illustrated film quiz; 300 questions and answers about
British and Hollywood films, directors and film stars.

London, Pendulum, 1946. unpaged. illus.

1238   NOBLE, Peter, 1917-

Screen quiz; 500 questions and answers on British
and Hollywood films.

London, Pendulum, 1947. unpaged.

1239   PAUL, Elliot Harold, 1891-

           Film flam.

           London, Muller, 1956. 160p. illus.

1240   THE PENGUIN FILM REVIEW

           London, Penguin Books, 1946-   v. illus.

           Editors: vol. 1: R.K. Neilson Baxter and others; vols. 2-9: Roger Manvell.

           A quarterly publication. Typical contents include twenty items on subjects ranging from film music to Soviet cinema and youth.

1241   PICTURE PARADE.   1949-

           London, Burke. v. illus. annual.

           Editor: 1949-   P. Noble.

1242   PICTUREGOER FILM ANNUAL.   1949-

           London, Odhams Press. v. illus. annual.

           Editor: 1949-   C. Chappell.

1243   PREVIEW.

           London, World Film Publications. v. illus. annual.

           Reviews of major films in year of publication.

1244   REED, Stanley

           The cinema. 5th ed.

           London, Educational Supply Association, 1959.

           122p. illus. *How things developed series.*

           An introduction to motion pictures for young readers.

1245   REYNOLDS, Frank, 1876-

Off to the pictures. Written and illustrated by Frank Reynolds.
London, Collins, 1937. 168p. illus.

Words and drawings from the famous Punch artist. Includes
visual impressions of Gracie Fields, Shirley Temple, Jessie
Matthews, etc.

RIVKIN, Allen, 1903-   **and** KERR, Laura, *comps.*

Hello Hollywood. A book about the movies by the people who
make them.

New York, Doubleday, 1962. 571p.

An anthology representing one hundred writers concerning
all aspects of Hollywood.

1246   ROBINSON, William Ronald, ed.

Man and the movies.

Baton Rouge, Louisiana State University Press, 1967.
371p.

A collection of essays written by twenty writers and critics,
presented in three groups:- The art and its forms.- The artist
and his work.- The personal encounter.

1247   ROBSON, Emanuel W., 1897-   **and** ROBSON, Mary Major, 1901-

In defence of moovie, by Sir Philip Sidney... transcribed from
In defense of poesie, by E.W. & M.M. Robson.

Edinburgh, Pillans & Wilson, 1940. 85p.

A defence of the cinema, mainly in the words of Sir Philip
Sidney's In defence of poesie. "An Elizabethan message for
these present times. Transcribed into modern English and
brought up to date." (cover)

ROTHA, Paul, 1907-

The film till now; a survey of world cinema. With an additional
section by Richard Griffith. Rev. ed.

London, Spring Books, 1967. 831p. illus.

*A standard critical survey originally published in 1930,
now greatly revised and enlarged, with additional chapters
by Richard Griffith. Informative and well illustrated.*

1248   ROTHA, Paul, 1907-

Rotha on the film; a selection of writings about the cinema.
London, Faber, 1958. 338p. illus.

*An anthology of the writings of the critic and film-maker.
Arranged in four sections:- Between the reels.- Films in
review.- Some problems of documentary.- The constant crisis.*

1249   SAMUELS, Charles Thomas, 1936-   ed.

A casebook on film.

New York, Van Nostrand Reinhold, 1970. 250p.

*Covers such topics as cinema as an art form; the writer
and the film; editing; a critical credo. Writers include
Sarris, Houston, Kael, Pudovkin, Deren, etc. Intended as a
student text.*

1250   SCHEUER, Steven H., ed.

           Movies on TV. 5th rev.   ed.

           New York, Bantam Books, 1969. 404p.

             An alphabetical listing of films likely to be shown on American television, with brief plot outlines, stars, release dates, and ratings. Earlier editions published under the following titles:- TV movie almanac and ratings 1958 & 1959 (1st ed., 1958); TV key movie reviews and ratings (2d rev.   ed., 1961); TV key movie guide (3d rev.   ed., 1966). The 4th rev.   ed. was published under the present title.

      SCREEN WORLD.   1949-

           New York, Greenberg, etc.   v. illus.   *annual*.

           Publisher varies.   Editor: 1949-1965: D. Blum: 1966- : J. Willis.

             The American equivalent to Film review, detailing films released in the United States during the year covered with detailed credits and a comprehensive index.

1251   SELDES, Gilbert Vivian, 1893-

           The great audience.

           New York, Viking, 1950.   299p.

             The book is concerned with films, radio and television, although the first 104 pages are devoted exclusively to film - the nature of the audience, its needs, and what it receives.

SELDES, Gilbert Vivian, 1893-

The public arts.

New York, Simon & Schuster, 1956. 303p.

A successor to the author's The 7 lively arts, examining films, radio and television. Emphasis is placed on their effects upon the American public. No index.

1252   SELDES, Gilbert Vivian, 1893-

The 7 lively arts.

New York, Sagamore Press, 1957. 306p.

A reprint of the work published in 1924, with a new introduction and added comments within the text by the author. Areas of film interest in the book, which is devoted to public entertainment forms, include chapters on Keystone films and Chaplin, and "An open letter to the movie magnates."

1253   SITNEY, P. Adams, *comp.*

Film culture reader.

New York, Praeger, 1970. 438p. illus.

A collection of articles from Film Culture, arranged in five sections:- The formative years, 1955-58.- The new American cinema.- The commercial cinema and the auteur theory.- The American avant-garde.- Overviews and theoretical considerations. The collection is of particular value as a survey of American avant-garde film, with many essays by the filmmakers themselves.

1254   SPEARMAN, Walter

...The film yesterday, today and tomorrow.

Chapel Hill, N.C., University of North Carolina Press, c1941.

36p.

1255   TALBOT, Daniel, ed.

Film: an anthology.

New York, Simon & Schuster, 1959. 649p.

An anthology arranged in three sections:- Aesthetics, social commentary and analysis.- Theory and technique.- History and personal. Contributors include many established film writers and critics. Also available in a slightly abridged form (University of California Press, 1969).

1256   TOWERS, Harry Alan, 1920-   and MITCHELL, Leslie Scott, 1920-
The march of the movies.

London, Sampson Low, Marston, 1947. 88p. illus.

Interviews with film personalities and an assortment of articles of general interest.

TYLER, Parker

Classics of the foreign film; a pictorial treasury.
New York, Citadel Press, 1962. 253p. illus.

Well written commentaries on 75 outstanding films produced outside the United States, ranging from The Cabinet of Dr. Caligari (1919) to La Notte (1961). With many stills.

TYLER, Parker

The Hollywood hallucination.
New York, Creative Age Press, 1944. 246p.

Examines the cinema as "the psychoanalytical clinic for the average worker's daydreams" and looks at Hollywood as a manufacturer of daydreams and hallucinations.

TYLER, Parker

Magic and myth of the movies.

New York, Holt, 1947. 283p. illus.

A development of the author's proposition that "the true field of the movies is not art but myth" and that this mythology and its effects must be understood.

TYLER, Parker

The three faces of the film: the art, the dream, the cult. New and revised edition.

South Brunswick, N.J., Barnes, 1967. 141p. illus.

Originally published in 1960, this book tries to illustrate the abstract meanings, often Freudian, behind films. Arranged in three sections:- The art: more or less fine.- The dream: more or less mythical.- The cult: more or less refined.

1257   U. S. COPYRIGHT OFFICE.

Motion pictures, 1912-1939-

Washington, Copyright Office, Library of Congress. v.

Continues Walls, Howard Lamarr. Motion pictures, 1894-1912 (q.v.) providing catalogue entries for films registered with the U.S. Copyright Office in the period covered. Various cumulations have been published, each containing a title sequence, with name and series indexes. The title entries provide details of production date, source of story, major credits, and name of company owning copyright.

1258   VEREKER, Barbara

    The story of films.

    London, Hutchinson, 1961. 128p. illus.

        A general introduction to film production and

    appreciation intended for adolescents.

1259   WALLS, Howard Lamarr, 1912-

    Motion pictures, 1894-1912, identified from the records of the

    United States Copyright Office.

    Washington, Copyright Office, Library of Congress, 1953.

    92p.

        Lists approximately six thousand titles registered

    with the Copyright Office. Continued by the U.S. Copyright

    Office as Motion pictures, 1912-1939 and by later cumulations

    (q.v.)

WEAVER, John T.

    Forty years of screen credits, 1929-1969.

    Metuchen, N.J. Scarecrow Press, 1970. 2v. (1458p.) illus.

        An alphabetical listing of film titles arranged by

    performer. Concentrates on American stars, but includes

    many British actors.

WEAVER, John T.

    Twenty years of silents, 1908-1928.

    Metuchen, N.J., Scarecrow Press, 1971. 514p.

        Film title listings arranged in two sequences:-

    The players.- The directors and producers. Arrangement

    of entries under each name is chronological. Also includes

    a list of silent film studio corporations and distributors.

1260   WHO'S WHO IN HOLLYWOOD.

          New York, Dell. v. illus.

              Editors: F. Epstein, C. Kane.

1261   WILSON, Albert Edward, 1885-

          Movie review.

          London, Hammond; Dewynters, 1948-49. 2v. illus.

1262   WISCONSIN FILM SOCIETY.

          Classics of the film. Edited by Arthur Lennig.

          Madison, Wis., 1965. 238p. illus.

              A collection of reviews of 30 films "which the authors feel significant and enduring" arranged under the following headings:- The American film.- The German film.- The French film.- The Scandinavian film.- Films of other countries.- The horror film.

1263   WISCONSIN FILM SOCIETY.

          Film notes of Wisconsin Film Society. Edited by Arthur Lennig. Madison, Wis., 1960. 139p. illus.

              Reviews of 26 films with notes on a further 31 titles. Arranged under the following headings:- The German film.- The Russian film.- The great comedians.- The Scandinavian film.- The American film.- Shorter reviews.

1264   WLASCHIN, Ken

          Bluff your way in the cinema.

          London, Wolfe, 1969. 64p.

              One of a series, intended to help the reader hold his own in conversation about film.

1265   WRIGLEY, Maurice Jackson, 1886-   and LEYLAND, Eric

The cinema: historical, technical and bibliographical; a

survey for librarians and students, by M. Jackson-Wrigley

and Eric Leyland.

London, Grafton, 1939. 198p. front.

A survey in three major sections: historical; technical;

educational and libraries. The book also includes a 31p.

bibliography, without annotations, arranged by subject, and 3

appendices: periodicals dealing with the cinema; some

outstanding films; historical data.

1266   ZINMAN, David H

50 classic motion pictures; the stuff that dreams are

made of.

New York, Crown, 1970.

A nostalgic survey of vintage Hollywood films.

MISCELLANY

1267   BESSIE, Alvah Cecil, 1904-

Inquisition in Eden.

New York, Macmillan, c1965. 278p.

An account of the 'Hollywood Ten' investigation in

1947 by the House Un-American Activities Committee.

Written in the form of a film scenario by one of the

screenwriters involved, the book also includes

reminiscences of Hollywood in the 1940's.

1268   BRUSSELS. CINEMATHEQUE DE BELGIQUE.

World list of film periodicals and serials. 2d ed.
Brussels, 1960. unpaged.

Includes references to 786 periodical titles published in 36 languages. Scope includes yearbooks and publications brought up-to-date periodically. With subject, title, and geographical indexes.

1269   CANADIAN FEDERATION OF FILM SOCIETIES

Handbook for Canadian film societies. Edited by Jean
Beauvais and Guy-L. Cote.

Ottawa, Canadian Federation of Film Societies, 1959. 116p.

Notes and hints on forming and running a film society in Canada.

1270   CARTER, S. B.

Ourselves and the cinema.

London Workers' Educational Association, 1948. 43p.

Suggested discussion topics on the cinema for W.E.A. groups. A revision of the author's The films, issued in 1945.

1271   CLYMER, Joseph Floyd, 1895-

Cars of the stars and movie memories, by Floyd Clymer.

Los Angeles, Clymer, 1954. 152p. illus.

With foreword by Cecil B. deMille.

1272   COGLEY, John

Report on blacklisting: 1. Movies.

New York, Fund for the Republic, c1956. 312p.

An account of the events concerning the Hollywood inquiries
of the Congressional Committee on Un-American Activities, based
on interviews with the people concerned and on research detailing
the extent and effect of blacklisting. A section written by
Dorothy B. Jones titled Communism and the movies is worthy of
note.

1273   COULTERAY, George de.

Sadism in the movies.

N.Y., Medical Press, 1965. 191p. illus.

A study of the numerous types of sadism in films,
illustrated by more than 250 stills. No index.

1274   GOW, Gordon

Suspense in the cinema.

London, Zwemmer, 1968. 167p. illus. *International film*
guide series.

Contents:- Precepts.- Isolation.- Irony.- Phobia.-
All in the mind.- Among thieves.- By accident.- The occult.-
Fantasy and reality. With filmography and brief bibliography.

1275   GRAHAM, Sheilah

The Garden of Allah.

New York, Crown, 1970. 258p. illus.

The story of the Hollywood hotel-retreat and of the
stars who frequented it.

1276   GREAT BRITAIN. COMMITTEE TO CONSIDER THE NEED FOR A NATIONAL
         FILM SCHOOL.

         National film school; report.

         London, H.M.S.O., 1967. 49p.

             *An official report issued by the Department of
         Education and Science covering all aspects of the
         establishment of a National Film School in Britain.*

1277   HUNTLEY, John, 1921-

         Railways in the cinema.

         London, Ian Allan, 1969. 168p. illus.

             *The result of research conducted for a railway film
         series presented at the National Film Theatre in England.
         Contents:- The silent film (1895-1928).- The sound film
         (1929-1969).- The short film: compilation films, poetic
         documentary, British Transport films, films for children,
         factual films and newsreels, television. Each major film
         entry includes credits, synopsis, and notes on the railway
         featured. A lengthy index provides English distribution
         sources for numerous railway films.*

1278   INTERNATIONAL FEDERATION OF FILM ARCHIVES.

         Union catalogue of books and periodicals published before 1914,
         held by the film archives members of the International Federatic
         of Film Archives. Provisional edition.

         Brussels, Royal Film Archive of Belgium for the F.I.A.F., 1967.
         89p.

             *Entries arranged in three parts:- Author index.- Title
         index.- Chronological list. Introduction in French and Englis*

1279   INTERNATIONAL FEDERATION OF FILM ARCHIVES.

Yearbook.   1964-

Paris, International Federation of Film Archives. v. *annual*.

Text in English and French. Includes general information on the Federation and its activities.

1280   INTERNATIONAL FEDERATION OF LIBRARY ASSOCIATIONS. INTERNATIONAL SECTION OF PERFORMING ARTS LIBRARIES AND MUSEUMS.

Performing arts libraries and museums of the world. 2d ed., rev. & enl.

Published with co-operation by the Centre National de la Recherche Scientifique (France) and by UNESCO, under the direction of Andre Veinstein in collaboration with Rosamond Gilder & others. Paris, Editions du Centre National de la Scientifique, 1967. 801p.

A guide to the major performing arts libraries and museums in thirty-seven countries, with information under each as to general characteristics, admission procedures and hours, assistance given to readers, history and nature of holdings, and other activities. Text in English and French.

1281   KAHN, Gordon.

Hollywood on trial; the story of the 10 who were indicted. New York, Boni and Gaer, 1948. 229p.

A contemporary account of the "Hollywood Ten" who were indicted by the House Committee On Un-American Activities. With an introduction by Thomas Mann.

KATZ, John Stuart, ed.

Perspectives on the study of film.

Boston, Little, Brown, 1971. 339p. illus.

Brings together articles dealing with the film medium and study, arranged under the following headings:- Film study and education.- The film as art and humanities.- The film as communications, environment and politics.- Curriculum design and evaluation in film study.

1282   KULA, Sam.

Bibliography of film librarianship.

London, Library Association, 1967. 68p.

A bibliography of 239 items "concerned with the collection, organization, and treatment of motion pictures in libraries" (introd.)

1283   LAHUE, Kalton C.

Collecting classic films.

New York, Hastings House/American Photographic Book Publishing Company, 1970. 159p. illus.

Advice for the would-be collector of classic films, with notes on sources of supply, suitable equipment, and methods of adding sound accompaniment to silent films.

1284   LEE, Raymond.

Fit for the chase; cars and the movies.

South Brunswick, N.J., Barnes, 1969. 237p. illus.

Consists mainly of photographs and stills illustrating the varied use of the automobile in American films and by Hollywood film stars. Brief text which sometimes fails to mention the films from which the stills are taken. No index.

1285   LOOK

Movie lot to beachhead: the motion picture goes to war

and prepares for the future, by the editors of Look,

with a preface by Robert St. John.

Garden City, N.Y., Doubleday, Doran, 1945.   291p.   illus.

LOVELL, Alan.

Anarchist cinema.

London, Peace News, 1962.   39p.   illus.

A pamphlet on the cinema of Bunuel, Vigo, and Franju

issued to coincide with a film series at the National Film

Theatre in London.

1286   MCCARTY, Clifford, 1929-

Published screenplays; a checklist.

Kent; Ohio, Kent State University Press, 1971.

127p.

A bibliography of screenplays published in English and

issued commercially, arranged alphabetically.   Information

includes production company and date, director, writer and source

of work if not original, and the bibliographical details of the

screenplay.

1287   MALLERY, David

The school and the art of motion pictures; a

discussion of practices and possibilities, with an

annotated list of new and old films of special interest to

schools and available either for theatre showings or

16mm rental.   Rev. ed.

Boston, National Association of Independent Schools,

1966.   147p.

Feature films suggested for high schools are listed

by categories such as comedy, musical, etc.

364

1288   MOTION

Violence and sadism in the cinema; a Motion monograph.

London, 1963. 55p. illus.

1289   MOVIES AT WAR.

New York, War Activities Committee of the Motion

Picture Industry, 1942-   v. illus. annual.

1290   MURRAY, Ken, 1903-

The golden days of San Simeon.

Garden City, N.Y., Doubleday, 1971. 163p. illus.

A nostalgic book about the estate owned by William

Randolph Hearst, and the celebrities, many from Hollywood,

who used to attend as guests.

1291   NOBLE, Peter, 1917-

The Negro in films.

London, Skelton Robinson, 1948. 288p. illus.

Examines "the way in which the Negro has been

depicted in certain films, from the early 1900s up to the

period of the Second World War, and particularly to point

out to what extent Hollywood's attitude to Negro film

characters has improved latterly." Appendices include

filmographies, bibliographies, and D.W. Griffith's defence

of The birth of a nation.

1292   ORR, James Edwin, 1912-

The inside story of the Hollywood Christian Group.

Grand Rapids, Zondervan, 1955. 134p.

1293   REILLY, Adam

Current film periodicals in English; an annotated
bibliography. Compiled under the direction of Mr.
William Sloan, Donnell Public Library, New York.
Revised, January 1970.
New York, 1970. 35 leaves.

SCHUSTER, Mel, *comp.*

**Motion picture performers; a bibliography of magazine and
periodical articles, 1900-1969.**

Metuchen, N.J., Scarecrow Press, 1971. 702p.

*Brief references without annotations, arranged chronologi-
cally under performers.*

1294   SPATZ, Jonas, 1935-

Hollywood in fiction; some versions of the American myth.
The Hague, Mouton, 1969. 148p.

1295   STARR, Cecile, ed.

Film society primer: a compilation of twenty-two articles
about and for film societies. Edited by Cecile Starr with the
assistance of Carolyn Henig.
Forest Hills, N.Y., American Federation of Film Societies, 1956.
84p.

1296   STARR, Cecile, ed.

Ideas on film; a handbook for the 16mm film user. 251p. illus.

*In addition to articles such as Documentary redefined,
production and sponsorship, experimental film, Getting the films
and screening them, etc., reviews of 200 films available to
societies on 16mm are included with lists of distributors and
film libraries.*

1297   THORPE, Edward

The other Hollywood.

London, Joseph, 1970.

173p. illus.

Not particularly relevant to film study, but an
interesting view of Hollywood in 1971 - the Hollywood of
the hustler, the hooker, and the hard-core pornography.
Written by an English observer.

UNESCO. *Department of Mass Communications.*

The influence of the cinema on children and adolescents;
an annotated international bibliography.

Paris, UNESCO, 1961. 106p.

1298   UNESCO. *Mass Communication Techniques Division*

World film directory; agencies concerned with educational,
scientific and cultural films.

Paris, UNESCO, 1962. 66p.

An international directory arranged by continent and
subdivided by county.

1299 UNESCO. *Statistical Division.*

Film and cinema statistics; a preliminary report on methodology with tables giving current statistics.

Paris, UNESCO, 1955. 111p.

A volume of useful statistics, with a summary in
French and Spanish.

1300   WEEGEE, *pseud.*   and HARRIS, Mel

         Naked Hollywood.

         New York, Pellegrini & Cudahy, 1953. unpaged. illus.

             Edited from photographs by Weegee (Arthur Fellig)

         with brief text by Mel Harris.

1301   WILK, Max, 1920-   comp.

         The wit and wisdom of Hollywood; from the squaw man to

         the hatchet man.

         New York, Atheneum, 1971. 329p.

             An "assortment of Hollywood jokes, toasts, anecdotes,

         letters, footnotes and feuilletons". (introd.)

1302   WISEMAN, Thomas

         The seven deadly sins of Hollywood.

         London, Oldbourne Press, 1957. 222p. illus.

             The sins are: Snobbery, gossip, sycophancy, shoptalk,

         egomania, salesmanship, and parochialism.

1303   WRITERS' PROGRAM. NEW YORK.

         The film index, a bibliography...vol. 1: The film as art.

         New York, The Museum of Modern Art Film Library and the

         H.W. Wilson Co., 1941.

         723p. illus.

             The major bibliography on the cinema. Only the

         first volume, The film as art, was ever published. 160

         major subject headings provide references to 8600 books

         and periodical articles, and to 3200 films. Thousands of

         authors, actors, directors, etc. are cited. Entries are

         often annotated in considerable detail. Coverage extends

         to books published to December 1935, although some later

         volumes are included. Editor of this major work was Harold

         Leonard.

INDEX

ASQUITH, Anthony, 1902-1968. 0354

ASSOCIATION FOR THE DIFFUSION OF
   JAPANESE FILMS ABROAD 113

ASSOCIATION OF CINEMATOGRAPH, TELE-
   VISION AND ALLIED TECHNICIANS
   1099

ASTAIRE, Fred, 1899-   0355,
   0356, 0357

UNE AUSSI LONGUE ABSENCE (Film)
   0750

AVERSON, Richard 01158

L'AVVENTURA (Film) 0741, 0773

AXEL, Gabriel 0808

AYFRE, Amédée 0389

BABITSKY, Paul 1196

BABY DOLL (Film) 0774

THE BACHELOR PARTY (Film) 0775

BACHLIN, Peter, 1916-   1053, 1149

BACHMANN, Gideon 0634

THE BACK OF BEYOND (Film) 0776

BADDELEY, Walter Hugh 0942

BAER, Arthur 0278

BAER, Bugs see BAER, Arthur

BAILY, F. E. 0279

BAIN, Donald 0565

BAINBRIDGE, John 0499

BALABAN, Abraham Joseph 0041

BALABAN, Carrie 0041

BALAZS, Bela 0188

BALCON, Sir Michael, 1896-   0097,
   0359, 0360

BALL, Robert Hamilton, 1902-
   0042

BALSHOFER, Fred J. 0361

BANASZKIEWICZ, Wladyslaw 0121

BANKHEAD, Tallulah 0362

BARABBAS (Film) 0777

BARBER, Rowland 0601

BARBOUR, Alan G. 0134, 0482, 0551,
   1084, 1085, 1086, 1087, 1088,
   1089, 1102, 1111

BARCLAY, John Bruce 1114

BARDECHE, Maurice 0001

BARDOT, Brigitte, 1934-   0363,
   0364, 0365, 0366

BARE, Richard L 0991

BARKAS, Natalie (Webb) 0367

BARKER, Felix 0630

BARNES, John 0032

BARNOUW, Eric see BARNOUW, Erik, 1908-

BARNOUW, Erik, 1908-   0101, 1017

BARR, Charles 0510, 0574

BARRY, Iris, 1895-   0001, 0517

BARRYMORE, John, 1882-1942. 0368

BARRYMORE, Lionel, 1878-1954. 0370

BARRYMORE FAMILY 0369, 0370

BARTOK, Eva 0371

BASKAKOV, Vladimir 0179

BASS, Ulrich 0941

BAST, William, 1931-   0441

BATTCOCK, Gregory, 1937-   1047

THE BATTLE OF BRITAIN (Film) 0778

THE BATTLESHIP POTEMKIN (Film) see
   POTEMKIN (Film)

BAUCHARD, Philippe 1032

BAXTER, John 0056, 0135, 1044, 1064

BAXTER, R. K. Neilson 1205, 1240

BAZIN, André, 1918-1958. 0189

THE BEACH OF FALESA (Film) 0779

BEAN, Robin 0632

BEATON, Cecil Walter Hardy, 1904-
   0880

LA BEAUTÉ DU DIABLE (Film) 0747

BEAUTY AND THE BEAST (Film) 0780,
   0781

372

HARDISON, O. B. 0753

HARDY, Forsyth 0097, 0124,
  1056

HARDY, Oliver Norvell, 1892-
  1957 see LAUREL AND HARDY
  (Comedy team)

HARDY, Phil 0491

HARIVEL, Jean Philippe le
  see LE HARIVEL, Jean
  Philippe

HARLEY, John Eugene, 1892-__
  1127

HARLOW, Jean, 1911-1937
  0523, 0524, 0525, 0526

HARMON, Francis Stuart 1895-__
  1190

HARRIS, Mel 1300

HART, Henry, 1903-__ 1236

HARWOOD, Ronald 0885

HASHIMOTO, Shinobu, 1918-__
  0846, 0899

HASTA LUEGO (Film) 0757

HAWKS, Howard, 1896-__
  0527, 0528

HAYAKAWA, Sessue 0529

HAYDEN, Nicola 0746, 0857

HAYDEN, Sterling 0530

HAYMES, Nora (Eddington) Flynn,
  1924-__ 0481

HAYNE, Donald 0444

HAYS, Will H., 1879-1954, 0531

HAYS OFFICE see MOTION PICTURE
  PRODUCERS AND DISTRIBUTORS OF
  AMERICA, INC.

HEAD, Edith 0532

HEARST, William Randolph,
  1863-1951. 1290

HECHT, Ben, 1893-__ 0592

HECKE, B.C. VAN see VAN HECKE,
  B.C., 1926-__

HELLINGER, Mark, 1903-1947. 0533

HELLMAN, Lillian 0884

HENDERSON, Robert M. 0520

HENDRICKS, Gordon 0036, 0037, 0038

HENIG, Carolyn 1295

HENNINGSEN, Poul, 1894-__ 1093

HENRY V (Film) 0753, 0838

HEPBURN, KATHARINE HOUGHTON,
  1907-__ 0534

HEPWORTH, Cecil M., 1874-__ 0535

HERDEG, Walter 1030

HERE COMES MR. JORDAN (Film)
  0756

HERMAN, Lewis Helmar 1011

HERNDON, Venable 0768

HERRING, Robert 1212

HIBBIN, Nina 0069

HIGH NOON (Film) 0753

HIGHAM, Charles 1931-__ 0150,
  0306, 0726, 1004

HILL, Jonathan 0387

THE HILL (Film) 0839

HIROSHIMA MON AMOUR (Film)
  0750, 0840

HIRST, Robert 0307

HITCHCOCK, Alfred Joseph, 1899-__
  0536, 0537, 0538, 0539

HOADLEY, Ray 0957

HOCURA, Ed 1171

HOELLERING, George 0879

HOFFMAN, William, 1937-__ 0643

HOFMANN, Charles 0047

HOLLYWOOD ALBUM 0308

HOLLYWOOD CHRISTIAN GROUP 1292

HOLLYWOOD STUDIO BLU-BOOK 0309

HOLMES, Winifred, 1903-__ 0053

IT HAPPENED ONE NIGHT (Film)
0755, 0756, 0760

IVAN THE TERRIBLE (Film)
0853, 0854

IVENS, Joris, 1898-   0549

JACOBS, Lewis, 1906-   0009,
0152, 0198, 0199

JACOPETTI, Gualtiero 0767

JACQUES, Richard 0746

JAIN, Rikhab Dass 1184

JAMES, David, 1919-   0909

JAN HUSS (Film) 0855

JANARO, Richard Paul 0219

JAPAN MOTION PICTURE ALMANAC
0112

JAPANESE FILMS 0113

JAPANESE MOTION PICTURE INDUSTRY
1186

JARRATT, Vernon 0106

JARVIE, I.C. 1131

JAY, John Mark, 1920-
0792

JEFFS, Waller 0085

JENNINGS, Dean Southern, 1905-
0718

JENNINGS, Humphrey, 1907-
1950. 0550, 0811

JENNINGS, Talbot 0902

JESSEL, George Albert, 1898-
0310

JENNINGS, Gary 1215

JENSEN, Paul M. 0569

JHABVALA, Ruth Prawer, 1927-
0841

JOAN OF ARC (Film) 0856

THE JOB (Film) 0763

JOBES, Gertrude 0153

JOHN, Errol 0757

JOHNSTON, Alva 0515

JOHNSTON, Winifred 1081, 1082

JONES, George William 0233

JONES, Jack Ray, 1934-   1070

JONES, Ken D. 0681

JONES, Lon 0777

JORDAN, Thurston C. 1216

LE JOUR SE LÈVE (Film) 0857

JOURNAL OF THE SOCIETY OF MOTION
PICTURE AND TELEVISION ENGINEERS
0007

JUAREZ (Film) 0756

JUDGMENT AT NUREMBERG (Film)
0858

JULES AND JIM (Film) 0859

JULIET OF THE SPIRITS (Film)
0860

KABIR, Alamgir, 1938-   0118

KAEL, Pauline 0234, 0235, 0236, 0802

KAHN, Gordon 1281

KANE, Christopher 1260

KANTOR, Bernard R. 0293

KARLOFF, Boris, 1887-1969
0551

KATZ, John Stuart 0237

KAUFFMANN, Stanley, 1916-
0238, 0239

KAYE, Danny, 1913-   0552

KEATON, Buster, 1895-1966
0316, 0553, 0554, 0555, 0556

KEATS, John, 1920-   0546

KEENE, Ralph 0807

KEHOE, Vincent J.R. 0999

KELLER, Hans Heinrich, 1919-
0240

KELLY, Gene, 1912-   0557

KELLY, Ron 0558

KELLY, Terence Peter 1178

KEMP'S INTERNATIONAL FILM &
TELEVISION DIRECTORY. 1217

LOCKWOOD, Margaret, 1916-
0582, 0583

LOLLOBRIGIDA, Gina, 1927-
0584

LONDON, Kurt, 1899-
1002

LONDON. NATIONAL FILM ARCHIVE.
1224

THE LONDONER (Film) 0762

LOOK 0688, 1285

LOOS, Anita, 1894-
0585

LOREN, Sophia, 1934-
0586, 0587

LORENTZ, Pare, 1905-
0588

LOSEY, Joseph, 1909-
0589, 0590

THE LOST WEEKEND (Film)
0754

THE LOVED ONE (Film)
0867

LOVELL, Alan 0315, 1225

LOW, Rachael 0092

LOWE, Thomas Alfred, 1888-
1226

LUBITSCH, Ernst, 1892-1947.
0591

LUC GODARD, Jean see GODARD,
Jean Luc, 1930-

LULU (Film) see PANDORA'S BOX
(Film)

LYNCH, William F., 1908-
1134

M (Film) 0868

MACALL, Martin 0758

McANAVY, Emile G. 1227

MACARTHUR, Charles, 1895-1956.
0592

McARTHUR, Colin 0716

MACARTNEY-FILGATE, Terence 0593

MACBETH (Film) 0869

McBRIDE, Jim 0810

McCABE, John 0576

McCAFFREY, Donald W. 0316, 0406

McCALLUM, John Dennis, 1924-
0425

MACCANN, Richard Dyer, 0157, 0204,
1135

McCARTY, Clifford, 1929- 0385,
0483, 0675, 1075, 1286

McCLELLAND, C. Kirk 0794

McCLURE, Arthur F. 0339, 0681

McCOY, Horace, 1897-1955. 0924

McCRINDLE, Joseph F. 0317

MACDONALD, Dwight 0244

McDONALD, Gerald Doan, 1905-
0407, 0408

MACGOWAN, Kenneth, 1888-1963.
1228

McGREGOR, Dion 0501

McGUIRE, Jeremiah C. 0245

McKAY, Marjorie 0058

McKENNA, Virginia, 1931-
0793

MACLAINE, Shirley 0594

MACLIAMMHOIR, Micheal, 1899-
0886

MACPHERSON, Sandy 0595

MACRAE, Arthur 0821

McVAY, James Douglas 1076

MADDUX, Rachel, 1913-
0936

MADE IN U.S.A. (Film) 0870

MADSEN, Axel 0732

MADSEN, Roy 0988

THE MAGICIAN (Film) 0743

MAJOR, Henry 0278

MAJOR BARBARA (Film) 0871

MAKE WAY FOR TOMORROW (Film)
0756

MALERBA, Luigi 0105

MALLERY, David 1287

MALTIN, Leonard 0318, 1229

MAMOULIAN, Rouben, 1898-
0596, 0597

MAN WHO COULD WORK MIRACLES
(Film) 0872

MANCHEL, Frank 0048

MANK, Charles, 1902-
0702

MANKIEWICZ, Herman Jacob,
1897-1953. 0802

MANKIEWICZ, Joseph L. 0769

MANN, Abby 0858

MANN, Anthony, 1906-1967.
1107

MANOOGIAN, Haig P. 0964

MANTZ, Paul 0598

MANVELL, Roger, 1909-
0019, 0070, 0083, 0092, 0093,
0097, 0158, 0254, 0759, 0965,
0986, 0989, 1003, 1029, 1049,
1136, 1205, 1230, 1231, 1232,
1240

MARCH, Fredric, 1897-   0283

MARCO POLO (Film) 0873

MARCUS, Fred Harold, 1921-
0205

MAREK, Kurt W. see CERAM, C.W.
pseud.

MARGRAVE, Seton 0829

MARION, Frances, 1890-   0873

MARILL, Alvin H. 0482, 0551

MARKOPOULOS, Gregory J. 0911

MARLOWE, Don 0159

THE MARRIED WOMAN (Film) 0874

MARSHALL, Herbert 0183

MARTIN, Bruce 0559

MARTIN, Olga Johanna 1014

MARTIN, Pete, pseud. 0319, 0453,
0619

MARX, Arthur, 1921-   0599

MARX, Groucho, 1891-   0599, 0600

MARX, Harpo, 1893-1964. 0601

MARX BROTHERS (Comedy team) 0602,
0603, 0604

MASCELLI, Joseph V. 0966

MASCULINE FEMININE (Film) 0875

MASON, James, 1900-   0605

MAST, Gerald, 1940-   0013

MAUGHAM, William Somerset, 1874-1965
0821, 0896, 0932

MAYER, Arthur, 1886-   0149, 0606

MAYER, Jacob Peter, 1903-   1137,
1138

MAYER, Louis B., 1885-1957. 0607

MAYER, Michael F. 0014

MAYERSBERG, Paul 0160

MAYSLES, Albert 0906

MAYSLES, David 0906

ME AND MY BIKE (Film) 0876

A MEDAL FOR BENNY (Film) 0754

MENJOU, Adolphe Jean 0608

MERCER, Ann 1220

MERCOURI, Melina, 1925-   0609

MEYERS, Warren B. 0320

MICHAEL, Paul 0161, 0386, 1165

MILDRED PIERCE (Film) 0758

MILESTONE, Lewis, 1895-
    0610

MILLAR, Gavin 0997

MILLE, Cecil Blount de see
    DE MILLE, Cecil Blount, 1881-1959

MILLER, Arthur C. 0361

MILLER, Diane (Disney) 0453

MILLER, Edwin, 1921-   0321

MILLER, Virgil E., 1886-   0611

MILNE, Tom 0459, 0590, 0597

MILNER, Michael 1097

MINNEY, Rubeigh James, 1895-
    0409, 1182, 1233

MINTON, Eric 0246, 1077

MIRACLE IN MILAN (Film) 0877

MIRACLE OF MORGAN'S CREEK (Film)
    0754

THE MISFITS (Film) 0878

MR. SMITH GOES TO WASHINGTON (Film)
    0756

MRS. MINIVER (Film) 0756

MITCHELL, Leslie Scott, 1920-
    1256

MIX, Olive (Stokes) 0612

MIX, Tom, 1880-1940. 0612

MIZOGUCHI, Kenji, 1898-1956.
    0613

MODERN CZECHOSLOVAK FILM: 1945-
    1965. 0064

MOISEIWITSCH, Maurice 0903

MOLEY, Raymond, 1886-   1192

MONAGHAN, John P. 0605

MONROE, Marilyn, 1926-1962
    0305, 0614, 0615, 0616, 0617,
        0618, 0619, 0620, 0621, 0878

MONTAGU, Ivor Goldsmid Samuel,
    1904-   0207, 0208, 0462,
    0854, 1234

MONTGOMERY, John, 1916-   1042

MONTI, Carlotta 0474

MOORE, Colleen, 1902-   0622

MORE, Kenneth, 1914-   0623

THE MORE THE MERRIER (Film) 0754

MORELLA, Joe 0322, 0507

MORGAN, Guy 0094

MORIN, Edgar 0162

MORLEY, Robert, 1908-   0624

MORRIS, Peter, 1937-   0059, 0060,
    0613

MOSLEY, Leonard, 1913-   0778

MOSS, Louis 1139

MOTION 1288

MOTION PICTURE ASSOCIATION OF
    AMERICA. 1193

MOTION PICTURE ASSOCIATION OF
    JAPAN 1186

MOTION PICTURE INDUSTRY OF JAPAN
    see JAPANESE MOTION PICTURE
    INDUSTRY

MOTION PICTURE PRODUCERS AND
    DISTRIBUTORS OF AMERICA, INC. 1192

MOTION PICTURE PRODUCTION
    ENCYCLOPEDIA. 0163

MOUSSINAC, Leon, 1890-1964.
    0463

MOUSSY, Marcel, 1924-   0827

MOVIES AT WAR 1289

MOVIES FOR TV: 6180 RATINGS... 1235

MULLER-STRAUSS, Maurice   1053

MUNDEN, Kenneth W.   0133

MURDER IN THE CATHEDRAL (Film)
   0879

MURRAY, Ken, 1903-   1290

MURRAY, Mae, 1889-1965.
   0625

MUSSELMAN, Morris McNeil   0608

MUSSMAN, Toby   0511

MY FAIR LADY (Film)   0880

MY MAN GODFREY (Film)   0756

MYERSCOUGH-WALKER, Raymond
   1008

NANOOK OF THE NORTH (Film)
   0861

NATIONAL BOARD OF REVIEW OF
   MOTION PICTURES, NEW YORK
   1236

NATIONAL COUNCIL OF WOMEN
   1117

NATIONAL FILM ARCHIVE, LONDON
   see LONDON. NATIONAL FILM
   ARCHIVE

NATIONAL SOCIETY OF FILM CRITICS
   0229

NAUMBERG, Nancy, 1911-   0967

NEERGAARD, Ebbe, 1901-1957.
   0066, 0067

NEFF, Hildegarde see KNEF,
   Hildegard

NEGRI, Pola, 1897-   0626

NEILSON-BAXTER, R.K.   see
   BAXTER, R.K. NEILSON

NELSON, AL P.   0786

NEMCEK, Paul L.   0398

NEMESKURTY, Istvan   0100

THE NEW YORK TIMES FILM REVIEWS
   0247

NEWMAN, Paul, 1925-   0627

NEWQUIST, Roy   0834

THE NEXT VOICE YOU HEAR (Film)
   0882

NICHOLS, Dudley, 1895-   0754,
   0755, 0756, 0918

NICOLL, Allardyce, 1894-   0270

NIGHT AND FOG (Film)   1113

THE NIGHT OF THE HUNTER (Film)
   0217

NIKLAUS, Thelma   0403

NILSEN, Vladimir S.   0206

NIVER, Kemp R.   0015, 0164, 0165,
   0166, 0641

NIZHNY, Vladimir B.   0207

NOA NOA (Film)   0217

NOBLE, Lorraine, 0760

NOBLE, Peter, 1917-   0086,
   0323, 0354, 0438, 0628, 0715,
   0727, 1237, 1238, 1241, 1291

NOBLE, Ronald   0629

NOBODY WAVED GOOD BYE (Film)
   0883

NOERDLINGER, Henry S.   0923

NOLAN, William F.   0547

NONE BUT THE LONELY HEART (Film)
   0754

THE PENGUIN FILM REVIEW
1240

PECKINPAH, Sam, 1926-
1107

PENN, Arthur 0638, 0768

PENNEBAKER, D.A. 0815

PENSEL, Hans 0324

PERIES, Lester James 0639

PERLMAN, William J. 1141

PERRY, Eleanor 0920, 0931

PERRY, Frank, 1930- 0931

PERRY, George 0537, 1178

PETERSON, Marcelene 0177

PETERSON, Roger C. 1903-
0700

LE PETIT SOLDAT (Film) 0890

PETRIE, Graham 0697

PICKFORD, Mary, 1893- 0640,
0641, 0642

PICTURE PARADE. 1241

PICTUREGOER FILM ANNUAL. 1242

PIERROT LE FOU (Film) 0891

PINCHOT, Ann 0508

PINTER, Harold 0761

PLATT, Frank C. 0325

POINT OF ORDER (Film) 0892

POITIER, Sidney, 1924- 0643

POLANSKI, Roman, 1933- 0644

POLITICAL AND ECONOMIC PLANNING
1052, 1175

POLLOCK, Eileen 0416

POLLOCK, Robert Mason 0416

PORTER, Hal 0057

PORTER, Vincent 1099

POTEMKIN (Film) 0893

POWDERMAKER, Hortense, 1903-
0645, 1194

POWELL, Dilys 0096

POWELL, Michael 0818, 0901, 0922

PRATLEY, Gerald 0488

PRATT, George C. 0017

PREJEAN, Albert 0646

PREMINGER, Otto, 1906- 0771

PREVERT, Jacques, 1900- 0799,
0857

PREVIEW 1243

PRICE, Ira 0249

PRIESTLEY, John Boynton, 1894-
0647

THE PRINCE AND THE SHOWGIRL (Film)
0894

PRYOR, Helen Sloman 0968

PRYOR, William Clayton 0968

PUBLIC LIBRARY INQUIRY see SOCIAL
SCIENCE RESEARCH COUNCIL. PUBLIC
LIBRARY INQUIRY.

PUDOVKIN, Vsevolod Illarionovich,
1893-1953. 0208

PULL MY DAISY (Film) 0895

PULMAN, Jack 0809

THE PUMPKIN EATER (Film) 0761

THE PURPLE HEART (Film) 0754

QUARTET (Film) 0896

QUE VIVA MEXICO (Film) 0897,
0898

QUEVAL, Jean 0397

QUIGLEY, Martin, 1890- 1142

QUIGLEY, Martin, 1917- 0039,
0167, 0969

SOCIAL SCIENCE RESEARCH COUNCIL.
  PUBLIC LIBRARY INQUIRY 1062
SOCIETY OF MOTION PICTURE AND
  TELEVISION ENGINEERS 0007
SOLDIERS THREE (Film) 0367
SOLMI, Angelo 0470
SOLT, Andrew P., 1916- 0856
SOLZHENITSYN, Aleksandr Isaevich,
  1918- 0885
SOME LIKE IT HOT (Film) 0914
SONS OF MATTHEW (Film) 0915
SONTAG, Susan, 1933-
  0258, 0259, 0816
SOUTH PACIFIC (Film) 0916
SOUTHERN, Terry 0817, 0867
THE SOUTHERNER (Film) 0754
THE SOVIET CINEMATOGRAPHY 0184
SOVIET FILMS, 1938-1939. 0185
SPAAK, Charles, 1903- 0832
SPATZ, Jonas, 1935- 1294
SPEARMAN, Walter 1254
SPEED, F. Maurice 0023, 0089,
  1110
SPELLBOUND (Film) 0754
SPENCER, Douglas Arthur, 1901-
  0972
SPLENDOR IN THE GRASS (Film) 0917
SPOTTISWOODE, Raymond, 1913- 0209,
  0973, 0974
SPRAOS, John 1183
SPRINGER, John Shipman, 1916-
  0484, 1078
STACK, Oswald, pseud. 0635
STAGECOACH (Film) 0755, 0756,
  0918
STANLEY, Robert, 1942- 1221
STARR, Cecile 1062, 1295,
  1296.

STAUFFACHER, Frank, 1916- 1046
STEDMAN, Raymond William 1092
STEELE, Joseph Henry 0381
STEENE, Birgitta 0377
STEIGER, Brad 0702
STEINBECK, John, 1902-1968.
  0679, 0826
STEPHENSON, Ralph 0210, 1031
STERNBERG, Josef von see VON
  STERNBERG, Josef, 1894-1969
STERNER, Alice P. 0260
STEVENS, George, 1904- 0680
STEWART, James, 1908- 0681
STILLER, Mauritz, 1883-1928
  0127, 0324
STOKES, Sewell, 1902- 0624
STORCK, Henri 1036
STORM IN THE WEST (Film) 0919
THE STORY OF LOUIS PASTEUR (Film)
  0760
STOUT, Wesley Winans 0581
STRAUSS, Maurice Muller- see
  MULLER-STRAUSS, Maurice
A STREETCAR NAMED DESIRE (Film)
  0753
STRICK, Philip 0351
STUART, Ray, 1899- 0335
STROHEIM, Erich von see VON
  STROHEIM, Erich, 1885-1957
SULLIVAN, Sister Bede 1101
SUMNER, Robert Leslie, 1922-
  0336
SUNDGREN, Nils Petter, 1929-
  0129
SUSSEX, Elizabeth 0346
SUTTER'S GOLD (Film) 0462
SVENSSON, Arne 0116, 0125
SWANSON, Gloria, 1898- 0289, 0682

WILLEMEN, Paul 0430

WILLIAMS, Chester 0498

WILLIAMS, Raymond 0275

WILLIAMS, Robert 1227

WILLIAMS, Tennessee, 1914-
0774

WILLIS, John A 0173

WILSON, Albert Edward, 1885-
1261

WILSON, Ivy Crane 0308

WILSON, Michael 0907

WILSON, Norman, 1906-
1055

WILSON (Film) 0754

WIND ACROSS THE EVERGLADES
(Film) 0940

WINDELER, Robert 0348

WINNINGTON, Richard 0267

WINQUIST, Sven G., 1924-
0131, 0132

WINTER LIGHT (Film) see
THE COMMUNICANTS (Film)

WISCONSIN FILM SOCIETY 1262,
1263

WISEMAN, Thomas 0028, 1302

WLASCHIN, Ken 1264

WOLFE, Maynard Frank 0766

WOLFENSTEIN, Martha, 1911-
1159

WOLLEN, Peter 0212, 0213, 0492

WOLLENBERG, Hans H. 0084, 0268

THE WOMEN (Film) 0756

WOOD, Alan 0648

WOOD, Leslie 0029, 0030

WOOD, Robin 0349, 0378,
0399, 0528, 0539, 0638

WOOD, Tom 0733

WOODHOUSE, Bruce 0977

THE WORD (Film) 0749

WRIGHT, Basil, 1907- 0477,
1063

WRIGLEY, Maurice Jackson, 1886-
1265

WRITERS CONGRESS, UNIVERSITY OF
CALIFORNIA AT LOS ANGELES, 1943.
1016

WRITERS GUILD OF AMERICA 1017

WRITERS' PROGRAM. NEW YORK.
1303

WUTHERING HEIGHTS (Film) 0756

WYLER, William, 1902- 0734

YEAR BOOK, CANADIAN ENTERTAINMENT
INDUSTRY. 1171

THE YEAR BOOK OF MOTION PICTURES
IN AMERICA see THE BEST
PICTURES...

THE YEAR'S WORK IN THE FILM. 0099

YELLOW JACK (Film) 0756

YOAKEM, Lola Goelet, 1017

YOUNG, Loretta, 1913- 0735

YOUNG, Vernon 0379

YOUNG APHRODITES (Film) 0941

YOUNGBLOOD, Gene, 1942- 0978

YURENEV, R. 0194

ZALMAN, Jan, pseud. 0065

ZANELLI, Dario 0908

ZANUCK, Darryl Francis, 1902-
0736

ZAVATTINI, Cesare, 1902- 0737

ZIEROLD, Norman J. 0342, 0343, 0505

- - - - - -

WITHDRAWN